Drinking
in Context

Drinking in Context

Patterns, Interventions, and Partnerships

Gerry Stimson ◆ Marcus Grant
Marie Choquet ◆ Preston Garrison

Routledge
Taylor & Francis Group
New York   London

Routledge is an imprint of the
Taylor & Francis Group, an informa business

Quoted material appearing in Chapter 10 within the section headed "Public-Private Partnerships, Research, and Policy" is from Hannum, H. (1998). Condemning the drinks industry rules out potentially useful research. *British Medical Journal*, 317, 335-336. Permission granted from BMJ Publishing Group.

Quoted material on page 219 is reprinted from *The Lancet*, 362, Greenberg, D. S., Conference deplores corporate influence on academic science, 302-303 (2003), with permission from Elsevier.

Tables 13.2A, 13.2B, and 13.3 are adapted from Gutjahr, E., Gmel, G., & Rehm, J. (2001). Relation between average alcohol consumption and disease: an overview. *European Addiction Research*, 7, 117-127. With permission from S. Karger AG.

Routledge
Taylor & Francis Group
270 Madison Avenue
New York, NY 10016

Routledge
Taylor & Francis Group
2 Park Square
Milton Park, Abingdon
Oxon OX14 4RN

© 2007 by Taylor & Francis Group, LLC
Routledge is an imprint of Taylor & Francis Group, an Informa business

Printed in the United States of America on acid-free paper
10 9 8 7 6 5 4 3 2 1

International Standard Book Number-10: 0-415-95447-9 (Hardcover)
International Standard Book Number-13: 978-0-415-95447-1 (Hardcover)

Library of Congress Cataloging-in-Publication Data

Drinking in context : patterns, interventions, and partnerships / Gerry V. Stimson, editor ; Barton Alexander ... [et al.].
   p. ; cm.
Includes bibliographical references and index.
ISBN 0-415-95447-9 (hardbound)
1. Drinking of alcoholic beverages. 2. Alcoholism. 3. Alcohol--Health aspects.   I. Stimson, Gerry V. (Gerry Vivian) II. Alexander, Barton.
   [DNLM: 1. Alcohol Drinking. 2. Alcoholic Intoxication--prevention & control. 3. Health Policy.   WM 274 D7795 2007]

QP801.A3D75 2007
362.292--dc22

2006019596

Visit the Taylor & Francis Web site at
http://www.taylorandfrancis.com

and the Routledge Web site at
http://www.routledgementalhealth.com

To the memory of Ed Pennington

Contents

List of Contributing Authors

Gerry Stimson*, International Harm Reduction Association, London, U.K.

Marcus Grant*, International Center for Alcohol Policies, Washington, D.C., U.S.

Marie Choquet*, Institut de Recherches Scientifiques sur les Boissons, Paris, France

Preston Garrison*, World Federation for Mental Health, Springfield, Virginia, U.S.

Barton Alexander*, Molson Coors Brewing Company, Denver, Colorado, U.S.

Mario Argandoña*, Consultant, Cochabamba, Bolivia (former Minister of Health of Bolivia)

Florence Baingana*, World Bank, Washington, D.C., U.S.

Linda Bennett*, University of Memphis, Memphis, Tennessee, U.S.

Brett Bivans, International Center for Alcohol Policies, Washington, D.C., U.S.

Russell Carvolth OAM, Consultant, Brisbane, Queensland, Australia (former Manager, Policy and Projects, Alcohol, Tobacco and Other Drugs, Queensland Department of Health)

Walter Gulbinat*, Global Network for Research in Mental and Neurological Health, Lichtenstein, Germany (former Director, Statistics, Information and Knowledge Management, United Nations International Drug Control Programme)

Hurst Hannum, University of Hong Kong, Hong Kong, China

---

* Members of the Editorial Advisory Group. The Group was chaired by Professor Norman Sartorius, University of Geneva, Geneva, Switzerland.

Mohan Isaac, University of Western Australia, Fremantle, Western Australia, Australia

Mark Leverton*, Diageo, London, U.K.

Marjana Martinic*, International Center for Alcohol Policies, Washington, D.C., U.S.

Sachio Matsushita, National Hospital Organization, Kurihama Alcoholism Center, Yokosuka, Kanagawa, Japan

Martin McKee, London School of Hygiene & Tropical Medicine, University of London, London, U.K.

John Orley*, Consultant, Guernsey, Channel Islands (former Programme Manager, Division of Mental Health, World Health Organization)

Crystal Park, University of Connecticut, Storrs, Connecticut, U.S.

Vikram Patel, London School of Hygiene & Tropical Medicine, University of London, London, U.K.

Gaye Pedlow*, Diageo, London, U.K.

Brian Quigley, Research Institute on Addictions, University at Buffalo, State University of New York, Buffalo, New York, U.S.

Godfrey Robson, Frontline Consultants, Edinburgh, U.K. (former Director of Health Policy for Scotland)

John Saunders*, University of Queensland, Brisbane, Queensland, Australia

Naotaka Shinfuku*, Seinan Gakuin University, Fukuoka, Japan (former Mental Health Advisor, World Health Organization Western Pacific Regional Office)

Daniya Tamendarova, International Center for Alcohol Policies, Washington, D.C., U.S.

Foreword

The impetus to write this book came from a shared conviction that the time had come to air some fresh approaches to alcohol policy. Hence the main title of our book: *Drinking*, because we think it is human behavior that is of greater interest, and *in Context*, because we are convinced that drinking is best viewed in relation to culture. The book focuses on the three key issues included in the subtitle: *patterns*, *interventions*, and *partnerships*. Together, these provide the context within which public policy relating to alcohol consumption can be developed in a way that respects the multiplicity of drinking cultures existing around the world.

These convictions are reflected in the diversity of the organizations that have helped to bring the book to print. The International Center for Alcohol Policies, which has taken the lead in the preparation of the book, is a think tank supported by major drinks companies. Three other organizations have also contributed their expertise to this process: the International Harm Reduction Association has extensive experience in the field of illicit drugs, the World Federation for Mental Health has a broad mandate to promote better mental health, and the Institut de Recherches Scientifiques sur les Boissons provides a welcome antidote to the Anglo-Saxon domination of the alcohol field.

In order to develop this book, an Editorial Advisory Group was formed under the chairmanship of Professor Norman Sartorius. That group met twice: once in Divonne-les-Bains, France, in April 2005 to produce the overall plan for the book; and then again in Mallorca, Spain, in March 2006 to review a draft manuscript. The writing of chapters was undertaken by individual authors and groups of authors in the period between these two meetings. Substantial revisions were then undertaken after the second meeting of the group.

The authorship of the book reflects this process*. Some authors contributed significantly to the development of the whole text; others provided shorter contributions to one or more chapters. Some of these individuals were members of the Editorial Advisory Group, and others were not. Under the overall guidance of the

---

* The opinions expressed in this book are those of the individual authors and do not necessarily reflect the views of the International Center for Alcohol Policies or its sponsoring companies, the International Harm Reduction Association, The World Federation for Mental Health, or the Institut de Recherches Scientifiques sur les Boissons.

main editor, Professor Gerry Stimson, these many contributions, some greater, some smaller, were woven together into the book as it is now. Technical editing was provided throughout by David Thompson.

This sense of collective responsibility—itself, as it happens, an underlying theme of the book—led to the decision not to attribute authorship of particular chapters to particular individuals, but rather to distinguish only between those who were the members of the Editorial Advisory Group, participating in all stages of the book's development, and those whose contributions, although important, had been more specific.

Following an introductory chapter that argues for a fresh approach to alcohol policy, we discuss how drinking patterns can provide a more nuanced way of describing drinking behavior than has been the case when the emphasis has been mainly on levels of consumption (Chapter 2). The importance of context in defining drinking patterns is repeatedly emphasized. Chapter 3 demonstrates how relatively simple assessment procedures can yield valuable insights that can form the basis for interventions.

Thus, in seeking solutions to the problems associated with inappropriate drinking behavior, the focus of this book is less on population-wide measures than on more targeted interventions that address particular issues in particular places. Chapter 4 provides an overview of these targeted interventions. A choice was made at the second Editorial Advisory Group meeting to focus in greater depth on three of these issues—alcohol-impaired driving (Chapter 5), public disorder (Chapter 6), and drinking among young people (Chapter 7)—because these are the issues that seem to be of most concern around the world and also because they have been successfully addressed with feasible interventions. We attempted in Chapter 8 to draw together the discussion of these three issues by providing an overall analytical framework that presents a pragmatic approach to assessment and to policy development (see especially Table 8.2).

The book then turns to a discussion of the relative contributions of key stake-holders and highlights the value of multi-stakeholder partnerships (Chapter 9). In Chapter 10, the issue of potential conflicts of interest is explored in order to demonstrate how to find the common ground that enables shared efforts to lead to shared solutions. The conclusion brings together some of the main themes of the book and suggests opportunities for further collaboration.

The book also includes a short annex discussing some methodological issues relating to the calculations used as the basis for the global burden of disease estimates and pointing to ways in which these could be made more useful by acknowledging the social benefits of drinking, as well as its health and social costs.

Preparing this book has been a challenging and dynamic process. Our hope is that its publication will move the debates on alcohol policy forward, both by helping to establish areas of consensus and by sharpening thinking about areas of disagreement. Clearly, nobody—least of all, the authors of this book—can pretend to have all the answers, but at least we may pride ourselves on having asked some of the right questions.

Gerry Stimson
International Harm Reduction
Association

Marcus Grant
International Center for Alcohol
Policies

Marie Choquet
Institut de Recherches Scientifiques sur
les Boissons

Preston Garrison
World Federation for Mental Health

1

New Solutions to Changing Problems

At the start of its Constitution, the World Health Organization (WHO; 2004d) defines health as "a state of complete physical, mental, and social wellbeing." This focus on the positive attributes of health as a resource for living, rather than on the presence or absence of disease and infirmity, has profound implications for health planning and for social policy generally. Although the definition distinguishes between physical, mental, and social wellbeing, it does not suggest that any one of these is preeminent. Thus, in considering any public policy related to health, its implications need to be assessed in all three of these domains.

Generally, the global trend has been toward embracing this broad definition of health. Although sudden outbreaks of infectious diseases, such as of severe acute respiratory syndrome (SARS) epidemic in 2002–2003, may temporarily focus attention upon immediate concerns for physical health, most significant health priorities of modern times are not treated as merely physical diseases. Cultural contexts and lifestyle issues are at the center of programs to prevent heart disease, the world's biggest killer, and underpin efforts to promote immunization programs. Initiatives to prevent accidents and injuries involve multi-stakeholder partnerships; and working to prevent the spread of HIV/AIDS requires the commitment of the whole of society.

The same is true of alcohol policy. Drinking beverage alcohol is a widespread source of individual and social pleasure in most countries around the world. Yet, some drinking patterns can lead to serious physical, mental, and social harms. Although the health sector has an important role in preventing these harms and providing treatment services, finding the most appropriate place for alcohol in society is a collective responsibility involving all sectors, both public and private.

DRINKING PROBLEMS IN A CHANGING SOCIAL CONTEXT

Although moderate or low alcohol consumption has been linked with clear health benefits (see, for example, National Institute on Alcohol Abuse and Alcoholism, 2003; Zakhari, 1997), certain drinking patterns are associated with a range of physical and social harms. These include both chronic health consequences (such as toxic effects on liver, heart, and other organs) and acute outcomes (such as traffic crashes, injuries, and alcohol poisoning). Clearly, the negative effects of harmful drinking are not confined to individual consumers but may have serious social impacts, affecting family and community functioning, public order, and economic productivity (for example, Blanchard & Kopp, 2001; Gmel & Rehm, 2003; Klingemann & Gmel, 2001).

Drinking patterns (described in greater detail in Chapter 2)—or how people drink and the social context in which they drink—are powerful predictors of drinking outcomes, whether positive or negative, and are influenced by culture. Culture, meanwhile, is hardly static. Globalization, urbanization, and other socioeconomic processes are transforming local conditions across borders and challenging traditional norms of behavior. The cultural context of drinking profoundly influences both problems and responses.

The prevalence of alcohol problems is changing globally, with increases in some areas and decreases in others. The 2004 *Global Status Report on Alcohol* published by WHO concluded that "globally, alcohol problems exert an enormous toll on the lives and communities of many nations" (WHO, 2004b, p. 67). According to recent research (Rehm et al., 2003; WHO, 2004b), the total national disease burden attributable to alcohol abuse is the highest in the transition economies of the former Soviet bloc, where heavy chronic and episodic drinking remains dangerously prevalent, followed by the established markets in Northern America, Europe, and the Western Pacific. WHO has also identified persistent and rising trends of detrimental drinking patterns in the populous developing countries of Asia, Latin America, and Africa, where means to address concomitant problems are limited, as well as among certain population groups internationally, especially the world's young people.

Although the international scope of the above data may obscure the diversity within each geographical grouping, these findings are in accord with recent country-level and regional work (for example, Connor, Broad, Rehm, Vander Hoorn, & Jackson, 2004; Grant, 1998; Hao, Chen, & Su, 2005; Norström, 2002; Parry, 2000; Parry et al., 2005; Saxena, 1997; U.S. Department of Health and Human Services, 2000). It must be noted, however, that the majority of available epidemiological studies originate in developed countries. Data from developing markets remain limited and inconsistent. Overall, the prevalence of alcohol-related problems internationally is changing, especially in regions with high levels of urbanization and growing disposable incomes (in developing countries) and among young people and women (in both developing and developed countries).

For example, increased urbanization in parts of Africa, Asia, and Latin America in the past several decades has diminished the influence of many traditional constraints on drinking behavior. In both urban and rural areas of the developing world, weakening or changing social controls allow for increased consumption within traditionally low-drinking or abstaining populations, such as young people and women.

Although the overall volume of drinking in emerging economies remains lower than in the developed countries, the prevalence of problem drinking is rising (Jernigan, 2001; Parry, 2000; Rehm, Greenfield, & Rogers, 2001; Riley & Marshall, 1999; Room et al., 2002; Saxena, 1997). The magnitude of resultant negative outcomes is hard to estimate. However, it is likely that they are growing in many countries, including China and India, the world's two most populous states (Benegal, 2005; Cochrane, Chen, Conigrave, & Hao, 2003; Hao et al., 2005; Isaac, 1998; Yucun & Zuxin, 1998). In China, for example, rates of alcohol-related chronic diseases and alcohol dependence have been increasing since the 1980s, particularly among the country's minority and urban communities. Epidemiological studies on the causes and scope of the country's alcohol-related problems, however, remain limited (Cochrane et al., 2003; Hao et al., 2005; Yucun & Zuxin, 1998).

Among the lower socioeconomic strata in poverty-stricken areas, excessive drinking may have substantial detrimental effects on productivity and thus on already meager family incomes. In many African countries, heavy alcohol consumption among such populations contributes to a variety of additional concerns, including domestic violence, an association between some excessive drinking patterns and the spread of HIV/AIDS, and health problems from counterfeit or low-quality alcohol (Haworth & Acuda, 1998; Haworth & Simpson, 2004; Riley & Marshall, 1999). Although the exact scale of these problems is unknown, it is reasonable to predict that they will worsen with further economic development and in the absence of adequate responses (for example, Room et al., 2002; WHO, 2004b).

Although endowed with more resources, developed countries face their own evolving set of challenges. As a result of growing gender equality, alcohol consumption among women is on the rise. Whereas the prevalence of alcohol-related problems among women and girls remains lower than among their male counterparts worldwide, this gender disparity is shrinking in many established economies, especially among the younger generations (for example, Bloomfield et al., 1999; Currie et al., 2004; Hibell et al., 2004; McPherson, Casswell, & Pledger, 2004). In some countries, such as Japan, this is a new cultural phenomenon that demands adjustments to established approaches to alcohol problems and prevention efforts (Higuchi, Suzuki, Matsushita, & Osaki, 2004; Suzuki et al., 2003).

As in developing countries, heavy episodic drinking among young people is a pressing concern. The negative consequences of youthful drinking are particularly evident in the statistics of acute health and social outcomes, such as traffic crashes, public disorder, and alcohol poisoning (for example, Brown & Tapert, 2004; Engels & Knibbe, 2000; Jernigan, 2001).

A number of large-scale studies in the United States and Europe have traced the status of and changes in this group's drinking behavior. In the United States, the overall consumption rates among high school and college-age youths remained fairly constant in the past 5 to 10 years (Johnston, O'Malley, Bachman, & Schulenberg, 2005; Substance Abuse and Mental Health Services Administration, 2004). The European data, meanwhile, exhibit broad cultural differences among young people in various countries and are a testament to the link between drinking patterns and drinking outcomes. According to the European School Survey Project on Alcohol and Other Drugs (ESPAD) (Hibell et al., 2004), alcohol-related problems among youths are the highest in areas where consumption is traditionally irregular but where drinkers often engage in episodes of excessive intake (for example, in northern European countries). Nevertheless, a trend toward harmonization of drinking habits is discernable among European youths (Currie et al., 2004; Hibell et al., 2004).

In broad terms, therefore, changing social conditions in both developing and developed countries are creating situations in which it is possible that alcohol problems could increase if appropriate public policies are not introduced. Given the range of problems and contexts, it is clear that there is no single solution, or even any fixed combination of solutions, that will be universally applicable. One size does not fit all.

MOVING BEYOND THE OLD SOLUTIONS

Because the world is changing and the place of drinking in society is being redefined, the old solutions to alcohol problems may no longer be adequate. In the past, much of the concern regarding alcohol was channeled through civil society, such as temperance movement organizations in Scandinavia and North America, where the focus was on public disorder. This perspective dominated much of the nineteenth century and the beginning of the twentieth century, leading, for example, to the introduction of Prohibition in the United States (Musto, 1997; Thornton, 1991). In the latter part of the twentieth century, the public health community became increasingly active in debates on alcohol policy, with a strong focus on the prevention of physical diseases and injuries attributable to excessive drinking. Most recently, as global concern about "binge" drinking by young people has grown, there has been a reemergence of attention to issues of social disorder.

There are important lessons to be learned from the efforts of the temperance movement and from the scientific work of the public health community. It is clear, however, that today's changing world of alcohol problems requires a balance between the freedom of individuals to drink and the need to protect those most at risk of harm. Because drinking beverage alcohol is deeply integrated into the values, cultures, and economies of so many societies, an adequate response is bound to reflect the diversity and complexity of these different contexts.

Thus, for example, a range of government departments—including trade, finance, agriculture, and education, as well as health—needs to be engaged, together with nongovernmental organizations representing a wide variety of civil society concerns. Equally, scientists and scholars from many different disciplines have insights to offer, as do professional associations. The private sector, including those involved in the production and distribution of beverage alcohol, also have important contributions to make to the process by which societies determine how best to arrange their priorities with respect to alcohol. And, of course, consumers (as well as those who choose not to consume) need to have a voice in this exchange of views. All have valid perspectives, even though some of them may not be easily compatible with each other. The challenge is to manage the collective responsibility so that the best interests of society as a whole are served.

The process of developing a new generation of alcohol policies is not based on a goal to achieve spurious consensus among parties with legitimate differences, but rather to promote full transparency in policy development, so that none of these differences is ignored. No one has a monopoly on alcohol policy. It is through partnerships, discussed in Chapters 9 and 10, that society can bring together the positive efforts by stakeholders who are not necessarily accustomed to working together, but who have much to teach each other. Such collective and complementary work can achieve much to advance public health.

Although the ongoing public debate about alcohol policy worldwide can leave the impression that population-level activities are at odds with more focused interventions, experience from other fields tells us that a combination of such initiatives can yield more positive results than a single approach. Indeed, public policy in a variety of arenas has evolved as a result of a continuum of activities from policy measures that address society at large to interventions more focused on practical solutions to emerging issues.

For instance, in the arena of environmental policy, much progress has been made over the past several decades as a result of a combination of special interest activism, government regulation, and collective industry action. Operating from a logical premise that pollution can be prevented, environmental groups across the globe have made steady progress in recent decades in establishing what has been described as the new "social ethos" that emphasizes the importance of protecting, conserving, and recycling natural resources.

This larger phenomenon of "green" mandates, both from governments and from the public at large, has been furthered both by public advocacy and by strident cleanup and cost recovery initiatives. The combination of this kind of collective responsibility—sometimes stimulated by governments, sometimes by consumers, and sometimes by the private sector—with steadfast pollution prevention campaigns has reinforced a new "green" social and consumer consciousness. Indeed, businesses around the globe now promote their environmentally conscious products and practices in marketing campaigns and coalesce in industry groups focused on responsible environmental practices and regulatory progress.

Another case in point is the public health issue of obesity and a range of related life-threatening medical conditions. Over the past several years, books such as *Fast Food Nation* (Schlosser, 2001) and documentaries such as *Super Size Me*

(Spurlock, 2004) have drawn global media attention to links between diet and health—and, more specifically, to obesity-related risk factors such as high blood pressure and high cholesterol and to conditions such as diabetes and cardio-vascular disease.

In response to this issue, at the public activism end of the spectrum, consumers have organized boycotts against companies whose products are viewed as linked to the obesity epidemic. Efforts to promote healthy dietary habits have also led to the establishment of coalitions such as the Partnership for Essential Nutrition, which launched a massive letter-writing campaign in 2004 to prevent marketers of low-carbohydrate diets from distributing information through U.S. schools. In addition, public health concerns about obesity have reached such high levels that, under a mandate from member states, WHO has developed an official *Global Strategy on Diet, Physical Activity and Health*, which was endorsed by the May 2004 World Health Assembly after detailed consultations with all relevant stakeholders, including the private sector (WHO, 2004c). Industry stakeholders have responded to public health concerns with commitments to take action—for example, the Grocery Manufacturers of America's (GMA) campaign to promote new federal dietary guidelines through school-based initiatives and to make packaged foods more healthful by incorporating more whole grains and lowering levels of saturated fat, trans fat, and sodium.

Here again, through a gamut of strategically different yet not necessarily con-flicting approaches—including consumer activism, new public policy guidelines, and an active industry involvement in health policy development—a positive evolu-tion in policy can be credited to a combination of activities. Strategies have moved away from resolutely focusing on restricting consumption toward initiatives target-ing informed and moderated consumption, so that various tactics can combine to prevent serious physical and social harms and to benefit public health.

These examples underscore a key premise that can apply to alcohol policy, whether global or local in nature: Various proposed solutions to alcohol-related problems are not necessarily at odds with one another and, on the contrary, can ultimately contribute to the combination of social, cultural, economic, and legislative changes that define true policy evolution. In recognition of the opportunities for harnessing a whole-of-society approach, a resolution adopted by the World Health Assembly in May 2005 calls for open consultations with all relevant sectors as an essential part of the development of comprehensive alcohol policy (WHO, 2005).

Given that a mix of measures is necessary to address the range and com-plexity of problems associated with harmful drinking patterns, policy-makers are faced with the task of determining which efforts are most likely to produce positive results—by preventing and mitigating physical, mental, and social harm at the same time as promoting healthier drinking patterns—in their particular societies, taking into account new trends and changing cultural contexts.

FINDING THE BEST POLICY MIX

Governments can and do influence the price and availability of alcohol, both for public health reasons and because alcohol taxation represents a significant source of government revenue in most societies where alcohol is legally sold. However, there is a danger in assuming that controls over price and availability represent an adequate solution in themselves or that, should they prove insufficient, all that is required is that they be made more rigorous. History teaches us that excessive restrictions ultimately alienate all but those ideologically committed to them. Most people expect to be able to lead their lives making choices from within a range of options that represent acceptable limits of social behavior. Each society needs to reach a broad understanding of what level of control appropriately balances freedom and protection, and this should be based on wide consultation among all interested parties.

Most governments are not particularly worried about alcohol as such. Rather, some sections of government tend to be worried about certain specific areas of alcohol-related harm. The justice department may be concerned about public disorder and underage drinking, the transport department about alcohol-impaired driving, the health department about increases in communicable and noncommunicable diseases, and so on. These concerns at government level both reinforce and are reinforced by public concerns, often expressed through the media or by special interest civil society organizations. Thus, for any particular society, there is likely to be a strong focus on a single issue, which could be teenage binge drinking, drink-driving, or an association between alcohol and AIDS. Chapters 5, 6, and 7 address in detail responses to the three issues that frequently feature in current concerns internationally: alcohol-impaired driving, public disorder, and drinking among young people.

Society expects measures to be proposed and implemented that will have the maximum impact upon whatever problem has been identified as having the highest priority. Governments increasingly look for "joined-up" solutions, which offer a broader benefit than merely the "quick fix" of attending to the concern of the day. It is exactly this combination of the specific and the general that presents an ideal opportunity to introduce a new generation of alcohol policies.

Different societies will doubtless have their own definitions of how much regulation is "reasonable." There are Islamic states that see little, if any, place for alcohol. There are countries, such as those in Scandinavia, that have long traditions of restrictive controls over the access citizens have to alcohol (see, for example, Norström, 2002). There are many countries with a workable but uncoordinated mixture of measures—some designed to encourage moderate consumption, and others to limit abuse and alcohol-related harm. And there are also countries that have few controls of any kind and no effective protection for individuals particularly at risk, such as children and young people (see WHO, 2004a). These definitions of the relative reasonableness of different levels of regulation reflect real and important cultural priorities.

Population measures, such as controls over price and availability, certainly have a legitimate place in the array of ways in which any society chooses to respond to the pleasures of drinking and the problems of immoderate consumption, but they are not in themselves a sufficient response. Just as it would be difficult to imagine a coherent alcohol policy that did not include such measures, so it would be insensitive to cultural differences to propose an alcohol policy that consisted only of such measures. Controls over price and availability are necessary, but not sufficient. The challenge is to describe the mix of other measures—all of which can be applied at the local level—that can provide the storehouse from which any society can select and adapt the approaches best suited to its own cultural preferences.

CULTURAL CONTEXT AND ALCOHOL POLICIES

In the development of alcohol policies that are intended to be relevant internationally, cross-cultural variation is of central importance. Currently, when attention *is* paid to the cultural traditions of countries participating in such endeavors, there is a strong tendency to consider mainly macropolitical and economic factors that distinguish nation-states. At the same time, there is a strong tendency to downplay cultural variation within particular national settings. This oversight, although understandable in light of the sheer effort necessary to rectify it, is a major hindrance to smooth and effective implementation of alcohol policies at the local level.

Two major flaws characterize many attempts to acknowledge the importance and relevance of culture in planning and implementing alcohol policies. First, nation-states are treated as "whole cultures" rather than a myriad of rich cultural variations. To view nations as representing a single "whole culture" is seldom an accurate or helpful depiction. Instead, it is essential to accommodate linguistic, religious, ethnic, kinship and family, gender, and age differences—among other cultural aspects—in setting forth alcohol policies intended to be applied to such groups.

Second, cultural features are viewed too often as hard and fast entities and as more or less permanent realities, rather than the result of a dynamic interaction among the people living within given cultural settings. In point of fact, cultures are constantly changing. This has been true historically, but with the phenomenal expansion of communication and transportation resources over the past century, the potential for culture change has accelerated greatly. Although it is unrealistic to expect to be able to constantly update our representation of a particular cultural milieu, we can anticipate that culture change will take place and that the relationships between groups within a society will be altered as well. This understanding can have an important impact on the effectiveness of alcohol policies.

On the one hand, lip service is often given to "cultural factors" in designing alcohol policy programs. On the other hand, the enormity of adequately addressing cultural variation, as it affects the receptivity to policy measures, typically leads to very limited attention and action. Thus, an oversimplified version of culture is often presented that really does not lead to greater effectiveness in implementation of new alcohol policies.

How do we arrive at the local-level cultural perspective on alcohol consumption that can meaningfully inform alcohol policies? In essence, to take culture seriously requires that we democratize the arena of developing alcohol policies. We need to assess—through firsthand contact—the perspectives and the behaviors of the cultural constituents whom given measures are supposed to engage. Guessing from afar or through "expert" opinions will not suffice. Observation, conversation, and interpretation from direct interaction with the people who will be affected by the policies must take place. Otherwise, such efforts are highly likely to be ineffective and possibly harmful with regard to intended outcomes.

An array of factors needs close consideration in developing culturally appropriate policy measures: linguistic differences, as they reflect understanding of alcohol consumption and its potentially positive and negative effects; religious variation and its perspective on alcohol; ethnic divisions, alliances, and shifts in ethnic identity; kinship and family ties; gender; age cohorts, especially in terms of the age at which drinking becomes acceptable; and informal controls on alcohol consumption and effects. In addition, any discussion of alcohol policy needs to take into account broader cultural views on the relationship between the individual and society, balancing personal freedoms with state controls. This is what an approach based on collective responsibility is seeking to achieve—the inclusion of all those who have a contribution to make to the process and outcome of alcohol policy development.

Equally, the exercise of individual responsibility is optimized by the ability to make informed choices. An informed choice implies that it is made on the basis of information provided for or otherwise acquired by the individual. Such information is, in part, available through education, be it formal education or the informal learning processes involving peers and family. People should be equipped with the knowledge and skills to make informed decisions about whether or not to drink. If they choose to drink, education and information should guide them, enabling them to obtain the benefits of drinking moderately while minimizing harm. Thus, an "informed choice" is most likely to occur when an individual has the skills to make decisions based on an ability to sift through the information and to weigh the risks and the benefits of alcohol consumption without being swayed by emotional pressures from others.

Individuals are assumed to be constantly making judgments about whether the pleasure derived from an activity is sufficient to undergo a certain level of risk. Individuals, however, are often not very good at assessing risk: At times, they may seem to overestimate risk (for example, from crime), and, at others, to underestimate it. Even then, a particular personal choice depends not just on whether there is risk, but also on the weight given to the risk. As one heavy drinker put it, "I'm here to enjoy life, not just to avoid dying" (Frederick, 1993, p. 5, as cited in MacAvoy & Mackenzie, 2005).

REFERENCES

Babor, T. F., Caetano, R., Casswell, S., Edwards, G., Giesbrecht, N., Graham, K., et al. (2003). *Alcohol: No ordinary commodity. Research and public policy.* Oxford: Oxford University Press.

Benegal, V. (2005). India: Alcohol and public health. *Addiction, 100,* 1051–1056.

Blanchard, N., & Kopp, P. (2001). Le coût social de l'alcool en France [The social cost of alcohol in France]. *Alcoologie et Addictologie, 23,* 125–129.

Bloomfield., K., Ahlström, S., Allamani, A., Choquet, M., Cipriani, F., Gmel, G., et al. (1999). *Alcohol consumption and alcohol problems among women in European countries.* Berlin, Germany: Institute for Medical Informatics, Biostatistics and Epidemiology, Free University of Berlin (EU BIOMED-II).

Brown, S. A., & Tapert, S. F. (2004). Health consequences of adolescent alcohol use. In National Research Council and Institute of Medicine, *Reducing underage drinking: A collective responsibility, background papers.* [CD-ROM]. Committee on Developing a Strategy to Reduce and Prevent Underage Drinking, Division of Behavioral and Social Sciences and Education. Washington, DC: National Academies Press.

Cochrane, J., Chen, H., Conigrave, K. M., & Hao, W. (2003). Alcohol use in China. *Alcohol and Alcoholism, 38,* 537–542.

Connor, J., Broad, J., Rehm, J., Vander Hoorn, S., & Jackson, R. (2004). *The burden of death, disease and disability due to alcohol: Report to ALAC.* Auckland: University of Auckland and Alcohol Advisory Council of New Zealand.

Currie, C., Roberts, C., Morgan, A., Smith, R., Settertobulte, W., Samdal, O., et al. (Eds.). (2004). *Young people's health in context. Health Behavior in School-aged Children (HBSC) study: International report from the 2001/2002 survey.* Copenhagen, Denmark: WHO Regional Office for Europe.

Engels, R. C. M. E., & Knibbe, R. A. (2000). Young people's alcohol consumption from a European perspective: Risks and benefits. *European Journal of Clinical Nutrition, 54*(Suppl. 1), S52–S55.

Gmel, G., & Rehm, J. (2003). Harmful alcohol use. *Alcohol Research and Health, 27,* 52–62.

Grant, M. (Ed.). (1998). *Alcohol and emerging markets: Patterns, problems, and responses.* Philadelphia: Brunner/Mazel.

Frederick, D. (1993). *The fun of alcohol: A rational defense of boozing against the anti-alcohol killjoys.* Political Notes No. 80. London: Libertarian Alliance.

Hao, W., Chen, H., & Su, Z. (2005). China: Alcohol today. *Addiction, 100,* 737–741.

Haworth, A., & Acuda, S. W. (1998). Sub-Saharan Africa. In M. Grant (Ed.), *Alcohol and emerging markets: Patterns, problems, and responses* (pp. 19–90). Philadelphia: Brunner/Mazel.

Haworth, A., & Simpson, R. (Eds.). (2004). *Moonshine markets: Issues in unrecorded alcohol beverage production and consumption.* New York: Brunner-Routledge.

Hibell, B., Andersson, B., Bjarnason, T., Ahlström, S., Balakireva, O., Kokkevi, A., et al. (2004). *The ESPAD Report 2003: Alcohol and other drug use among students in 35 European countries.* Stockholm: Swedish Council for Information on Alcohol and Other Drugs (CAN) and the Pompidou Group at the Council of Europe.

Higuchi, S., Suzuki, K., Matsushita, S., & Osaki, Y. (2004). *Young people's drinking behavior in Japan*. Paper presented at Symposium 40, "Young People's Drinking—International Perspective," 18th World Congress of the World Association for Social Psychiatry, Kobe, Japan. Retrieved April 7, 2005, from http://www.icap.org/download/Kobe/Higuchi_WASP.pdf.

Isaac, M. (1998). India. In M. Grant (Ed.), *Alcohol and emerging markets: Patterns, problems, and responses* (pp. 145–175). Philadelphia: Brunner/Mazel.

Jernigan, D. H. (2001). *Global status report: Alcohol and young people*. Geneva, Switzerland: World Health Organization.

Johnston, L. D., O'Malley, P. M., Bachman, J. G., & Schulenberg, J. E. (2005). *Monitoring the Future: National results on adolescent drug use. Overview of key findings 2004*. Bethesda, MD: National Institute on Drug Abuse.

Klingemann, H., & Gmel, G. (Eds.). (2001). *Mapping the social consequences of alcohol consumption*. Dordrecht, the Netherlands: Kluwer.

MacAvoy, M., & Mackenzie, M. (2005). Government regulation, corporate responsibility, and personal pleasure: A public health perspective from New Zealand. In M. Grant & J. O'Connor (Eds.), *Corporate social responsibility and alcohol: The need and potential for partnership* (pp. 81–96). New York: Routledge.

McPherson, M., Casswell, S., & Pledger, M. (2004). Gender convergence in alcohol consumption and related problems: Issues and outcomes from comparisons of New Zealand survey data. *Addiction, 99*, 738–748.

Musto, D. F. (1997). Alcohol control in historical perspective. In M. Plant, E. Single, & T. Stockwell (Eds.), *Alcohol: Minimising the harm. What works?* (pp. 10–25). New York: Free Association Books.

National Institute on Alcohol Abuse and Alcoholism. (2003). *State of the science report on the effects of moderate drinking*. Rockville, MD: U.S. Department of Health and Social Services.

Norström, T. (Ed.). (2002). *Alcohol in postwar Europe: Consumption, drinking patterns, consequences and policy responses in 15 European countries*. Stockholm: National Institute of Public Health.

Parry, C. D. H. (2000). Alcohol problems in developing countries: Challenges for the new millennium. *Suchtmedizin in Forschung und Praxis, 2*, 216–220.

Parry, C. D. H., Plüddemann, A., Steyn, K., Bradshaw, D., Norman, R., & Laubscher, R. (2005). Alcohol use in South Africa: Findings from the first Demographic and Health Survey (1998). *Journal of Studies on Alcohol, 66*, 91–97.

Rehm, J., Greenfield, T. K., & Rogers, J. D. (2001). Average volume of alcohol consumption, patterns of drinking, and all-cause mortality: Results from the U.S. National Alcohol Survey. *American Journal of Epidemiology, 153*, 6471.

Rehm, J., Rehn, N., Room, R., Monteiro, M., Gmel, G., Jernigan, D., et al. (2003). The global distribution of average volume of alcohol consumption and patterns of drinking. *European Addiction Research, 9*, 147–156.

Riley, L., & Marshall, M. (1999). *Alcohol and public health in 8 developing countries*. Geneva, Switzerland: World Health Organization.

Room, R., Jernigan, D., Carlini-Marlatt, B., Gureje, O., Mäkelä, K., Marshall, M., et al. (2002). *Alcohol in developing societies: A public health approach*. Helsinki, Finland: Finnish Foundation for Alcohol Studies.

Saxena, S. (1997). Alcohol, Europe and the developing countries. *Addiction, 92*(Suppl. 1), S43–S48.

Schlosser, E. (2001). *Fast food nation*. New York: Houghton Mifflin.

Spurlock, M. (Director/Producer). (2004). *Super size me* [Motion picture]. Los Angeles: Roadside Attractions.

Substance Abuse and Mental Health Services Administration. (2004). *Overview of findings from the 2003 National Survey on Drug Use and Health*. Rockville, MD: Author.

Suzuki, K., Osaki, Y., Minowa, M., Wada, K., Ohida, T., Doi, Y., et al. (2003). Japanese national survey of adolescent drinking behavior: Comparison between 1996 and 2000 surveys. *Japanese Journal of Alcohol Studies and Drug Dependence, 38*, 425–433.

Thornton, M. (1991). *The economics of prohibition*. Salt Lake City: University of Utah Press.

U.S. Department of Health and Human Services. (2000). *Tenth special report to the U.S. Congress on alcohol and health: Highlights from current research*. Bethesda, MD: Author.

World Health Organization (WHO). (2004a). *Global status report: Alcohol policy*. Geneva, Switzerland: Author.

World Health Organization (WHO). (2004b). *Global status report on alcohol 2004*. Geneva, Switzerland: Author.

World Health Organization (WHO). (2004c). *Global strategy on diet, physical activity and health*. Retrieved July 24, 2006, from http://www.who.int/dietphysicalactivity/strategy/eb11344/strategy_english_web.pdf.

World Health Organization (WHO). (2004d). *World Health Organization: Basic texts*. 44th ed. Retrieved July 24, 2006, from http://www.who.int/governance/en/.

World Health Organization (WHO). (2005, May). *WHA58.26. Public-health problems caused by harmful use of alcohol*. Retrieved July 24, 2006, from http://www.who.int/nmh/WHA58.26en.pdf.

Yucun, S., & Zuxin, W. (1998). China. In M. Grant (Ed.), *Alcohol and emerging markets: Patterns, problems and responses* (pp. 123–143). Philadelphia: Brunner/Mazel.

Zakhari, S. (1997). Alcohol and the cardiovascular system: Molecular mechanisms for beneficial and harmful action. *Alcohol Health and Research World, 21*, 21–29.

2

Patterns of Drinking and Their Outcomes

When examining the available data on alcohol consumption across populations and levels of attributed problems, one might expect that countries where consumption is generally high would also show high levels of alcohol-related harm. Conversely, where consumption is lower, mortality and morbidity levels attributable to alcohol might be expected to be lower as well. However, this seemingly intuitive relationship is not consistently found. Countries with high levels of alcohol consumption are not necessarily those in which alcohol-related mortality and morbidity are also high, and vice versa.

The relationship between drinking and outcomes is complex. This chapter reviews the available evidence on the many facets that help understand who the drinkers are, how their drinking relates to the benefits and harms they are likely to experience, and the contexts that shape their drinking behavior. Implications for how this knowledge can be applied to interventions are addressed in Chapter 4.

DRINKING PATTERNS: POPULATIONS, CONTEXTS, AND BEHAVIORS

The average amount of alcohol consumed per person in a country (known as *per capita consumption*) is a long-accepted measure of the extent of drinking. It has formed the basis for epidemiological research in the alcohol field, dating back to the work of Ledermann in the 1950s (Ledermann & Tabah, 1951). More recently, measures of per capita consumption have formed the basis of one of the most ambitious attempts to quantify the contribution alcohol makes to deaths and disease states. An analysis of this effort, the World Health Organization's (WHO) Global Burden of Disease project (Murray & Lopez, 1996), is offered in the Annex at the end of this volume.

Although per capita consumption measures are a convenient way of collecting relevant data, they are crude indicators, offering an overview of general trends across populations but failing to capture the myriad ways in which individuals drink. Whereas some people drink little or rarely become intoxicated, others have frequent bouts of heavy consumption. Still others—whether by choice, necessity, religious observance, or personal conviction—abstain from alcohol (International Center for Alcohol Policies [ICAP], 2000). Despite their short-comings, population-level measures provide a useful gross indicator of drinking. However, to completely understand the way in which people drink, the harms and benefits that may accompany their drinking, and interventions to minimize harm, it is necessary to understand the *patterns* of drinking. Over the past two decades, research into drinking patterns has yielded a wealth of information about drinkers, their behaviors, and the likely consequences of their consumption. Drinking patterns comprise a number of facets:

- the quantity of alcohol consumed per occasion;
- types of beverages being consumed;
- the duration and frequency of drinking;
- the characteristics of individual drinkers;
- the settings in which drinking takes place and activities that accompany drinking; and
- the cultural role and significance of alcohol and the social mores that surround it.

At a general level, drinking patterns describe three important aspects of alcohol consumption: *populations*, individuals or groups sharing common traits or drinking practices; *contexts* within which drinking takes place; and *behaviors* that may accompany drinking and have bearing on outcomes.

Populations

As a first step to understanding drinking patterns and their impact on outcomes, it is necessary to understand who the consumers of alcohol are. There is great variation across countries and cultures in who drinks alcohol and who does not, and why.

Several dimensions define populations of drinkers and have an impact on both how they drink and the consequences they are likely to experience. Among them are gender, age and how drinking evolves across the life span (also known as *drinking trajectories*), socioeconomic factors and educational level, and individual factors related to health and genetic predisposition to problems.

Gender. Gender plays an important role in shaping drinking behavior. In general, men are more likely than women to drink and to drink more. This difference between the sexes is in part due to social and cultural factors and the relative acceptability of drinking for men and women, and in part to physiological differences in the ability to metabolize alcohol. As a result of their physiology (body mass and water content) and generally smaller size, women experience the effects of alcohol quicker than men and at lower doses (Nolen-Hoeksema, 2004). Alcohol abuse and problems among women are also more likely to be linked with mental illness and compulsive behavior than they are in men (Plant, Miller, & Plant, 2005). However, drinking patterns, especially among women, are gradually changing in many societies as gender roles evolve. A general convergence of drinking among men and women has been described in some countries (Bloomfield et al., 1999; McPherson, Casswell, & Pledger, 2004; Wilsnack & Wilsnack, 1997).

Alcohol and Indian Women

Traditionally, men have been the predominant consumers of beverage alcohol in India, as in most societies around the world. In many developed countries, the proportions of men and women who drink have been converging over the past decades. This trend is also becoming apparent in some developing and transition economies. This shift is in part related to the changing roles of women, their growing presence in the workforce, and the gradual acceptance of women's drinking, even in traditionally nonpermissive societies.

Over recent years, drinking by women in India and alcohol abuse among them seem to be steadily increasing. Although neither has been systematically studied, hospital-based data for persons seeking help for alcohol-related neuropsychiatric problems give an indirect indication of the growing use and abuse of alcohol by women (Murthy, Benegal, & Murthy, 1999). According to statistics from the National Institute of Mental Health and Neurosciences (NIMHANS), Bangalore, for example, there was a fourfold increase in women registering with alcohol-related problems over a period of 12 years (from January 1983 to July 1994).

A NIMHANS report on the profile of women treated for alcohol-related problems during that period showed that 85% of them were of lower socio-economic status. A significantly large proportion of those women (65.8%) had a family history of alcohol-related problems in a first-degree relative, and 65% had an alcohol-dependent spouse. There was also a high prevalence of either preceding or concurrent psychiatric and/or medical morbidity. Bingeing and solitary drinking were common. Although female patients typically began drinking later in life than men, there is evidence that the age at which both men and women developed the various problems that prompted consultation was similar (Murthy et al., 1999).

Age. Age is another important influence on how people drink. Drinking patterns generally change over the course of an individual's lifetime. Because of their inexperience with alcohol, general propensity for risk taking, and physiological susceptibility, young people are considered to be at particular risk for harm from drinking (for example, Brown & Tapert, 2004; Brown, Tapert, Granholm, & Delis, 2000; Spear, 2004). Much effort has been devoted to addressing how young people drink, as well as to the influences that may modify their consumption patterns. The relationship between young people and alcohol is discussed in detail in Chapter 7.

Age is a factor not only in the young but also in older adults. In general, older people drink less than their younger counterparts, and older individuals tend to drink less as they age (Moore et al., 2005; Moos, Schutte, Brennan, & Moos, 2004). Retirement from active employment, loss of a life partner, and changes in lifestyle associated with old age modify the drinking habits of older adults.

Research suggests that older people who continue to drink moderately are generally more active, possess stronger social networks, and are less likely to suffer from cognitive impairments than nondrinkers (Hajat, Haines, Bulpitt, & Fletcher, 2004). At the same time, physiological changes, health status, and the increased need for medications may require that older individuals limit their alcohol consumption.

Social and Economic Factors. The interaction of social class, education, marital status, and ethnicity with drinking patterns has been described for various cultures around the world. It contributes to how people drink, their views on alcohol, its role in society, and, to some degree, the outcomes they may experience. Social and economic status, for example, are instrumental in shaping drinking behavior. In some cultures, certain drinking behaviors are thought to reflect manliness, valor, upward social mobility, and boundaries between ethnic groups (Heath, 1995, 2000). The implications of these relationships for prevention, particularly through behavioral changes, are significant.

The affordability of alcohol relates closely to patterns. For example, in countries throughout the developing world, Western-type commercially produced beverages are generally confined to more affluent urban populations. Traditional non-commercial beverage types are prevalent in rural communities, as well as among the urban poor, and may present a public health problem in terms of low quality or contamination (Haworth & Simpson, 2004). In some societies, particularly in developed countries, higher income and education levels appear to be associated with more frequent drinking (for example, Almeida-Filho et al., 2005; Oksuz & Malhan, 2005). Being married and employed also correlates with more frequent alcohol consumption, although not necessarily with heavier drinking (Moore et al., 2005; Zins, Gueguen, Leclerc, & Goldberg, 2003). Whereas alcohol intake may be less frequent among those in lower socioeconomic categories, data show that their drinking is likely to be heavier on a given occasion and is likely to occur as a group activity (Burger, Mensink, Bergmann, & Pietrzik, 2003; Casswell, Pledger, & Hooper, 2003).

There is some indication that patterns of excessive consumption may be closely related to social and economic factors in countries undergoing rapid social and economic change (Kopp, Skrabski, & Szekely, 2002). Thus, high unemployment, poverty, and resulting frustration have been linked to heavy and excessive drinking in cultures from Micronesia (Marshall, 1979; Plange, 1998) to Eastern Europe (Makinen, 2000; Walberg, McKee, Shkolnikov, Chenet, & Leon, 1998).

The outcomes of drinking, especially of heavy drinking, are also modified by social and economic factors. Low social and economic status are often associated with poor nutrition and health, resulting in heightened risk for harm (for an overview, see Marmot & Wilkinson, 1999). Socioeconomic status may determine access to adequate health care. Those at the bottom of the social and economic scales are often denied access to screening, guidance, and treatment available to individuals who are better off.

Genetic and Biomedical Factors. Much research has been conducted on the genetic underpinnings of increased sensitivity to alcohol and predisposition to alcohol dependence. Both human and animal studies have contributed to the body of knowledge (Haber, Jacob, & Heath, 2005; Heilig & Sommer, 2004; Schuckit, 2000; Wilhelmsen & Ehlers, 2005). Currently, over 60 genes have been found to respond in a significant way to alcohol and may be involved in mediating dependence. Many of these genes are related to the neurochemical responses to alcohol within the central nervous system (Javors, Tioururine, & Prihoda, 2000; Lingford-Hughes et al., 2005).

Genetic factors also underlie why some individuals who are not alcohol-dependent experience greater adverse outcomes from drinking than do others. These predisposing factors may manifest themselves as low tolerance to alcohol and differential metabolism of alcohol through the enzymes alcohol dehydrogenase (ALH) and aldehyde dehydrogenase (ALDH), which reduce the ability to break down alcohol. This trait has been observed in certain Asian populations (Edenberg et al., 2004; Wall, Horn, Johnson, Smith, & Carr, 2000), among some Ashkenazi Jews (Neumark et al., 2004), as well as among some Native Americans and certain indigenous populations in South America (Gill, Eagle Elk, Liu, & Dietrich, 1999). Individuals who have inherited this trait exhibit the well-known "flushing reaction" after drinking even a small quantity of alcohol. This response may confer a protective effect against dependence.

Certain medical conditions—such as diabetes, hypertension, and hepatitis C—may also modify the likely effects of drinking (Beilin, 1995, 2004; Regev & Jeffers, 1999; Wakim-Fleming & Mullen, 2005). Similarly, the interaction of alcohol with a range of medications may increase risk for alcohol-related harm, reduce the drugs' effectiveness, or even trigger dangerous reactions to the medications (see, for example, Ramskogler et al., 2001). In particular, adverse interactions have been described for analgesics, antihistamines, psychopharma-cologically active drugs, anticoagulants, antihypertensive drugs, and antibiotics (Weathermon & Crabb, 1999).

Contexts

The second dimension of drinking patterns relates to the context within which an individual finds him- or herself with regard to drinking—namely, the prevailing culture around alcohol in a given society, its acceptability and the general social mores around it, as well as what types of beverages are consumed. Context also includes the various external influences that help shape views on drinking and behaviors that may accompany it.

Culture. The role and significance of alcohol vary across cultures, as do tolerance of drinking, its social impact, and the acceptability of drinking among different groups, including women, older adults, and young people (Heath, 1995, 2000; MacAndrew & Edgerton, 1969). Cultural differences play a significant role in the potential outcomes of drinking.

Most cultures where alcohol is consumed may be divided into three broad categories: wine cultures, as in the Mediterranean region; beer cultures, as throughout much of Europe and Africa; and spirits cultures, including Eastern Europe, the Scandinavian countries, and regions of Asia. The preferred choice of beverage often relates to the drinking style prevalent in a particular country or region. Whereas the Mediterranean pattern, for example, is generally associated with drinking in moderation and with meals, the Scandinavian pattern is known as one of binge drinking.

In recent years, however, the clear delineation between various drinking cultures has been disappearing. Traditionally wine-drinking cultures are increasingly showing a taste for beer, whereas those characterized by their preference for spirits are consuming more wine (Simpura & Karlsson, 2001). Across Europe, traditional drinking patterns are slowly converging (see Österberg & Karlsson, 2003; Simpura, 2001). In addition, various novelty drinks are growing in popularity among some groups (for example, young people and women). In many developing countries, particularly in urban areas, "Western" beverages and consumption patterns have displaced traditional drinks and behaviors. The resulting outcomes are attributable to more than just changes in tastes, but to changing norms around alcohol and its integration into the social fabric.

Cultural differences in drinking patterns can also be found within individual countries. Attitudes toward drinking, traditions, and cultural values are often preserved among ethnic and national groups in multicultural societies. Even where the level of acculturation is high, drinking patterns may differ. In the United States, for example, Whites drink more than other ethnic groups (Moore et al., 2005). Similarly, in the United Kingdom, Black and Asian groups are less likely to drink than Whites (Rodham, Hawton, Evans, & Weatherall, 2005). Acculturation, shifts in population demographics, and evolving gender roles eventually influence changes in drinking patterns. However, these changes are slow, and traditions and norms linger over generations (McCambridge, Conlon, Keaney, Wanigaratne, & Strang, 2004; Orford, Johnson, & Purser, 2004; Schiff, Rahav, & Teichman, 2005).

Noncommercial Alcohol. What people drink is an important element of their pattern of drinking and may influence drinking style, as well as potential outcomes. Beverage alcohol can be divided into two basic categories: commercial products and those made outside of commercial settings, or noncommercial alcohol. Within the category of commercially produced alcohol, wine, beer, and distilled spirits are the most common, and are all subject to regulation and standards of quality and purity. These beverages are taxed, and their sale is officially recorded, furnishing both revenue and government statistics.

The category of noncommercial alcohol is less straightforward. The production and consumption of such beverages are steeped in tradition and culture and have been an integral part of many societies the world over (Haworth & Simpson, 2004). Some noncommercial alcohol is illicitly produced and available only through the black market, whereas other beverages are produced specifically for home consumption or for limited local trade.

Noncommercial alcohol is used widely around the world. It ranges from traditionally brewed beverages such as opaque beers, consumed throughout large parts of Africa, to distilled *urrack* and arrack in India, and to home-produced wines and fruit distillates such as grappa, *Obstler*, and *palinka* in European countries. According to some estimates, roughly half of all alcohol consumed around the world can be classified as "noncommercial" (Haworth & Simpson, 2004).

Noncommercial Alcohol: India and Sri Lanka

According to official statistics, percentages of drinkers are low and those of abstainers are high in the countries of Southeast Asia, including India and Sri Lanka (World Health Organization [WHO], 2004). However, it is believed that official data on per capita consumption do not reveal a complete picture of prevailing drinking patterns. According to some estimates, about half of all beverage alcohol consumed around the world is noncommercial, and this figure may be significantly higher in developing regions. Noncommercial beverages include both legally produced and illicit products that are brewed, distilled, or fermented in different ways according to traditional recipes or as counterfeit beverages to be sold on the black market.

In India, traditional spirits ("country liquor") and Indian-made commercial products, particularly whisky, account for more than 90% of all the alcohol consumed (Benegal, 2005; Gupta, Saxena, Pednekar, & Maulik, 2003). *Country liquor* includes distilled beverages made from locally available cheap raw materials, such as sugar cane, rice, or wheat, with alcohol content between 25 and 45% pure ethanol. The most commonly consumed beverage type is arrack, which is comparatively cheap and is sold through a government-licensed countrywide network of outlets.

Data from Karnataka State show that more than 40% of all alcohol consumed in that state is unrecorded (Benegal, Gururaj, & Murthy, 2003). Much of it is illicit distilled spirits, produced clandestinely in small production units. Illicit liquor is popular among the poorer sections of the population, as it is cheaper than government-licensed arrack (WHO, 2004). Mohan, Chopra, Ray, and Sethi (2001) noted that in many parts of India, production and marketing of liquor form a cottage industry, in which each village has one or two units operating illegally.

Patterns of consumption of both licit and illicit beverage alcohol are highly variable across India. Policies on the production, quality control, taxation, and distribution of alcohol vary from state to state, and whereas the sale of alcohol is officially prohibited in some states, it is legal in others. However, the noncommercial beverage alcohol market is thriving. Socioeconomic factors, actual cost of the beverage, and ease of access contribute to variations in the patterns of consumption (Gaunekar et al., 2004).

Few cross-sectional surveys have reported the prevalence of alcohol use in Sri Lanka during the past decade. A survey among 1,200 people in Gampaha District showed that 37.7% of men and 1.6% of women had consumed alcohol during the fortnight preceding the interview; these men and women were classified as "regular drinkers." The per capita annual consumption of alcohol in the sample was 5.6 liters for men and 0.055 liters for women (WHO, 2004). However, it is believed that—as in other Asian countries—official data on per capita consumption in Sri Lanka do not reveal the true drinking pattern. Much of the alcohol consumed in the country is an illicit brewed drink, *kasippu*. According to some estimates, about 90% of the total alcohol consumed in the country is unrecorded and consists of *kasippu*. *Kasippu* drinkers outnumber licit drinkers by 20 to 1.

Sri Lanka is a country with relatively high suicide rates compared to the rest of the world. Abeyasinghe (2002) noted that more than 60% of male suicides in Sri Lanka were related to alcohol dependence, particularly on *kasippu*. Baklien and Samarasinghe (2003), who studied the relationship between alcohol and poverty in nine marginalized communities throughout Sri Lanka, reported that *kasippu* was the most frequently used beverage alcohol across the country. A substantial proportion of the income of low-income families was spent on alcohol, with 7% of men reporting that their alcohol expenditure was greater than their income. The authors also noted that the highest proportion of daily drinkers was among those with the least formal education.

The noncommercial alcohol market has been linked with a number of important health and social outcomes. Alcohol-related road traffic crashes and domestic violence have been associated with abusive drinking patterns involving noncommercial beverages. Adulteration of products occurs in both India and Sri Lanka, as in other countries. Contamination and low-quality production related to the absence of enforceable standards and deaths from adulterated illicit products have been reported.

Home-produced beverages are not subject to the same controls as commercially produced alcohol. Contamination with methanol, heavy metals, bacteria, and other undesirable ingredients is a common cause of poisoning and health problems, especially in developing and transition countries (Holstege, Ferguson,

Wolf, Baer, & Poklis, 2004; Silverberg, Chu, Nelson, Morgan, & Todd, 2001; Szücs, Sárváry, McKee and Ádány, 2005). Illicit alcohol—often counterfeit or produced to circumvent high taxation or bans on production—is frequently reported as a source of health problems and has been linked with organized crime in a number of countries.

Although the consumption of home-produced beverages cuts across classes and groups in many countries, noncommercial alcohol is largely consumed in rural areas and may be preferred among certain ethnic or socioeconomic groups (reviewed in Haworth & Simpson, 2004). For example, ethnicity is linked to consumption of *cachaça*, a local cane spirit in Brazil. In Russia, *samogon*, a home-produced spirit, although widely consumed, is most prevalent in rural areas and among blue-collar workers, retirees, and the unemployed.

The production of noncommercial alcohol, like its consumption, is often the domain of particular groups. Women are frequently the brewers in Africa, which enables them to contribute economically to their families (Pietila, 2002). A social phenomenon in Russia, resulting from economic necessity, has been the emergence of the elderly poor—particularly retirees—as producers and sellers of *samogon* in order to supplement their income (Zaigraev, 2004).

Surrogate Alcohol in the Former Soviet Union

In countries of the former Soviet bloc, the 19th century saw the emergence of many companies engaged in large-scale commercial production of alcohol in its various forms. At the same time, in rural areas throughout this region, there is a persisting tradition of home production.

However, commercially produced beverage alcohol and noncommercial homemade products are only part of the picture. There is growing evidence that, especially in the countries of the former Soviet Union, consumption of a range of surrogate spirits is relatively widespread. These products include cheap aftershaves, perfumes, and other alcohol-containing products not intended for drinking. Yet, the low cost of these various substances, their high alcohol content, and their general availability make them attractive to those individuals who are poor and suffer from alcohol abuse or dependence.

In a study in Izhevsk, Russia, 7% of a representative sample of men aged between 25 and 54 years admitted to drinking surrogate alcohols at least weekly. The products consumed included aftershaves sold in attractively packaged 250 ml bottles, as well as a range of medicinal tinctures, sold in 30 to 50 ml containers. The former typically contain about 96% ethanol, and the latter about 66%. This compares with 44% ethanol in commercially produced Russian vodka (McKee et al., 2005). Many individuals also have access to a wide variety of alcohol-based products by virtue of their occupation. Reported examples range from surgical teams sharing surgical spirits at the end of an operating session to the aircraft engineers draining de-icing fluid from the tanks of MiG fighters. Indeed, the fuel for the R2, one of the Soviet Union's first ballistic missiles, was changed from ethanol to methanol because those guarding the missile were drinking it (White, 1995).

Settings and Venues. Alcohol is consumed in a variety of settings and venues, including private homes, bars and taverns, restaurants, sporting events, and public celebrations. As Heath (2000) pointed out, the distinction between private (or living) and public space is important in many cultures, influencing drinking behavior. In some societies, drinking is well integrated into everyday life as part of meals and social gatherings, while in others it represents a discrete activity, often to be carried out in well-defined locations. For example, alcohol consumption among the Navajo of North America is unlikely to occur near living quarters. Scandinavian drinking patterns traditionally include drinking in communal baths and saunas. Pubs and taverns are common and often primary venues for traditional drinking patterns in the United Kingdom and Ireland, and drinking in open spaces from shared vessels characterizes drinking practices in parts of Africa.

The characteristics of various drinking settings and venues—for instance, lighting, seating, crowd control, and the availability of food and beverage types—have a bearing on both consumption and potential outcomes. Certain venues, such as restaurants, are more likely to encourage drinking at a leisurely pace. Food, the key factor in how alcohol is absorbed, is less likely to accompany drinking in bars and pubs, where consumption may also be heavier and faster paced than in restaurants. The influence on drinking of certain regulations governing licensing hours has also been described. For example, an unintended consequence in some countries—for instance, in Australia (Briscoe & Donnelly, 2003; Chikritzhs & Stockwell, 2002) and Iceland (Ragnarsdottir, Kjartansdottir, & Daviosdottir, 2002)—has been to encourage heavy drinking patterns among patrons attempting to beat the clock at closing time.

Within drinking venues, various factors determine who drinks and how. Often, the patrons of drinking venues self-select. Live music or entertainment is likely to attract particular audiences, especially young people. Shebeens in South Africa, for example, are likely to cater to certain ethnic and socioeconomic groups (see Chapter 3). Martini bars, a phenomenon in urban areas in some countries, are likely to be frequented by a more affluent and upwardly mobile clientele.

Drinking settings and venues offer a powerful opportunity for intervention. A range of modifications has been identified that allows for a safer drinking environment. These modifications also offer convenient points for implementing other approaches that can help target those individuals whose drinking places them at particular risk for harm (see Chapter 6 for further discussion).

Behavior

The third dimension of drinking patterns is behavior, including both how people drink and various other activities that may accompany their drinking. Drinking culture and the general acceptability of alcohol are reflected to a large extent in drinking behavior.

Drinking and Leisure. For many people, drinking is associated with leisure time and represents a "time-out" that accompanies pleasurable activities and relaxation. In some contexts, time-out includes drinking at mealtimes and family gatherings, marking the end of the workday and the beginning of personal time. Patterns that integrate drinking within the context of normal daily leisure are characteristic of the Mediterranean drinking style and are less likely to be associated with problematic outcomes (for example, Brodsky & Peele, 1999). Where drinking is an isolated activity, engaged in for its own sake and with the end goal of drunkenness, the potential for harm is much greater.

The concept of time-out can be extended to seasonal fluctuations in alcohol consumption. In many countries, the highest consumption levels occur during summer months or holidays and may take the form of binge drinking (for example, Leifman & Gustafsson, 2004). In some cultures, drinking is reserved almost exclusively for special events and occasions, such as celebrations and festivals, although these patterns may be changing with shifts in traditional drinking (Heath, 1995, 2000).

Fiesta

In Bolivia, Ecuador, Mexico, and Peru, the traditional Andean fiesta was confined to indigenous peasants in rural and isolated villages, but is now a tourist attraction reaching beyond those communities. Traditionally, a fiesta began with a Catholic mass, followed by a procession, communal singing, and dancing. The community then indulged—for a few days—in eating, drinking, sexual licentiousness, and occasional outbursts of drunken violence. Both men and women drank heavily during the period of the local fiesta, which happened two to four times each year. However, they remained dry the rest of the year, and rarely became problematic or dependent drinkers.

The traditional Andean fiesta has now become a pattern of alcohol consumption that has permeated the whole society. This is reflected, for example, in western Bolivia, where thousands of tourists and local people, joined by the president, attend the huge fiestas in the principal cities. During these occasions, commercially produced beer and spirits are plentiful and compete with cheap, traditional, homemade fermented beverages. The choice of beverages among modern fiesta participants depends on cultural background and economic situation, but heavy episodic drinking is common, along with such consequences as car crashes, violence, unprotected sexual activity, and littering. Both the Catholic Church and the indigenous people disapprove of these transformations of the traditional fiesta, but despite their severe criticism the problems grow every year. Unfortunately, adoption of the periodic and sacred fiesta by the wider community in the Andean countries does not include the consequent abstinence for several months afterwards.

For urban and more modernized groups in Latin America, the word *fiesta* has a different meaning than for rural peasants; this difference in meaning is reflected in different patterns of drinking. For the Latin American urban middle classes, the Spanish word *fiesta* is the equivalent of the English terms *party* and/or *social gathering*. Social gatherings on occasions such as weddings, births, baptisms, birthdays, anniversaries, and funerals rely on drinks to ease the mourners' grief or enliven the celebration. Apart from such special occasions, most homes keep well-stocked bars that help to encourage impromptu gatherings and welcome visitors. Acute alcohol intoxication is commonplace when friends meet at any time. Many people believe that the only problems caused by alcohol are alcohol dependence (Sharman, 2005) and its sequels, particularly liver cirrhosis and other chronic conditions. They dismiss the risks of acute intoxication, which is not seen as a matter for concern but is rather an incentive for further drinking, as a demonstration of bravery (especially among men) and as a way of having fun and gaining love and prestige.

Heavy Drinking Episodes. A critical component of drinking behavior is the *rhythm* of heavy drinking—the extent to which heavy drinking episodes are isolated or spread out, and how frequently they occur. Together with the amount consumed on each occasion, rhythm of drinking is a likely predictor for harm (Grant & Litvak, 1998).

Heavy episodic or binge drinking is a pattern associated with elevated risk for a range of health and social harms. Across cultures, this pattern is more prevalent among men than women (for example, Carlini-Marlatt, Gazal-Carvalho, Gouveia, & Souza, 2003; Kuntsche, Rehm, & Gmel, 2004). One reason for the gender difference may relate to the acceptability of heavy drinking and intoxication—both are generally more tolerated in men (Fillmore et al., 1997; Heath, 2000). Recent findings, however, suggest that binge drinking in some countries is increasing among girls and young women (for example, Hibell et al., 2004; McPherson et al., 2004).

First experiences with heavy episodic drinking often occur in early adolescence, a period of general experimentation and risk taking. Its effects may linger into later years, and heavy episodic drinking is often predictive of later problems in adulthood (for example, Hingson & Kenkel, 2004; McCarty et al., 2004; Oesterle et al., 2004). Because of young people's vulnerability to harm, binge drinking is an issue of considerable concern for public health and the focus of much attention.

Culture plays a role, which is not explained simply by how much alcohol is consumed across a given population or in a given society. Rather, it relates to the consumption of large amounts on single occasions and is generally observed among certain groups of drinkers. There is evidence that, at least among young people, peer norms and influences and consequent pressure to adhere to perceived normative behavioral rituals may motivate binge drinking (Coleman & Cater, 2005a; Durkin, Wolfe, & Clark, 2005; Kypri & Langley, 2003).

Heavy episodic drinking is often associated with other high-risk behaviors and a range of harmful outcomes, including personal injury, unsafe sexual practices, and health problems. Emergency room admissions, drink-driving crashes, and other episodes are more frequently reported for individuals who have been drinking excessively (Quinlan et al., 2005; Savola, Niemela, & Hillbom, 2005). Various risky sexual practices combined with heavy drinking have been described, including unprotected sex and having multiple partners (Coleman & Cater, 2005b; Guo et al., 2002). Studies have also linked some heavy drinking patterns to sexual assaults (Champion et al., 2004; Mohler-Kuo, Dowdall, Koss, & Wechsler, 2004) and involvement in fights (Swahn, Simon, Hammig, & Guerrero, 2004).

Drinking and Other Behaviors. The combination of alcohol consumption with other activities plays an important role in determining potential outcomes. Similarly, drinking increases the likelihood that certain behaviors may occur; harmful relationships are often associated with heavy drinking and episodes of intoxication.

An example of a possibly harmful interaction that immediately comes to mind is that of drinking and driving, addressed at length in Chapter 5. Alcohol consumption is known to impair the ability to react quickly and to adequately judge risky situations. As a result, drivers who have consumed alcohol are more likely to be involved in traffic crashes and have a greater likelihood of experiencing fatal outcomes than those who have not been drinking. Young drivers have been found to be at particular risk, because they are inexperienced with both alcohol and driving and are more likely than adults to engage in risky consumption behaviors, such as binge drinking.

However, other activities—for example, playing sports and operating machinery, boats, or airplanes—are similarly affected by alcohol consumption. It should also be noted that pedestrians and cyclists make up a large proportion of road traffic fatalities, especially in developing countries (see, for example, International Integrated Information Networks, 2005; Transport Research Centre, 2005). In many instances, it is they, and not the drivers of motorized vehicles, who are intoxicated. Recognizing the potential risk associated with drinking settings, venues, and activities allows the development of appropriate response measures.

There has been concern, particularly in urban areas, about the incidence of public disorder and violence that are associated with particular drinking patterns. Chapter 6 addresses this issue in detail, offering opportunities for intervention that can be applied to reduce the potential for harm. It is clear that social disruption is generally related to heavy drinking episodes and intoxication. The reduction of inhibitions that comes with such drinking may open the door for violent behavior and disturbance among certain people.

Yet, there are also behaviors that mix well with drinking, and others that are encouraged by moderate alcohol consumption. These relate to social situations where drinking is part of an enjoyable and balanced lifestyle, contributing to enhanced interactions between individuals. Increased sociability, relaxation, and, ultimately, pleasure are invariably cited among the main reasons why people drink. In some drinking cultures—for example, those in southern Europe and the Mediterranean—drinking is an integral part of family gatherings and meals, and alcohol is generally regarded as food. It is important to bear in mind the social functions of alcohol and to give these positive attributes their due, as they often become obscured by the strong focus on health and the potential for harm.

RELATING PATTERNS TO OUTCOMES

The diversity of drinking patterns is reflected in the range of health, social, and economic outcomes that have been related to alcohol consumption (San Jose, van Oers, van de Mheen, Garretsen, & Mackenbach, 2000). A substantial body of evidence is now available relating some dimensions of drinking patterns—including abstention from alcohol—to particular chronic (long-term) and acute (short-term) effects (Gruenewald et al., 2002; Rehm, Room, Graham, et al., 2003). In general, harms have been linked to heavy and abusive drinking patterns, whereas benefits are generally associated with moderate drinking.

However, there is a caveat to relating drinking patterns to their possible outcomes: An association does not necessarily imply a *causal* link. Where such associations are made, other confounding influences that may modify the effects of drinking on a particular individual should also be taken into consideration. These relationships are summarized in Table 2.1.

Health Outcomes

Patterns of drinking have an impact both on physical (somatic) and mental health, and on whether the outcome is likely to be harmful or beneficial. In general, negative outcomes are primarily associated with heavy drinking, whether chronic or in the form of isolated occasions of heavy consumption that occur within an otherwise moderate pattern. Although the outcomes of each may be different, both scenarios pose a risk to health. The harmful effects of drinking have been described in detail and include both chronic and acute outcomes.

Somatic Health. Chronic harm to somatic or physical health linked to alcohol consumption is usually associated with long-term heavy drinking. It includes increased risk for a range of disease states, such as alcohol dependence, liver cirrhosis, cardiomyopathy and congestive heart failure, hemorrhagic stroke, alcoholic psychosis, cognitive and neurological impairment, and some forms of upper digestive tract and oral cancers (Blanc, Joomaye, Perney, Roques, & Chapoutot, 2001; Diehl, 1998; Jarvenpaa, Rinne, Koskenvuo, Raiha, & Kaprio,

Table 2.1 Relationship Between Drinking Pattern and Physical, Mental, and Social Outcomes, and the Role of Confounders

Drinking Pattern	Physical Health	Mental Health	Social Health	Confounding Factors
			Increased Risk for Harm	
Harms				
Heavy Drinking Sustained (A) or episodic (B)	Alcohol dependence (A) Neurological damage (A) Liver cirrhosis (A) Esophageal and laryngeal cancer (A) Colon cancer (A) Breast cancer (A) Ischemic stroke (A, B) Fetal alcohol syndrome (FAS) (A, B) Alcoholic gastritis (A) Intentional and unintentional injuries (e.g., related to traffic crashes, workplace trauma, falls, and assault) (A, B)	Dementia (A) Alcoholic psychosis (B)	Absenteeism (A, B) Suicide, depression (A, B) Family disruption (A) Crime and violence (A, B) Unwanted/unintended sexual activity (A, B) Social costs of chronic harm (A) Social costs of acute harm (A, B)	Physical and mental health outcomes Nutritional deficits (e.g., thiamine deficiency) Genetic predisposition/family history Hepatitis C Contamination and infection from low-quality beverages Smoking Diet Stress Lifestyle Access to health care (prevention and treatment) Social health outcomes Cultural permissiveness and acceptability Association not equal to causation Lifestyle Socioeconomic factors Stress

continued

Table 2.1 (continued) Relationship Between Drinking Pattern and Physical, Mental, and Social Outcomes, and the Role of Confounders

Drinking Pattern	Physical Health	Mental Health	Social Health	Confounding Factors
Benefits		**Decreased Risk for Harm**		
Moderate Drinking Sustained (A) or episodic (B)	Type II diabetes mellitus (A) Coronary heart disease (A) Hemorrhagic stroke (A) Pancreatitis (A) Osteoporosis (A) Macular degeneration (A) Cholelithiasis (gall bladder disease) (A)	Improved cognitive function and memory (especially in older adults) (A) Vascular dementia (A) Wellbeing, pleasure, and relaxation (A, B)	Quality of life (A, B) Sociability and social integration (A, B) Reduced mortality and morbidity across populations (A) Symbol of adulthood and maturity	Diet and exercise Lifestyle Socioeconomic factors Access to health care

Note: Heavy and moderate drinking patterns are associated with a number of harms and benefits that relate to physical, mental, and social health. Some are related to sustained drinking patterns (A), and others to episodic drinking (B). However, each of these outcomes may also be influenced with a range of factors external to drinking that contribute to eventual outcomes; in many cases, these factors work together to influence the final health implications.

2005; Leevy & Moroianu, 2005; Lieber, 2004; Murray et al., 2002; Puddey, Rakic, Dimmitt, & Beilin, 1999; Rehm, Sempos, & Trevisan, 2003). For women, an elevated risk for breast cancer has been described. The risk for fetal alcohol syndrome and related conditions is also elevated for children of women who are chronic heavy drinkers during pregnancy (Abel, 1998; Coles, Russell, & Schuetze, 1997). For young people undergoing developmental changes, heavy chronic or episodic ("binge") drinking may have an effect on neurological development and lead to problems later in life (Spear, 2004).

Not all health outcomes develop over the long term. Many are acute and the result of isolated drinking episodes. For example, heavy episodic drinking has been linked with cardiovascular problems, such as atrial fibrillation (Freestone & Lip, 2003; Frost & Vestergaard, 2004; Koul, Sussmane, Cunill-De Sautu, & Minarik, 2005). For pregnant women, binge drinking has been correlated with harm to the developing fetus, especially in the early stages of pregnancy (Abel, 1998; Coles et al., 1997).

Acute outcomes, including unintended injuries, make up a significant proportion of the burden of disease attributable to alcohol and correlate with heavy episodic drinking (Boutayeb & Boutayeb, 2005; Chisholm, Rehm, van Ommeren, & Monteiro, 2004; Connor, Broad, Rehm, Vander Hoorn, & Jackson, 2005; McKenna, Michaud, Murray, & Marks, 2005; Rehm, Rehn, et al., 2003; Rehm, Room, Graham, et al., 2003; Rehm, Room, Monteiro, et al., 2003; Rodgers et al., 2004). Analyses of emergency room data suggest that the severity of injuries sustained in association with drinking may depend on drinking patterns: Heavier drinking is likely to result in more severe injury (for example, Cherpitel, 1996). The risk of automobile crashes or boating accidents is also related to drinking behavior, as is the risk for injuries in the workplace and while participating in sports and other recreational activities (Chochinov, 1998).

At the same time, research evidence shows that light to moderate drinking may confer health benefits for some groups of individuals. Moderate drinkers have been found to have lower mortality rates than both abstainers and heavy drinkers (Doll & Peto, 1995; Holman, English, Milne, & Winter, 1996; Trevisan, Schisterman, Mennotti, Farchi, & Conti, 2001). The impact of moderate drinking on specific health outcomes has been described in a comprehensive overview produced by the National Institute on Alcohol Abuse and Alcoholism in the United States (Gunzerath, Faden, Zakhari, & Warren, 2004). Somatic benefits include the well-described cardio-protective effect, particularly for middle-aged men and postmenopausal women, for whom the onset of osteoporosis may also be delayed (Hines & Rimm, 2001; Mukamal, 2003; Mukamal & Rimm, 2001; Murray et al., 2002; Rehm, Sempos, et al., 2003; Trevisan, Ram, et al., 2001). The risk for ischemic stroke appears to be reduced among moderate drinkers, as is the risk for type II diabetes mellitus (Nakanishi, Suzuki, & Tatara, 2003; Wannamethee, Camargo, Manson, Willett, & Rimm, 2003). Similarly, the incidence of pancreatic disease and macular degeneration is lower among moderate drinkers. Finally, there is evidence that cognitive function and memory are improved among older individuals who drink moderately, and that the risk of vascular dementia is lowered (Luchsinger, Tang, Siddiqui, Shea, & Mayeux, 2004; Mukamal et al., 2003; Ruitenberg et al., 2002; Stampfer, Kang, Chen, Cherry, & Grodstein, 2005).

The long-term benefits and harms from alcohol consumption occur on a continuum, largely determined by pattern. The case of coronary heart disease (CHD) illustrates this relationship particularly well. Whereas chronic heavy drinking is associated with an increase in CHD risk, low or moderate levels of consumption can confer benefits, especially for middle-aged men and postmenopausal women. This relationship appears to be particularly modified by the frequency of drinking.

In examining the relationship between pattern and outcomes, it is important not to lose sight of the fact that drinking is one of many dimensions of an individual's lifestyle. As a result, the impact of a particular pattern on outcome is also shaped by other influences: age and general health or other lifestyle choices, such as stress, diet, exercise, or obesity. The relationship between excessive alcohol consumption and, particularly, oral cancers, for example, is strongly influenced by smoking (Goldenberg et al., 2004; Poschl & Seitz, 2004; Sturgis, Wei, & Spitz, 2004; Zeegers, Kellen, Buntinx, & van den Brandt, 2004).

Mental Health. Alcohol problems and mental health problems often coincide, and depression, schizophrenia or schizoaffective disorders, anxiety, and bipolar disorder may place individuals at greater risk for developing alcohol dependence. Recent research has attempted to shed light on the relationship between alcohol dependence and mental disorders, as defined by the *Diagnostic and Statistical Manual of Mental Disorders*, fourth edition (*DSM-IV*; American Psychiatric Association, 1994). Data from several countries suggest that alcohol dependence is more common among individuals suffering from affective disorder (notably, depression) than among the general population. Individuals who suffer from depression are several times more likely to also abuse alcohol than those who do not (Lukassen & Beaudet, 2005; Sullivan, Fiellin, & O'Connor, 2005). A role in this relationship has been suggested for ethnicity, age, gender, and socioeconomic standing, which are also factors in access to adequate screening and treatment services for both sets of disorders. Recent evidence suggests that individuals who are younger, homeless, and male are at elevated risk for comorbid alcohol abuse and mental health disorders (Montross et al., 2005).

Mental health problems can also be the long-term result of alcohol abuse. Neurological damage and mental health impairments often develop among heavy drinkers (Deshmukh, Rosenbloom, De Rosa, Sullivan, & Pfefferbaum, 2005). Especially among older adults, long-term alcohol abuse has been shown to result in dementia (Pinder & Sandler, 2004).

Treatment of comorbid patients is a difficult prospect, and the relapse rates for alcohol abuse are high (Oslin, 2005; Sullivan et al., 2005). In addition, the effects of certain medications to treat mental disorders may be negated by alcohol use, compromising the success of treatment (Oslin). Finding successful ways of treating patients suffering from both alcohol abuse and mental health problems requires methods that may have to be tailored to the particular needs of patients. However, signs of alcohol abuse in persons suffering from mental disorders occur early on (Baethge et al., 2005) and may be helpful for early identification and other targeted interventions.

Mental Health and Alcohol in Developing Countries

At any time globally, about 1 in 10 adults in general population and about 1 in 3 adults attending a primary health center suffers from a mental disorder. Depression and anxiety (referred to as the *common mental disorders*, or CMD) and alcohol and drug abuse (referred to as the *substance abuse disorders*) are the most frequent of all mental disorders. Psychotic disorders such as schizophrenia and bipolar disorder, although relatively less common, are profoundly disabling. It is no surprise, then, that mental disorders figure prominently in the list of leading global causes of disability (Murray & Lopez, 1996). The burden is greatest during the most productive years of life, young adulthood, when about 75% of all mental disorders seen in adults begin (Kessler, Bergland, Demler, Jin, & Walters, 2005).

Developing countries, categorized as low or middle income in the World Bank's classification, account for over 80% of the world's population. Of the 400 million people with mental disorders, the vast majority lives in poor countries. Despite the enormous burden and impact of mental disorders (which include substance abuse disorders in this discussion), over 90% of global mental health resources are concentrated in rich countries. In many developing countries, for example, there is about one psychiatrist for every million people (WHO, 2005). It is not surprising, then, that the majority of individuals suffering from mental disorders do not seek professional help, and families bear the brunt of the untreated morbidity and disability.

Formal health care in the developing countries often takes the form of primary or traditional medical care, where mental disorders typically go undetected. Instead, patients may receive a cocktail of treatments targeting the various *symptoms* of mental disorders, for instance, sleeping pills for sleep problems and vitamins for fatigue (Linden et al., 1999). Psychosocial treatments are rarely provided. Typically, only persons with psychotic disorders with disturbed behavior are brought to specialist mental health services (if these are available). Here, care is heavily biased toward drug therapies. Mental illness is strongly associated with stigma (Jamison, 2006), and human rights violations and institutionalization characterize services for severe mental disorders (National Human Rights Commission, 1999).

More developing countries are turning their attention to raising the profile of mental health by designing mental health policies and increasingly implementing them (WHO, 2005). More donors are supporting mental health–related work, and interest among public health professionals and policy-makers in mental health issues is also growing. The pace of reform is excruciatingly slow, however, and with every new challenge facing the public health sector, mental health is once more relegated to the shadows. Thus, for example, mental health is completely absent from the Millennium Development Goals (MDGs) (Sachs & McArthur, 2005), which set out a vision for development focusing on health and education, in spite of mental health's close link with many of the individual MDGs (Miranda & Patel, 2005). Virtually all population-based studies of the risk factors for mental disorders—particularly, depressive and anxiety disorders and substance abuse disorders—consistently show higher prevalence among the poor and marginalized. Mental disorders also impoverish people through the costs of health care and as a result of lost employment opportunities (Patel & Kleinman, 2003); treatment may, therefore, help people rise out of poverty.

For many years, we lacked evidence that anything could be done for mental disorders in poor countries. However, a number of clinical trials have been published recently from across the developing world, demonstrating the efficacy and cost-effectiveness of locally feasible treatments for depression, schizophrenia, and substance abuse. Studies have demonstrated that community care for schizophrenia is feasible and leads to superior clinical and disability outcomes. Both antidepressant and psychosocial treatments are efficacious for depression (Patel, Araya, & Bolton, 2004). Community initiatives can help reduce the rates of substance abuse disorders (Wu, Detels, Zhang, Li, & Li, 2002). Perhaps the best examples that management of suffering is possible derive not from trials, but from the remarkable work of grassroots organizations implementing mental health interventions (Patel & Thara, 2003).

Despite the growing number of studies on the prevalence of alcohol consumption and alcohol use disorders in developing countries (for example, Riley & Marshall, 1999; WHO, 2004), much remains to be done. There is wide variation in the study methods used, including how alcohol use and various disorders are defined, as well as in the sampling strategies. These variations make comparisons difficult. Typically, surveys target populations considered to be at high risk, for example, young people, individuals in primary health care, or those in psychiatric facilities. The very weak evidence base on the association of alcohol use and mental health in developing countries, particularly from a population perspective, needs to be acknowledged from the outset. Investigating the adverse mental health correlates of alcohol use must adequately account for the possible role of confounders. If there is little evidence on the associations between mental health and alcohol abuse, there is even less on the associations between moderate drinking and mental health in developing countries.

However, a number of important studies indicate moderate levels of comorbidity between alcohol abuse and mental illness in developing countries.

In a study from India, a linear relationship was found between comorbidity of mental disorders and alcohol and poorer quality of life (Singh, Mattoo, Sharan, & Basu, 2005). Studies carried out in population-based settings also reveal a strong association among hazardous drinking, poor mental health (especially, depressive and anxiety disorders), and suicide. In particular, two studies on the association of alcohol use and mental health were carried out on a sample of male industrial workers in Goa, India. A survey of 1,013 workers found that a fifth of all respondents were hazardous drinkers (Silva, Gaunekar, Patel, Kukalekar, & Fernandes, 2003). In general, these men had begun drinking at an earlier age and had lower educational levels than nonhazardous drinkers. Although hazardous drinkers were significantly more likely to recognize that they had a drinking problem, only a small proportion (14%) had sought help for their problem. Hazardous drinkers were significantly more likely to be suffering from a common mental disorder (depressive or anxiety disorders) or to have experienced an adverse health outcome, such as hospital admission. Thus, this study demonstrated a significant degree of comorbidity between CMD and hazardous drinking, similar to that reported by researchers in developed countries (Hickie, Koschera, Davenport, Naismith, & Scott, 2001; Lynskey, 1998).

In a subsequent case-control investigation of the impact of alcohol consumption, two groups of drinkers (hazardous and nonhazardous or moderate drinkers) were compared with a group of abstinent men (Gaunekar, Patel, & Rane, 2005). Hazardous drinkers reported a higher number of sick leave days, increased rates of tobacco use, more frequent injury in the form of fractures, higher disability scores, more money spent on health, and poorer mental health. Whereas hazardous drinkers did not report any financial difficulties, their spouses were more likely to attribute financial difficulties to their husbands' drinking. As compared to moderate drinkers, hazardous drinkers tended to drink alone and in bars, and preferred noncommercial alcoholic beverages, which are cheaper and have relatively high alcohol concentration. These findings suggest that the adverse association between Indian male alcohol use and mental health is concentrated among men who drink hazardously.

Similar relationships have been reported elsewhere in the world. In some Eastern European countries, a strong association between per capita alcohol consumption and suicide rates has been reported (WHO, 1999). In Chile, in the early 1980s, 38.6% of suicides were reported to be "alcohol-related"; a more recent study from Ethiopia reported a linear relationship between adolescent suicide attempts and alcohol consumption (WHO, 1999). Several causal explanations have been cited. For example, alcohol may disinhibit suicidal impulses (and aggression in general), whereas chronic and heavy alcohol use may lead to a gradual disintegration of the person's social life, depression, and, thus, an elevated risk of suicide.

Another important consequence of drinking in developing countries is related to the mental health of individuals living with problem drinkers.

Several studies from developing countries have shown higher levels of family dysfunction and family violence among alcohol-dependent individuals and alcohol abusers (Gaunekar et al., 2005). Spouses (most often, female) of alcoholics were reported to suffer from significant stress levels and various physical and mental health problems. It should be noted, however, that these studies were conducted either with samples of alcohol-dependent subjects or in clinical populations.

Studies carried out among individuals in primary care in India showed significantly higher rates of depressive and anxiety disorders among women (Patel et al., 1998). In this population, concerns about spousal drinking behavior and the related experience of domestic violence were key risk factors. Higher rates of common mental disorders in women have been found in virtually all studies from developing countries (and, indeed, also in developed countries); gender disadvantage, intimate partner violence, and alcoholism were cited as major factors to explain this increased risk (Patel, Araya, Lima, Ludermir, & Todd, 1999). A recent community survey of women in India has confirmed these hypotheses: Depressive and anxiety disorders were strongly—and independently—associated with intimate partner violence and concerns about husbands' drinking habits (Patel et al., 2006).

Social Outcomes

Drinking patterns are also strong predictors of certain social and economic outcomes (Stockwell, Chikritzhs, & Brinkman, 2000). Heavy chronic and episodic drinking has been found to contribute to the risk for interpersonal violence and aggression for some people (Britton et al., 2003; Caetano, Schafer, Clark, Cunradi, & Raspberry, 2000; Krug, Dahlberg, Mercy, Zwi, & Lozano, 2002; Wells & Graham, 2003). In addition, excessive alcohol consumption may result in impaired job performance, loss of productivity, and loss of employment (Anderson & Larimer, 2002; McFarlin & Flas-Stewart, 2002), whereas moderate drinking that is integrated into a healthy lifestyle correlates with higher earning potential when compared to both heavy drinking and abstention (French & Zarkin, 1995).

There is evidence suggesting that individuals in certain professions are more likely to have risky drinking patterns. This association may reflect an amalgam of consumption, demographics, and situational contexts rather than a neat relationship, but it is worth noting. For example, journalists and bartenders often appear to have drinking patterns that place them at higher risk for harm (Brewer, 2001). Particular attention has been paid to drinking patterns among physicians (Rosta, 2002; Rosta & Aasland, 2005), pilots (Cook, 1997), and others whose performance in the workplace may be impaired by alcohol and have an impact on others around them.

Drinkers themselves are not the only ones affected by heavy chronic and episodic consumption. Secondary effects have also been described: They include violence; difficulties with drunken associates, family members, or friends; and a lowered quality of life because of public disorder and safety issues (for example, Single et al., 1997; Wechsler, Lee, Hall, Wagenaar, & Lee, 2002).

Calculations have been made of the social cost of abusive and heavy patterns of drinking (Blanchard & Kopp, 2001; Klingemann & Gmel, 2001; Murray & Lopez, 1996, 1999), including the disease burden due to lost productivity and life years—disability adjusted life years, or DALYs (Rehm, Rehn, et al., 2003; Rehm, Room, Graham, et al., 2003; Rehm, Room, Monteiro, et al., 2003). However, the picture remains incomplete. A comprehensive analysis requires attention to both costs and benefits—harms weighed against the positive effects of moderate drinking for health and social issues (see the Annex for further discussion). In addition, although data exist for developed countries, there remains a dearth of information about developing countries around the world (Grant, 1998; Murray & Lopez, 1996). A reliable picture of the global social cost of alcohol consumption must include calculations of both harms and benefits and a reasonable estimation of the actual burden attributable to alcohol (without myriad confounding factors) in developing countries.

Just as certain drinking patterns confer health benefits upon some individuals, they can also contribute to social wellbeing and carry with them positive cultural connotations, such as symbolizing maturity or adulthood. For many people, drinking is a means of achieving relaxation and reducing stress (Grant & Peele, 1999; Peele & Brodsky, 2000), and subjective assessments of quality of life may include drinking as one of a number of pleasurable activities (Orley, 1999; Strandberg, Strandberg, Salomaa, Pitkälä, & Miettinen, 2004). To date, there is no means of assessing the value of this contribution of alcohol in a quantitative fashion. As addressed in the Annex, the inability to include the positive psychosocial contribution of alcohol to health and wellbeing in any calculations of net benefit and harm represents a significant confounder in the available analyses.

FROM PATTERNS TO POLICY

Drinking patterns vary significantly across countries and cultures. Across centuries and across national borders, humankind has found myriad ways to consume alcohol. If alcohol is no ordinary commodity, nor is it an ordinary risk factor for health and social problems (see Annex). Drinking alcohol confers benefits as well as harms. Indeed, drinking is not just a risk to the physical, mental, and social aspects of health, but it also contributes to physical, mental, and social wellbeing.

The rich variation in drinking patterns, and how they change over time, must give the public and the policy-maker cause for sober thought. First, drinking patterns are not set in stone. It might seem quite "normal and natural" in some countries that young men get drunk and fight. In others, such behavior would be seen as unnatural. Drinking is malleable, and hence can be changed for the better so as to maximize social and individual benefits and minimize harms. Second, there is no single quick policy "fix." Population-level interventions (such as pricing and availability) are insensitive to local variation in drinking behavior. For the purposes of policy and prevention, a comprehensive alcohol policy needs population-level interventions, but there is also a need to disaggregate populations in order to develop a more nuanced and comprehensive approach to reducing alcohol-related harms. A focus on drinking patterns offers opportunities to create interventions that specifically target harm; fit the needs of particular populations, cultures, and settings; and create safer drinking environments. An understanding of such patterns also opens the door to approaches that are proactive, aiming to minimize risk rather than simply responding to harm. Selecting the interventions that are right for particular populations, contexts, or behaviors requires getting beneath the data on overall population consumption. We turn to that in the next chapter.

REFERENCES

Abel, E. L. (1998). *Fetal alcohol abuse syndrome*. New York: Plenum.

Abeyasinghe, R. (2002). *Illicit alcohol: Drinking culture in Colombo*. Colombo, Sri Lanka: Vijitha Yapa.

Almeida-Filho, N., Lessa, I., Magalhaes, L., Araujo, M. J., Aquino, E. A., Kawachi, I., et al. (2005). Alcohol drinking patterns by gender, ethnicity, and social class in Bahia, Brazil. *Revista De Saude Publica, 38*, 45–54.

American Psychiatric Association. (1994). *Diagnostic and statistical manual of mental disorders*, 4th ed. Washington, DC: Author.

Anderson, B. K., & Larimer, M. E. (2002). Problem drinking and the workplace: An individualized approach to prevention. *Psychology of Addictive Behaviors, 16*, 243–251.

Baethge, C., Baldessarini, R. J., Khalsa, H. M., Hennen, J., Salvatore, P., & Tohen, M. (2005). Substance abuse in first-episode bipolar I disorder: Indications for early intervention. *American Journal of Psychiatry, 162*, 1008–1010.

Baklien, B., & Samarasinghe, D. (2003). *Alcohol and poverty in Sri Lanka*. Colombo, Sri Lanka: FORUT.

Beilin, L. J. (1995). Alcohol, hypertension and cardiovascular disease. *Journal of Hypertension, 13*, 939–942.

Beilin, L. J. (2004). Update on lifestyle and hypertension control. *Clinical and Experimental Hypertension, 26*, 739–746.

Benegal, V. (2005). India: Alcohol and public health. *Addiction, 100*, 1051–1056.

Benegal, V., Gururaj, G., & Murthy, P. (2003). *WHO Collaborative project on unrecorded consumption of alcohol: Karnataka, India*. Bangalore, India: National Institute of Mental Health and Neurosciences (NIMHANS).

Blanc, F., Joomaye, Z., Perney, P., Roques, V., & Chapoutot, C. (2001). Troubles somatiques [Somatic disorders]. *Alcoologie et Addictologie, 23*, 319–333.

Blanchard, N., & Kopp, P. (2001). Le coût social de l'alcool en France [The social cost of alcohol in France]. *Alcoologie et Addictologie, 23*, 125–129.

Bloomfield., K., Ahlström, S., Allamani, A., Choquet, M., Cipriani, F., Gmel, G., et al. (1999). *Alcohol consumption and alcohol problems among women in European countries*. Berlin, Germany: Institute for Medical Informatics, Biostatistics and Epidemiology, Free University of Berlin (EU BIOMED-II).

Boutayeb, A., & Boutayeb, S. (2005). The burden of non-communicable diseases in developing countries. *International Journal for Equity in Health, 4*, 2.

Brewer, C. (2001). Alcohol: The media are in denial. *British Medical Journal, 7312*, 580.

Briscoe, S., & Donnelly, N. (2003). Problematic licensed premises for assault in inner Sydney, Newcastle and Wollongong. *Australian and New Zealand Journal of Criminology, 36*, 18–33.

Britton, A., Nolte, E., White, I. R., Gronbaek, M., Powles, J., Cavallo, F., et al. (2003). Comparison of the alcohol-attributable mortality in four European countries. *European Journal of Epidemiology, 18*, 643–651.

Brodsky, A., & Peele, S. (1999). Psychosocial benefits of moderate alcohol consumption: Alcohol's role in a broader conception of health and wellbeing. In S. Peele & M. Grant (Eds.), *Alcohol and pleasure: A health perspective* (pp. 187–207). Philadelphia: Brunner/Mazel.

Brown, S. A., & Tapert, S. F. (2004). Health consequences of adolescent alcohol use. In National Research Council and Institute of Medicine, *Reducing underage drinking: A collective responsibility, background papers.* [CD-ROM]. Committee on Developing a Strategy to Reduce and Prevent Underage Drinking, Division of Behavioral and Social Sciences and Education. Washington, DC: National Academies Press.

Brown, S. A., Tapert, S. F., Granholm, E., & Delis, D. C. (2000). Neurocognitive functioning of adolescents: Effects of protracted alcohol use. *Alcoholism: Clinical and Experimental Research, 24*, 164–171.

Burger, M., Mensink, G. B. M., Bergmann, E., & Pietrzik, K. (2003). Characteristics associated with alcohol consumption in Germany. *Journal of Studies on Alcohol, 64*, 262–269.

Caetano, R., Schafer, J., Clark, C. L., Cunradi, C. B., & Raspberry, K. (2000). Intimate partner violence, acculturation, and alcohol consumption among Hispanic couples in the United States. *Journal of Interpersonal Violence, 15*, 30–45.

Carlini-Marlatt, B., Gazal-Carvalho, C., Gouveia, N., & Souza, M. (2003). Drinking practices and other health-related behaviors among adolescents of São Paulo City, Brazil. *Substance Use and Misuse, 38*, 905–932.

Casswell, S., Pledger, M., & Hooper, R. (2003). Socioeconomic status and drinking patterns in young adults. *Addiction, 98*, 601–610.

Champion, H. L., Foley, K. L., Durant, R. H., Hensberry, R., Altman, D., Wolfson, M., et al. (2004). Adolescent sexual victimization, use of alcohol and other substances, and other health risk behaviors. *Journal of Adolescent Health, 35*, 321–328.

Cherpitel, C. J. (1996). Alcohol in fatal and nonfatal injuries: A comparison of coroner and emergency room data from the same county. *Alcoholism: Clinical and Experimental Research, 20*, 338–342.

Chikritzhs, T., & Stockwell, T. (2002). Impact of later trading hours for Australian public houses (hotels) on levels of violence. *Journal of Studies on Alcohol, 63*, 591–599.

Chisholm, D., Rehm, J., van Ommeren, M., & Monteiro, M. (2004). Reducing the global burden of hazardous alcohol use: A comparative cost-effectiveness analysis. *Journal of Studies on Alcohol, 65*, 782–793.

Chochinov, A. (1998). Alcohol "on board," man overboard: Boating fatalities in Canada. *Canadian Medical Association Journal, 159,* 259–260.

Coleman, L., & Cater, S. (2005a). Underage "binge" drinking: A qualitative study into motivations and outcomes. *Drugs: Education, Prevention and Policy, 12,* 125–136.

Coleman, L., & Cater, S. (2005b). A qualitative study of the relationship between alcohol consumption and risky sex in adolescents. *Archives of Sexual Behavior, 34,* 649–661.

Coles, C. D., Russell, C. L., & Schuetze, P. (1997). Maternal substance use: Epidemiology, treatment outcome, and developmental effects. An annotated bibliography, 1995. *Substance Use and Misuse, 32,* 149–168.

Connor, J., Broad, J., Rehm, J., Vander Hoorn, S., & Jackson, R. (2005). The burden of death, disease, and disability due to alcohol in New Zealand. *New Zealand Medical Journal, 118,* U1412.

Cook, C. C. H. (1997). Alcohol and aviation. *Addiction, 92,* 539–555

Deshmukh, A., Rosenbloom, M. J., De Rosa, E., Sullivan, E. V., & Pfefferbaum, A. (2005). Regional striatal volume abnormalities in schizophrenia: Effects of co-morbidity for alcoholism, recency of alcoholic drinking, and antipsychotic medication type. *Schizophrenia Research, 79,* 189–200.

Diehl, A. M. (1998). Alcoholic liver disease. *Clinical Advances in Liver Disease, 2,* 103–118.

Doll, R., & Peto, R. (1995). Mortality and alcohol consumption. *British Medical Journal, 310,* 470.

Durkin, K. F., Wolfe, T. W., & Clark, G. A. (2005). College students and binge drinking: An evaluation of social learning theory. *Sociological Spectrum, 25,* 255–272.

Edenberg, H. J., Dick, D. M., Xuei, X., Tian, H., Almasy, L. Bauer, L. O., et al. (2004). Variations in GABRA2, encoding the alpha2 subunit of the $GABA_A$, are associated with alcohol dependence and with brain oscillations. *American Journal of Human Genetics, 74,* 705–714.

Fillmore, K. M., Golding, J. M., Leino, E. V., Motoyoshi, M., Shoemaker, C., Terry, H., et al. (1997). Patterns and trends in women's and men's drinking. In R. W. Wilsnack & S. C. Wilsnack (Eds.), *Gender and alcohol: Individual and social perspectives* (pp. 21–48). New Brunswick, NJ: Rutgers Center of Alcohol Studies.

Freestone, B., & Lip, G. Y. (2003, December) Atrial fibrillation (acute). *Clinical Evidence,* (10), 76–94.

French, M. T., & Zarkin, G. A. (1995). Is moderate alcohol use related to wages? Evidence from four worksites. *Journal of Health Economics, 14,* 319–344.

Frost, L., & Vestergaard, P. (2004). Alcohol and risk of atrial fibrillation or flutter: A cohort study. *Archives of Internal Medicine, 164,* 1993–1998.

Gaunekar, G., Patel, V., Jacob, K. S., Vankar, G., Mohan, D., Rane, A., et al. (2004). Drinking patterns of hazardous drinkers: A multicenter study in India. In A. Haworth & R. Simpson (Eds.), *Moonshine markets: Issues in unrecorded alcohol beverage production and consumption* (pp. 125–144). New York: Brunner-Routledge.

Gaunekar, G., Patel, V., & Rane, A. (2005). The impact and patterns of hazardous drinking amongst male industrial workers in Goa, India. *Social Psychiatry and Psychiatric Epidemiology, 40,* 267–275.

Gill, K., Eagle Elk, M., Liu, Y., & Dietrich, R. A. (1999). Examination of ALDH2 genotypes, alcohol metabolism and the flushing response in Native Americans. *Journal of Studies on Alcohol, 60,* 149–158.

Goldenberg, D., Lee, J., Koch, W. M., Kim, M. M., Trink, B., Sidransky, D., et al. (2004). Habitual risk factors for head and neck cancer. *Otolaryngology—Head and Neck Surgery, 131,* 986–993.

Grant, M. (Ed.). (1998). *Alcohol and emerging markets: Patterns, problems, and responses.* Philadelphia: Brunner/Mazel.

Grant, M., & Litvak, J. (Eds.). (1998). *Drinking patterns and their consequences.* Washington, DC: Taylor & Francis.

Grant, M., & Peele, S. (Eds.). (1999). *Alcohol and pleasure: A health perspective.* Philadelphia: Brunner/Mazel.

Gruenewald, P. J., Russell, M., Light, J., Lipton, R., Searles, J., Johnson, F., et al. (2002). One drink to a lifetime of drinking: Temporal structures of drinking patterns. *Alcoholism: Clinical and Experimental Research, 26,* 916–925.

Gunzerath, L., Faden, V., Zakhari, S., & Warren, K. (2004). National Institute on Alcohol Abuse and Alcoholism report on moderate drinking. *Alcoholism: Clinical & Experimental Research, 28,* 829–847.

Guo, J., Chung, I. J., Hill, K. G., Hawkins, J. D., Catalano, R. F., & Abbott, R. D. (2002). Developmental relationships between adolescent substance use and risky sexual behavior in young adulthood. *Journal of Adolescent Health, 31,* 354–362.

Gupta, P. C., Saxena, S., Pednekar, M. S., & Maulik, P. K. (2003). Alcohol consumption among middle-aged and elderly men: A community study from Western India. *Alcohol and Alcoholism, 38,* 327–331.

Haber, J. R., Jacob, T., & Heath, A. C. (2005). Paternal alcoholism and offspring conduct disorder: Evidence for the "common genes" hypothesis. *Twin Research and Human Genetics, 8,* 120–131.

Hajat, S., Haines, A., Bulpitt, C., & Fletcher, A. (2004). Patterns and determinants of alcohol consumption in people aged 75 years and older: Results from the MRC trial of assessment and management of older people in the community. *Age and Ageing, 33,* 170–177.

Haworth, A., & Simpson, R. (Eds.). (2004). *Moonshine markets: Issues in unrecorded alcohol beverage production and consumption.* New York: Brunner-Routledge.

Heath, D. B. (Ed.). (1995). *International handbook on alcohol and culture.* Westport, CT: Greenwood.

Heath, D. B. (2000). *Drinking occasions: Comparative perspectives on alcohol and culture.* Philadelphia: Brunner/Mazel.

Heilig, M., & Sommer, W. (2004). Functional genomics strategies to identify susceptibility genes and treatment targets in alcohol dependence. *Neurotoxicology Research, 6,* 363–372.

Hibell, B., Andersson, B., Bjarnason, T., Ahlström, S., Balakireva, O., Kokkevi, A., et al. (2004). *The ESPAD Report 2003: Alcohol and other drug use among students in 35 European countries.* Stockholm: Swedish Council for Information on Alcohol and Other Drugs (CAN) and the Pompidou Group at the Council of Europe.

Hickie, I. B., Koschera, A., Davenport, T. A., Naismith, S. L., & Scott, E. M. (2001). Comorbidity of common mental disorders and alcohol or other substance misuse in Australian general practice. *Medical Journal of Australia, 175,* S31–S36.

Hines, L. M., & Rimm, E. B. (2001). Moderate alcohol consumption and coronary heart disease: A review. *Postgraduate Medical Journal, 77,* 747–752.

Hingson, R., & Kenkel, D. (2004). Social, health, and economic consequences of underage drinking. In National Research Council and Institute of Medicine, *Reducing underage drinking: A collective responsibility, background papers*. [CD-ROM]. Committee on Developing a Strategy to Reduce and Prevent Underage Drinking, Division of Behavioral and Social Sciences and Education. Washington, DC: National Academies Press.

Holman, C. D. J., English, D. R., Milne, E., & Winter, M. G. (1996). Meta-analysis of alcohol and all-cause mortality: A validation of NHMRC recommendations. *Medical Journal of Australia, 164*, 141–145.

Holstege, C. P., Ferguson, J. D., Wolf, C. E., Baer, A. B., & Poklis, A. (2004). Analysis of moonshine for contaminants. *Journal of Toxicology—Clinical Toxicology, 42*, 597–601.

International Center for Alcohol Policies (ICAP). (2000). *Who are the abstainers?* ICAP Reports 8. Washington, DC: Author.

International Integrated Information Networks. (2005). *Southern Africa: Special report on road traffic injury prevention*. Retrieved August 18, 2005, from http://www.irinnews.org/S_report.asp?ReportID=41686&SelectRegion=Southern_Africa.

Jamison, K. R. (2006). The many stigmas of mental illness. *Lancet, 367*, 533–534.

Jarvenpaa, T., Rinne, J. O., Koskenvuo, M., Raiha, I., & Kaprio, J. (2005). Binge drinking in midlife and dementia risk. *Epidemiology, 16*, 766–771.

Javors, M., Tioururine, M., & Prihoda, T. (2000). Platelet serotonin uptake is higher in early-onset than in late-onset alcoholics. *Alcohol and Alcoholism, 35*, 390–393.

Kessler, R., Bergland, P., Demler, O., Jin, R., & Walters, E. E. (2005). Lifetime prevalence and age-of-onset distributions of *DSM-IV* disorders in the national Comorbidity Survey Replication. *Archives of General Psychiatry, 62*, 593–602.

Klingemann, H., & Gmel, G. (Eds.). (2001). *Mapping the social consequences of alcohol consumption*. Dordrecht, the Netherlands: Kluwer Academic.

Kopp, M. S., Skrabski, A., & Szekely, A. (2002). Risk factors and inequality in relation to morbidity and mortality in a changing society. In G. Weidner, M. S. Kopp, & M. Kristenson (Eds.), *Heart disease: Environment, stress, and gender* (pp. 101–113). Washington, DC: IOS Press.

Koul, P. B., Sussmane, J. B., Cunill-De Sautu, B., & Minarik, M. (2005). Atrial fibrillation associated with alcohol ingestion in adolescence: Holiday heart in pediatrics. *Pediatric Emergency Care, 21*, 38–39.

Krug, E. G., Dahlberg, L. L., Mercy, J. A., Zwi, A. B., & Lozano, R. (Eds.). (2002). *World report on violence and health*. Geneva, Switzerland: World Health Organization.

Kuntsche, E., Rehm, J., & Gmel, G. (2004). Characteristics of binge drinking in Europe. *Social Science and Medicine, 59*, 113–127.

Kypri, K., & Langley, J. D. (2003). Perceived social norms and their relation to university student drinking. *Journal of Studies on Alcohol, 64*, 829–834.

Ledermann, S., & Tabah, F. (1951). Nouvelles données sur la mortalité d'origine alcoolique [New data on alcohol-related mortality]. *Population, G*, 41–56.

Leevy, C. M., & Moroianu, S. A. (2005). Nutritional aspects of alcoholic liver disease. *Clinical Liver Disease, 9*, 67–81.

Leifman, H., & Gustafsson, N. K. (2004). Drickandets temporala struktur: Analyser av alkoholkonsumtionens och berusningsdrickandets månatliga variationer i Sverige [Temporal variations in drinking: Analysis of monthly variations in alcohol consumption and binge drinking in Sweden]. *Nordisk Alcohol- & Narkotikatidskrift, 21*, 5–21.

Lieber, C. S. (2004). Alcoholic fatty liver: Its pathogenesis and mechanism of progression to inflammation and fibrosis. *Alcohol, 34*, 9–19.

Linden, M., Lecrubier, Y., Bellantuono, C., Benkert, O., Kisely, S., & Simon, G. (1999). The prescribing of psychotropic drugs by primary care physicians: An international collaborative study. *Journal of Clinical Psychopharmacology, 19*, 132–140.

Lingford-Hughes, A. R., Wilson, S. J., Cunningham, V. J., Feeney, A., Stevenson, B., & Brooks, D. J. (2005). GABA-benzodiazepine receptor function in alcohol dependence: A combined 11C-flumazenil PET and pharmacodynamic study. *Psychopharmacology (Berlin), 180*, 595–606.

Luchsinger, J. A., Tang, M., Siddiqui, M., Shea, S., & Mayeux, R. (2004). Alcohol intake and risk of dementia. *Journal of the American Geriatric Society, 52*, 540–546.

Lukassen, J., & Beaudet, M. P. (2005). Alcohol dependence and depression among heavy drinkers in Canada. *Social Science and Medicine, 61*, 1658–1667.

Lynskey, M. T. (1998). The comorbidity of alcohol dependence and affective disorders: Treatment implications. *Drug and Alcohol Dependence, 52*, 201–209.

MacAndrew, C., & Edgerton, R. E. (1969). *Drunken comportment: A social explanation.* Chicago: Aldine.

Makinen, I. H. (2000). Eastern European transition and suicide mortality. *Social Sciences & Medicine, 51*, 1405–1420.

Marmot, M., & Wilkinson, R. G. (Eds.) (1999). *Social determinants of health.* Oxford: Oxford University Press.

Marshall, M. (Ed.). (1979). *Beliefs, behaviors and alcoholic beverages: A cross-cultural survey.* Ann Arbor: University of Michigan Press.

McCambridge, J., Conlon, P., Keaney, F., Wanigaratne, S., & Strang, J. (2004). Patterns of alcohol consumption and problems among the Irish in London: A preliminary comparison of pub drinkers in London and Dublin. *Addiction Research and Theory, 12*, 373–384.

McCarty, C. A., Ebel, B. E., Garrison, M. M., DiGiuseppe, D. L., Christakis, D. A., & Rivara, F. P. (2004). Continuity of binge and harmful drinking from late adolescence to early adulthood. *Pediatrics, 114*, 714–719.

McFarlin, S. K., & Flas-Stewart, W. (2002). Workplace absenteeism and alcohol use: A sequential analysis. *Psychology of Addictive Behaviors, 16*, 17–21.

McKee, M., Szücs, S., Sárváry, A., Ádány, R., Kiryanov, N., Saburova, L., et al. (2005). The composition of surrogate alcohols consumed in Russia. *Alcoholism: Clinical and Experimental Research, 29*, 1884–1888.

McKenna, M. T., Michaud, C. M., Murray, C. J., & Marks, J. S. (2005). Assessing the burden of disease in the United States using disability-adjusted life years. *American Journal of Prevention Medicine, 28*, 415–423.

McPherson, M., Casswell, S., & Pledger, M. (2004). Gender convergence in alcohol consumption and related problems: Issues and outcomes from comparisons of New Zealand survey data. *Addiction, 99*, 738–748.

Miranda, J. J., & Patel, V. (2005). Achieving the Millennium Development Goals: Does mental health play a role? *PLoS Medicine, 2*, e291.

Mohan, D., Chopra, A., Ray, R., & Sethi, H. (2001). Alcohol consumption in India: A cross-sectional study. In A. Demers, R. Room, & C. Bourgault (Eds.), *Surveys of drinking patterns and problems in seven developing countries* (pp. 103–114). Geneva, Switzerland: World Health Organization.

Mohler-Kuo, M., Dowdall, G. W., Koss, M., & Wechsler, H. (2004). Correlates of rape while intoxicated in a national sample of college women. *Journal of Studies on Alcohol, 65,* 37–45.

Montross, L. P., Barrio, C., Yamada, A. M., Lindamer, L., Golshan, S., Garcia, P., et al. (2005). Tri-ethnic variations of co-morbid substance and alcohol use disorders in schizophrenia. *Schizophrenia Research, 79,* 297–305.

Moore, A. A., Gould, R., Reuben, D. B., Greendale, G. A., Carter, M. K., Zhou, K., et al. (2005). Longitudinal patterns and predictors of alcohol consumption in the United States. *American Journal of Public Health, 95,* 458–465.

Moos, R. H., Schutte, K., Brennan, P., & Moos, B. S. (2004). Ten-year patterns of alcohol consumption and drinking problems among older women and men. *Addiction, 99,* 829–838.

Mukamal, K. J. (2003). Alcohol use and prognosis in patients with coronary heart disease. *Preventive Cardiology, 6,* 93–98.

Mukamal, K. J., Kuller, L. H., Fitzpatrick, A. L., Longstreth, W. T., Mittleman, M. A., & Siscovick, D. S. (2003). Prospective study of alcohol consumption and risk of dementia in older adults. *Journal of the American Medical Association, 289,* 1405–1413.

Mukamal, K. J., & Rimm, E. B. (2001). Alcohol's effects on the risk for coronary heart disease. *Alcohol Research and Health, 25,* 255–261.

Murray, C. J. L., & Lopez, A. D. (1999). Global mortality, disability, and the contribution of risk factors: Global Burden of Disease Study. *Lancet, 349,* 1436–1442.

Murray, C. J. L., & Lopez, A. D. (Eds.). (1996). *Global burden of disease: A comprehensive assessment of mortality and disability from diseases, injuries, and risk factors in 1990 and projected to 2020.* Cambridge, MA: Harvard School of Public Health.

Murray, R. P., Connett, J. E., Tyas, S. L., Bond, R., Ekuma, O., Silversides, C. K., et al. (2002). Alcohol volume, drinking pattern and cardiovascular morbidity and mortality: Is there a U-shaped function? *American Journal of Epidemiology, 155,* 242–248.

Murthy, P. J. N. V., Benegal, V., & Murthy, P. (1999). *Alcohol dependence in Indian women: A clinical perspective.* Retrieved October 24, 2005, from http://www.nimhans.kar.nic.in/deaddiction/Publications.html.

Nakanishi, N., Suzuki, K., & Tatara, K. (2003). Alcohol consumption and risk for development of impaired fasting glucose or type 2 diabetes in middle-aged Japanese men. *Diabetes Care, 26,* 48–54.

National Human Rights Commission (NHRC). (1999). *Quality assurance in mental health.* New Delhi, India: Author.

Neumark, Y. D., Friedlander, Y., Durst, R., Leitersdorf, E., Jaffe, D., Ramchandani, V. A., et al. (2004). Alcohol dehydrogenase polymorphisms influence alcohol-elimination rates in a male Jewish population. *Alcoholism: Clinical and Experimental Research, 28,* 10–14.

Nolen-Hoeksema, S. (2004). Gender differences in risk factors and consequences for alcohol use and problems. *Clinical Psychology Review, 24,* 981–1010.

Oesterle, S., Hill, K. G., Hawkins, J. D., Guo, J., Catalano, R. F., & Abbott, R. D. (2004). Adolescent heavy episodic drinking trajectories and health in young adulthood. *Journal of Studies on Alcohol, 65,* 204–212.

Oksuz, E., & Malhan, S. (2005). Socioeconomic factors and health risk behaviors among university students in Turkey: Questionnaire study. *Croatian Medical Journal, 46,* 66–73.

Orford, J., Johnson, M., & Purser, B. (2004). Drinking in second generation Black and Asian communities in the English Midlands. *Addiction Research and Theory, 12,* 11–30.

Orley, J. (1999). Pleasure and quality of life. In M. Grant & S. Peele (Eds.), *Permission for pleasure: A health perspective* (pp. 329–340). Philadelphia: Brunner/Mazel.

Oslin, D. W. (2005). Treatment of late-life depression complicated by alcohol dependence. *American Journal of Geriatric Psychiatry, 13,* 491–500.

Österberg, E., & Karlsson, T. (2003). *Alcohol policies in EU member states and Norway: A collection of country reports.* Brussels: Directorate General for Health and Consumer Affairs (DG SANCO).

Patel, V., Araya, R., & Bolton, P. (2004). Treating depression in developing countries. *Tropical Medicine and International Health, 9,* 539–541.

Patel, V., Araya, R., Lima, M. S., Ludermir, A., & Todd, C. (1999). Women, poverty and common mental disorders in four restructuring societies. *Social Science and Medicine, 49,* 1461–1471.

Patel, V., Kirkwood, B. R., Pednekar, S., Pereira, B., Barros, P., Fernandes, J., et al. (2006). Gender disadvantage and reproductive health risk factors for common mental disorders in women: A community survey in India. *Archives of General Psychiatry, 63,* 404–413.

Patel, V., & Kleinman, A. (2003). Poverty and common mental disorders in developing countries. *Bulletin of the World Health Organization, 81,* 609–615.

Patel, V., Pereira, J., Coutinho, L., Fernandes, R., Fernandes, J., & Mann, A. (1998). Poverty, psychological disorder and disability in primary care attenders in Goa, India. *British Journal of Psychiatry, 171,* 201–209.

Patel, V., & Thara, R. (Eds.). (2003). *Meeting mental health needs of developing countries: NGO innovations in India.* New Delhi: Sage.

Peele, S., & Brodsky, A. (2000). Exploring psychological benefits associated with moderate alcohol use: A necessary corrective to assessments of drinking outcomes? *Drug and Alcohol Dependence, 60,* 221–247.

Pietila, T. (2002). Drinking mothers feeding children: Market women and gender politics in Kilimanjaro, Tanzania. In D. F. Bryceson (Ed.), *Alcohol in Africa: Mixing business, pleasure, and politics* (pp. 197–212). Portsmouth, NH: Heinemann.

Pinder, R. M., & Sandler, M. (2004). Alcohol, wine and mental health: Focus on dementia and stroke. *Journal of Psychopharmacology, 18,* 449–456.

Plange, N. K. (1998). Social and behavioral issues related to drinking patterns. In M. Grant & J. Litvak (Eds.), *Drinking patterns and their consequences* (pp. 89–102). Washington, DC: Taylor & Francis.

Plant, M. L., Miller, P., & Plant, M. A. (2005). The relationship between alcohol consumption and problem behaviors: Gender differences among British adults. *Journal of Substance Use, 10,* 22–30.

Poschl, G., & Seitz, H. K. (2004). Alcohol and cancer. *Alcohol and Alcoholism, 39,* 155–165.

Puddey, I. B., Rakic, V., Dimmitt, S. B., & Beilin, L. J. (1999). Influence of drinking on cardiovascular disease and cardiovascular risk factors: A review. *Addiction, 94,* 649–663.

Quinlan, K. P., Brewer, R. D., Siegel, P., Sleet, D. A., Mokdad, A. H., Shults, R. A., et al. (2005). Alcohol-impaired driving among U.S. adults, 1993–2002. *American Journal of Preventive Medicine, 28,* 346–350.

Ragnarsdottir, P., Kjartansdottir, A., & Daviosdottir, S. (2002). Effect of extended alcohol serving-hours in Reykjavik. In R. Room (Ed.), *Effect of Nordic alcohol policies: What happens to drinking and harm when alcohol controls change?* (pp. 145–154). Helsinki, Finland: Nordic Council for Alcohol and Drug Research (NAD).

Ramskogler, K., Hertling, I., Riegler, A., Semler, B., Zoghlami, A., Walter, H., et al. (2001). Mögliche Interaktionen zwischen Ethanol und Pharmaka und deren Bedeutung für die medikamentöse Therapie im Alter [Possible interaction between ethanol and drugs and their significance for drug therapy in the elderly]. *Wiener Klinische Wochenschrift, 113,* 363–370.

Regev, A., & Jeffers, L. J. (1999). Hepatitis C and alcohol. *Alcoholism: Clinical and Experimental Research, 23,* 1543–1551.

Rehm, J., Rehn, N., Room, R., Monteiro, M., Gmel, G., Jernigan, D., et al. (2003). The global distribution of average volume of alcohol consumption and patterns of drinking. *European Addiction Research, 9,* 147–156.

Rehm, J., Room, R., Graham, K., Monteiro, M., Gmel, G., & Sempos, C. T. (2003). Relationship of average volume of alcohol consumption and patterns of drinking to burden of disease: An overview. *Addiction, 98,* 1209–1228.

Rehm, J., Room, R., Monteiro, M., Gmel, G., Graham, K., Rehn, N., et al. (2003). Alcohol as a risk factor for the global burden of disease. *European Addiction Research, 9,* 157–164.

Rehm, J., Sempos, C. T., & Trevisan, M. (2003). Alcohol and cardiovascular disease—more than one paradox to consider. Average volume of alcohol consumption, patterns of drinking and risk of coronary heart disease: A review. *Journal of Cardiovascular Risk, 10,* 15–20.

Riley, L., & Marshall, M. (Eds.). (1999). *Alcohol and public health in eight developing countries.* Geneva, Switzerland: World Health Organization.

Rodgers, A., Ezzati, M., Vander Hoorn, S., Lopez, A. D., Lin, R. B., & Murray, C. J. (2004). Distribution of major health risks: Findings from the Global Burden of Disease Study Comparative Risk Assessment Collaborating Group. *Public Library of Science—Medicine, 1,* e27.

Rodham, K., Hawton, K., Evans, E., & Weatherall, R. (2005). Ethnic and gender differences in drinking, smoking and drug taking among adolescents in England: A self-report school-based survey of 15 and 16 year olds. *Journal of Adolescence, 28,* 63–73.

Rosta, J. (2002). Drinking patterns of doctors: A comparison between Aarhus in Denmark and Mainz in Germany. *Drugs: Education, Prevention and Policy, 9,* 367–376.

Rosta, J., & Aasland, O. G. (2005). Female surgeons' alcohol use: A study of a national sample of Norwegian doctors. *Alcohol and Alcoholism, 40,* 436–440.

Ruitenberg, A., van Swieten, J. C., Witteman, J. C., Mehta, K. M., van Duijn, C. M., Hofman, A., et al. (2002). Alcohol consumption and risk of dementia: The Rotterdam Study. *Lancet, 359,* 281–286.

Sachs, J. D., & McArthur, J. W. (2005). The millennium project: A plan for meeting the Millennium Development Goals. *Lancet, 365,* 347–353.

San Jose, B., van Oers, J. A. M., van de Mheen, H., Garretsen, H. F., & Mackenbach, J. P. (2000). Drinking patterns and health outcomes: Occasional versus regular drinking. *Addiction*, *95*, 865–872.

Savola, O., Niemela, O., & Hillbom, M. (2005). Alcohol intake and the pattern of trauma in young adults and working aged people admitted after trauma. *Alcohol and Alcoholism*, *40*, 269–273.

Schiff, M., Rahav, G., & Teichman, M. (2005). Israel 2000: Immigration and gender differences in alcohol consumption. *American Journal of Addictions*, *14*, 234–247.

Schuckit, M. A. (2000). Genetics of the risk for alcoholism. *American Journal on Addictions*, *9*, 103–112.

Sharman, C. H. (2005). The problem with drinking. *Perspectives in Health*, *10*. Retrieved December 15, 2005, from http://www.paho.org/English/DD/PIN/Number21_article04.htm.

Silva, M. C., Gaunekar, G., Patel, V., Kukalekar, D. S., & Fernandes, J. (2003). Prevalence and correlates of hazardous drinking in industrial workers: A study from Goa, India. *Alcohol and Alcoholism*, *38*, 79–83.

Silverberg, M., Chu, J., Nelson, L., Morgan, B. W., & Todd, K. H. (2001). Elevated blood lead levels in urban moonshine drinkers. *Annals of Emergency Medicine*, *38*, 460–461.

Simpura, J. (2001). Trends in alcohol consumption and drinking patterns: Sociological and economic explanations and alcohol policies. *Nordisk Alkohol- & Narkotikatidskrift*, *18*(Suppl.), 3–13.

Simpura, J., & Karlsson, T. (2001). Trends in drinking patterns among adult population in 15 European countries, 1950 to 2000: A review. *Nordisk Alkohol- & Narkotikatidskrift*, *18*(Suppl.), 31–53.

Singh, J., Mattoo, S. K., Sharan, P., & Basu, D. (2005). Quality of life and its correlates in patients with dual diagnosis of bipolar affective disorder and substance dependence. *Bipolar Disorders*, *7*, 187–191.

Single, E., Beaubrun, M., Mauffret, M., Minoletti, A., Moskalewicz, J., Moukolo, A., et al. (1997). Public drinking, problems and prevention measures in twelve countries: Results of the WHO project on public drinking. *Contemporary Drug Problems*, *24*, 425–448.

Spear, L. P. (2004). Biomedical aspects of underage drinking. In *What drives underage drinking? An international analysis* (pp. 25–38). Washington, DC: International Center for Alcohol Policies.

Stampfer, M. J., Kang, J. H., Chen, J., Cherry, R., & Grodstein, F. (2005). Effects of moderate alcohol consumption on cognitive function in women. *New England Journal of Medicine*, *352*, 245–253.

Stockwell, T., Chikritzhs, T., & Brinkman, S. (2000). Role of social and health statistics in measuring harm from alcohol. *Journal of Substance Abuse*, *12*, 139–154.

Strandberg, A. Y., Strandberg, T. E., Salomaa, V. V., Pitkälä, K., & Miettinen, T. A. (2004). Alcohol consumption, 29-y total mortality, and quality of life in men in old age. *American Journal of Clinical Nutrition*, *80*, 1366–1371.

Sturgis, E. M., Wei, Q., & Spitz, M. R. (2004). Descriptive epidemiology and risk factors for head and neck cancer. *Seminars in Oncology*, *31*, 726–733.

Sullivan, L. E., Fiellin, D. A., & O'Connor, P. G. (2005). The prevalence and impact of alcohol problems in major depression: A systematic review. *American Journal of Medicine*, *118*, 330–341.

Swahn, M. H., Simon, T. R., Hammig, B. J., & Guerrero, J. L. (2004). Alcohol-consumption behaviors and risk for physical fighting and injuries among adolescent drinkers. *Addictive Behaviors, 29,* 959–963.

Szűcs, S., Sárváry, A., McKee, M., & Ádány, R. (2005). Could the high level of cirrhosis in Central and Eastern Europe be due partly to the quality of alcohol consumed? An exploratory investigation. *Addiction, 100,* 536–542.

Transport Research Centre. (2005). *Road traffic accidents in the Czech Republic in 2003. Prague, Czech Republic.* Retrieved August 18, 2005, from http://www.cdv.cz/english/text/branch/road/accid_03.htm.

Trevisan, M., Ram, M., Hovey, K., Russell, M., Freudenheim, J., Muti, P., et al. (2001). Alcohol drinking patterns and myocardial infarction. *American Journal of Epidemiology, 153,* S97.

Trevisan, M., Schisterman, E., Mennotti, A., Farchi, G., & Conti, S. (2001). Drinking pattern and mortality: The Italian risk factor and life expectancy pooling project. *Annals of Epidemiology, 11,* 312–319.

Wakim-Fleming, J., & Mullen, K. D. (2005). Long-term management of alcoholic liver disease. *Clinical Liver Disease, 9,* 135–149

Walberg, P., McKee, M., Shkolnikov, V., Chenet, L., & Leon, D. A. (1998). Economic change, crime, and mortality crisis in Russia: A regional analysis. *British Medical Journal, 317,* 312–318.

Wall, T. L., Horn, S. M., Johnson, M. L., Smith, T. L., & Carr, L. G. (2000). Hangover symptoms in Asian Americans with variations in the aldehyde dehydrogenase (ALDH2) gene. *Journal of Studies on Alcohol, 61,* 13–17.

Wannamethee, S. G., Camargo, C. A., Manson, J. E., Willett, W. C., & Rimm, E. B. (2003). Alcohol drinking patterns and risk of type 2 diabetes mellitus among younger women. *Archives of Internal Medicine, 163,* 1329–1336.

Weathermon, R., & Crabb, D. W. (1999). Alcohol and medication interactions. *Alcohol Research and Health, 23,* 40–54.

Wechsler, H., Lee, J. E., Hall, J., Wagenaar, A. C., & Lee, H. (2002). Secondhand effects of student alcohol use reported by neighbors of colleges: The role of alcohol outlets. *Social Science and Medicine, 55,* 425–435.

Wells, S., & Graham, K. (2003). Aggression involving alcohol: Relationship to drinking patterns and social context. *Addiction, 98,* 33–42.

White, S. (1995). *Russia goes dry: Alcohol, state and society.* Cambridge: Cambridge University Press.

Wilhelmsen, K. C., & Ehlers, C. (2005). Heritability of substance dependence in a Native American population. *Psychiatric Genetics, 15,* 101–107.

Wilsnack, R. W., & Wilsnack, S. C. (Eds.). (1997). *Gender and alcohol: Individual and social perspectives.* New Brunswick, NJ: Rutgers Center of Alcohol Studies.

World Health Organization (WHO). (1999). *Global status report on alcohol 1999.* Geneva, Switzerland: Author.

World Health Organization (WHO). (2004). *Global status report on alcohol 2004.* Geneva, Switzerland: Author.

World Health Organization (WHO). (2005). *Mental health atlas.* Geneva, Switzerland: Author.

Wu, Z., Detels, R., Zhang, J., Li, V., & Li, J. (2002). Community base trial to prevent drug use amongst youth in Yunnan, China. *American Journal of Public Health, 92,* 1952–1957.

Zaigraev, G. (2004). The Russian model of noncommercial alcohol consumption. In A. Haworth & R. Simpson (Eds.), *Moonshine markets: Issues in unrecorded alcohol beverage production and consumption* (pp. 31–40). New York: Brunner-Routledge.

Zeegers, M. P., Kellen, E., Buntinx, F., & van den Brandt, P. A. (2004). The association between smoking, beverage consumption, diet and bladder cancer: A systematic literature review. *World Journal of Urology, 21,* 392–401.

Zins, M., Gueguen, A., Leclerc, A., & Goldberg, M. (2003). Alcohol consumption and marital status of French women in the GAZEL cohort: A longitudinal analysis between 1992 and 1996. *Journal of Studies on Alcohol, 64,* 784–789.

3

Selecting the Right Interventions: The Need for Assessment

The focus of this book—on patterns of drinking, targeted interventions, and a multisector partnership approach to reducing alcohol-related harm—encourages a new look at what information is required in order to develop interventions that are acceptable, appropriate, and effective. Reducing alcohol-related harms and promoting the positive functions of alcohol through a focus on specific patterns of drinking and on particular target groups require appropriate information about those patterns and groups in order to tailor interventions. However, planners at local and national levels often find themselves in a "data desert," lacking the information necessary to make decisions.

In developed countries, there may be a relative abundance of national data on per capita consumption, some health outcomes (for instance, alcohol-related morbidity and mortality), and alcohol-impaired driving (Connor, Broad, Rehm, Hoorn, & Jackson, 2005; Nolte, Britton, & McKee, 2003; Ridolfo & Stevenson, 2001; Sjögren, Eriksson, Broström, & Ahlm, 2000; U.S. National Highway Traffic Safety Administration, 2005; White, Altmann, & Nanchahal, 2004; Zureik & Ducimetière, 1996). These data lend themselves to sophisticated population-level analyses of the links, for example, between consumption and chronic disease (Rehm, Patra, & Popova, 2006; Singh & Hoyert, 2000), consumption and price changes, or price changes and alcohol-related diseases (Chaloupka, Grossman, & Saffer, 2002; Sloan, Reilly, & Schenzler, 1994). Such data have informed the WHO Global Burden of Disease study (Murray & Lopez, 1996), which includes a calculation of the contribution of alcohol to a variety of diseases. The assumptions on which such calculations are made, and the strengths and weaknesses of the data, are examined in the Annex. These population-level analyses have inclined many public health workers to focus on the reduction of alcohol consumption as the mainstay of public policy on alcohol: A population-level approach to reducing alcohol-related harm is tied to a focus on population-level data on alcohol consumption and alcohol problems. There is somewhat of a circular relationship between the availability of certain types of evidence (for example, consumption and price) and the appeal of certain types of interventions (for example, taxation). A "one size fits all" approach to alcohol policy is linked to a relatively narrow focus on data collection.

In many parts of the world, especially in developing and transitional countries, there is often a lack of population-level data with which to inform decisions. This may encourage reliance on findings from epidemiological analyses conducted in other, richer countries. It may further encourage conventional solutions to reducing alcohol-related harms without examining national and local need and relevance. Globally, compared with epidemiological data, there is a relative lack of information on variations in drinking patterns and behaviors and on drinking in specific populations (see Annex). This has drawbacks for countries and communities that want to develop more targeted and nuanced approaches to reducing alcohol-related harm.

WHY ASSESS DRINKING BEHAVIOR?

The increasing emphasis on an evidence base for alcohol policy highlights the need for good epidemiological surveillance data. It has also enhanced our understanding of which interventions are likely to be effective and at what cost. Because of research costs and methodological complexities, only a small amount of epidemiological information is available in most countries, and only a relatively small range of interventions has been subject to intensive evaluation. Policy-makers in countries without their own evidence base must make a judgment about whether epidemiological findings and evaluation data from rich countries can be extrapolated to areas with very different resource contexts and traditions.

Another aspect of the need for evidence tends to go unnoticed, certainly in the scientific literature, because it is local and of limited generalizability. It is that interventions should be "evidence informed," that is, developed and implemented in cognizance of the characteristics of a particular pattern of drinking, social context, or target group.

Drinking behaviors are diverse and vary from country to country, between areas within countries, between social groups, and across different time periods. There are huge variations in those who drink, what they drink, when they drink, whom they drink with, how they drink, and what they do while they are drinking (Heath, 1995, 2002). Contrast, for example, "toasting" in Russia (Sverdlov, 2001), "round buying" in the United Kingdom (Dorn, 1981) and in Zimbabwean beerhalls (Woelk, Fritz, Bassett, Todd, & Chingono, 2001), the Australian "shout" (Hall & Hunter, 1995; Sargent, 1979), the American cocktail party (Gusfield, 1987; Mandelbaum, 1965), or drinking in religious ceremonies and cults (Adams, 1995;

Leacock, 1979; Trenk, 2001). These styles of drinking are deeply embedded in custom and etiquette, and represent very different ways of influencing the pacing of drinking, overall volume of consumption, and positive and negative outcomes. The interventions required to change these practices are likely to vary as well— and certainly cannot be implemented without knowing the drinking behavior in some detail.

"Off-the-shelf" solutions to reducing alcohol-related harm do not necessarily suit the diversity of drinking patterns and problems within a community, nor might they be relevant to a particular target population. The task of influencing drinking for the better requires interventions that facilitate changes in both individual consumption behaviors and the cultural norms about appropriate and inappropriate drinking styles. The challenge of changing drinking behaviors and drinking cultures, in turn, requires knowledge about those behaviors and cultures, what influences them, and what opportunities there are for intervening so as to maximize enjoyment and minimize private and public harms.

Take, for example, drinking and unsafe sexual behavior, an important issue in the prevention of sexually transmitted infections, including HIV/AIDS. Evidence for a link between some drinking patterns and risky sexual behaviors can be established from surveys of particular populations—for example, migrants (Lin et al., 2005), men who have sex with sex workers (Madhivanan et al., 2005), or patients attending sexually transmitted infection clinics (Kalichman & Cain, 2004; Simbayi et al., 2004). But such data are often insufficiently detailed to assist the development of local interventions to reduce alcohol-related risks. This will require an understanding of the role of drinking in different sectors of the population. For instance, "beerhalls" play a key function in the social lives of men in Zimbabwe. A conventional epidemiological study might reveal links, for example, between the number of drink units consumed and sexual risk, but the description of the role of the beerhall goes far deeper than a correlation of consumption and risk. It is clear that any attempt to change drinking patterns among men in Zimbabwe will have to be made in the context of the role that beerhalls play within the population that frequents them.

Social Significance of Beerhalls in Zimbabwe

Research conducted for the World Health Organization (WHO) and the Joint United Nations Programme on HIV/AIDS (UNAIDS) studied the relationship between substance use and high-risk sexual behavior in Zimbabwe, a country with one of the world's highest prevalences of HIV/AIDS (Woelk et al., 2001). As well as exploring the social dynamics that link alcohol and drug use with HIV risk behavior, the report provides an interesting insight into the social significance of beerhalls.

"Beerhalls" are the most widely patronized drinking establishments in contemporary Zimbabwe, especially among Black African men. A legacy of the British campaign to control alcohol consumption among this population in the early 1900s, beerhalls are large courtyards with tables and benches (capable of hosting several hundred patrons at a time), surrounded by a high wall of 6 to 8 feet. At the center of the yard is a large, one-room concrete building (the hall) with more benches and tables. Beer is sold at the "bar," a metal counter with no seats around, located in one corner of the hall.

The halls trade in a variety of beers. Traditional opaque African beers (made from maize or other grains) are the most popular products. Chibuku, a brand of opaque beer commercially brewed in Harare and at other locations in Zimbabwe, is overwhelmingly the drink of choice among beerhall patrons. Chibuku is usually sold in "mugs" (a single large, open container, shared among several people). Interestingly, Chibuku's advertising slogan is "Hari Yemadzisahwira" ["Mug of friends"]. Although not as popular among the patrons as Chibuku, a variety of clear beers, more familiar to the Westerners, is sold by the bottle at beerhalls.

Beer is usually bought in rounds: "Men who have more expendable income on a given day will purchase more of the beer but others usually return the favor . . . . Sharing is the social norm at the beerhall and no one drinks alone" (Woelk et al., 2001, p. 9).

Apart from drinking, beerhalls offer a variety of social activities for the patrons, including board games (which many patrons bring with them) and gambling (for example, dart or draft games and off-track horse race betting). Importantly, beerhalls may also fulfill the role of community centers for certain groups: "On Sunday mornings, for example, one often sees banking cooperative members or funeral society members meeting at a beerhall to conduct business" (Woelk et al., 2001, p. 9).

The initiatives taken to reduce alcohol-related harms and the resources available for their implementation vary between and within countries. They are influenced by social, cultural, political, religious, and economic factors. Views on public health and social issues also vary. Some countries have invested substantially in developing a public health framework for analyzing and responding to health problems; in others, it is rare or absent. New interventions must therefore be designed in the context of the available resources.

The development of interventions should be based on an assessment of drinking, which calls for the collation of evidence that aids decision-making. A suitable slogan might be "No intervention without assessment."

LINKING EVIDENCE AND ACTION

There are considerable obstacles to linking research evidence with policy and intervention development (Black, 2001; Jacobson, Butterill, & Goering, 2003; Weiss, 1979). Government officials, health service planners, and industry and NGO staff may be exasperated at the time it takes to deliver research. The time horizon of these actors is usually limited to the next election, the next annual funding, or the business cycle. Policy-makers, planners, activists, and people in industry tend to be "information minimalists," needing just enough of the right kind of information to make decisions: Adequacy and relevance prevail over scientific perfection.

Researchers, on the other hand, are renowned for maximizing information collection and analysis. Conventional social science and epidemiology often fail to deliver relevant information. Scientists often lack skills pertinent to helping the development of policy and practice and are not rewarded for the policy or practical relevance of their work. Much of science—including social science—is methodologically narrow and insensitive to the scope of issues associated with public problems, including those connected with alcohol. Few researchers have been trained in using a variety of research methods, insights, and sources of evidence that might be needed for an assessment of a local, regional, or national situation.

At the same time, the policy-makers' competence in an evidence-informed approach to policy and intervention development may be questionable. First, much of alcohol policy is driven by political or economic expediency, intermittently spiced with moral panics (such as about underage drinking or public drinking), rather than by dispassionate and pragmatic appraisal. Second, there is a tendency to get locked into conventional responses. Reasons for this include, for example, the assumption that it is quicker and simpler to borrow interventions that have been developed elsewhere—or a competition between agencies where their survival depends on promoting their own product, even though it may not be the most appropriate and effective. There is also a connection with constraints built into public funding, where "vertical systems" in education, health, and law enforcement discourage cross-sector sponsorship or monetary transfers (between, for instance, health and policing). Some solutions are not implemented because the costs fall on one sector, and the savings on another: For example, changes to the built environment that separate traffic from people in entertainment districts have costs for the municipal authority, but the savings accrue to hospital and emergency services.

Despite these difficulties, the design and delivery of effective interventions require forging better links between assessment and action. This entails better partnership between data gatherers and policy-makers and new ways of thinking about the collection and use of data (International Center for Alcohol Policies, 2002).

INFORMATION FOR POLICY PLANNING

The initial impetus for "doing something about drinking" may emerge in a number of ways. For example, it may follow from a local crisis (such as a spate of youth overdoses with alcohol); public health researchers or clinicians may identify a significant health burden (such as fetal alcohol syndrome); a review of public health programming may discover significant gaps (such as limited services for ethnic minorities); there may be demands from the public or specific interest groups (such as action groups against alcohol-impaired driving); dedicated funding for a specific activity may become available; a national or international campaign may stir local attention; or politicians, media, community groups, or other decision-makers may raise the issue (Stimson et al., 2003).

What, then, can be done where there is a clear need to develop interventions to reduce alcohol-related harm? If it is desire to have interventions informed by evidence (and this is not always the case), the conventional starting point is to undertake an epidemiological needs assessment. This might involve analysis of existing information that profiles alcohol consumption, variation in consumption by different demographic groups, statistics on alcohol-related morbidity and mortality, and data on adverse outcomes.

Countries and communities will be at different starting points in terms of the awareness of drink-related issues and the availability of relevant information. Globally, the most commonly available information is national aggregate data on per capita alcohol consumption. An estimate of annual adult per capita consumption is available for 185 countries from WHO's *Global Status Report on Alcohol* (World Health Organization [WHO], 2004). Such data are commonly derived from sales, production, and taxation statistics for "recorded alcohol" and exclude cross-border sales, smuggling, homemade alcohol, and tourist consumption. In many parts of the world, however, unrecorded consumption is significant: It is estimated at almost four fifths of all alcohol consumed in India and some other countries of Southeast Asia, about half of all alcohol consumption in Africa, and about one third in Eastern Europe and Latin America (Rehm et al., 2003).

National consumption data are of some use to national policy development, but have limited value for developing programs to reduce specific alcohol-related harms. National data from sales, production, and taxation cannot be analyzed to show drinking patterns of different sectors of the population or local variations in drinking behaviors (WHO, 2004). Developed countries will also have other data on alcohol consumption and associated problems, including health services diagnoses records, mortality data, and police and court records.

More relevant to policy-makers commissioning an epidemiological needs assessment are data from population surveys, either surveys specifically on alcohol (Grant, Kaplan, Shepard, & Moore, 2003; Osaki, Matsushita, Shirasaka, Hiro, & Higuchi, 2005) or, more commonly, conducted as part of bigger health or crime surveys (for example, Macpherson, 2002; Parry et al., 2005). In addition, the alcohol beverage industry has market research data on sales and consumption, but these data are not usually shared for commercial reasons. Survey data can describe the social distribution of drinking, patterns of drinking, and related health and social problems. Surveys are useful for measuring health and social problems that do not show up in police or health statistics (such as family and work problems), and they have the advantage over aggregate national consumption data because they enable analysis of the links between different variables.

**Common Sources of Information Used in
Epidemiological Needs Assessment**

Population consumption data: production, sales, and taxation data
Arrest and conviction data: for example, records on alcohol-impaired driving and public drunkenness
Alcohol-related mortality data: for example, death certificate data and fatal accident reports
Alcohol-related morbidity data: for example, data from inpatient and outpatient treatment facilities
General population surveys: health, crime, and market research
Surveys of special populations: for example, surveys of young people, indigenous populations, arrestees, migrants, particular occupational groups, hospital patients, people attending accident and emergency services, and homeless people

One hundred and forty-eight countries have some survey data on population drinking (WHO, 2004), although in many countries the amount of information is rather scant. As discussed in the Annex, the extent and quality of the data are better for developed than developing countries. Some countries might also have available surveys describing drinking among specific groups, such as young people (Child and Adolescent Health Research Unit, 2005; Currie et al., 2004; Hibell et al., 2004; Johnston, O'Malley, Bachman, & Schulenberg, 2004; King, Ball, & Carroll, 2001; Uehata et al., 2002), arrestees (Holloway & Bennett, 2004; Martin, Bryant, & Fitzgerald, 2001), and medical patients (Chen, Yi, & Hilton, 2005). For instance, the European School Survey Project on Alcohol and Other Drugs (ESPAD) looks at drinking among representative samples of 15- to 16-year-old school students in 35 European countries (Hibell et al., 2004).

Surveys are clearly an important resource but are not without their own challenges. The caveat is that self-report surveys consistently underreport actual consumption figures: For example, comparison of data from national sales or taxation with survey reports suggests that people tend to underreport their consumption of beverage alcohol (Harford et al., 1988; Nevitt & Lundak, 2005; White et al., 2005). Surveys need to be properly conducted, paying due attention to the representativeness of the sample with regard to the population studied, the reliability and validity of responses, and comparability with other surveys.

However, many aspects of drinking are not measured. There is a dearth of information on significant alcohol-related harms that are not readily measurable though treatment data and mortality statistics, such as acute health problems and public order and public nuisance problems. It has been estimated that acute problems (including alcohol-related motor vehicle injuries, other transport and water accidents, falls, suicides, deaths in fires, and assaults) account for two thirds of total potential years of life lost in Australia and Canada (English et al., 1995; Single, Robson, Xie, & Rehm, 1998). Measurement of acute problems is important for monitoring the impact of policy and interventions, because these respond more rapidly to policy change and are not subject to the time lags inherent in using chronic diseases as a marker for policy impact. Yet such data (with the possible exception of alcohol-impaired driving fatalities) are rarely collected systematically. WHO's *International Guide for Monitoring Alcohol Consumption and Related Harm* (WHO, 2000), designed to facilitate policy formation, provides extensive advice on the collection of national data about alcohol consumption and chronic health problems associated with alcohol use, but has only a few pages on measuring acute problems.

A municipality interested in reducing public nuisance related to alcohol consumption—such as noise, hooliganism, and litter—would be hard put to find relevant national or local data. Acts of domestic violence, for example, may be brought to the attention of police, but in many countries the police prefer to stay out of such matters, or there may be major disincentives for women to report them for fear of social disapproval or loss of family rights and income. Even when such cases are reported to police, the link between domestic violence and alcohol may not be investigated or is unlikely to be entered into a database that would allow proper analysis. Some injury consequent to alcohol-related fights may be treated in accident and emergency departments, but the link with alcohol is unlikely to be recorded in patient case notes or in the statistical returns of accident and emergency services (Dill, Wells-Parker, & Soderstrom, 2004). Many alcohol-related problems—as other social and health problems—go unreported and unrecorded. On the other hand, the reports might refer to alcohol, but lack the specificity necessary to determine how related drinking was to the injury.

Moreover, the positive roles of alcohol in facilitating sociability, aiding relaxation, enhancing leisure, and aiding celebration (Heath, 1999) are rarely touched upon when assessing drinking behavior. Positive outcomes may be of interest to municipalities that wish to reduce problems associated with drinking while at the same time maximizing community benefits from alcohol consumption.

RAPID METHODS FOR ASSESSING DRINKING BEHAVIOR AND PROBLEMS

Clearly, it is important to improve routine national data systems and surveys to collect information on alcohol consumption and problems. There needs to be better collection of epidemiological data for strategic planning at a national level. The WHO (2000) guidelines suggest some of what needs to be done. However, the financial implications are considerable: For example, resource-poor countries may face a difficult choice between, on the one hand, developing systems that contribute to global and national monitoring and, on the other hand, collecting local intelligence information that is directly linked to policy-making and developing local interventions.

The absence of data does not put a hold on the need to develop interventions. Given the challenges identified above, international agencies have become increasingly interested in rapid methods for assessing health and social problems, specifically in order to design interventions. Collectively known as *rapid assessment*, these methods have been developed as a practical tool for measuring health and social problems. They have gained popularity in areas where policy-makers, health and social planners, and practitioners need to gather information quickly; where there may be limited resources and capacity to collect information; and where conventional epidemiological, social science, and public health assessment methods (such as population surveys) may be difficult to undertake (Manderson, 1996). Rapid assessment approaches have been driven by necessity; as a consequence, they are probably more familiar to people working in developing countries than in developed ones, although they are relevant to both.

Rapid assessment methods go under a variety of names. Studies devoted to rural development (agricultural development, sanitation, and disease control) are often called *rapid rural appraisals* (Chambers, 1980; Rhoades, 1992). Other common terms are *situational analyses* (Unwin & Aspray, 2002) and *contextual assessments* (Larson & Manderson, 1997). Rapid assessments have been undertaken in fields as diverse as nutrition (Scrimshaw & Hurtado, 1987; WHO, 1995), water hygiene (Almedon, Blumenthal, & Manderson, 1997), reproductive health, disaster response (Glass & Noji, 1992), HIV/AIDS, sexual behavior, malarial control, and situational crime control (Eck, 2002; Scott, 2002).

The approach has been extensively used in the illicit drugs field, especially when there is a dearth of epidemiological data. Rapid assessments have been utilized, for example, in developing measures to control the illicit production of drugs and in understanding drug use behaviors to implement HIV prevention programs (United Nations International Drug Control Programme, 1998). They have been undertaken in a wide range of countries and settings (DeJong, Tsagarelli, & Schouten, 1999; Dorabjee & Samson, 2000; Kumar et al., 2000; Mwenesi, 1996). At least 83 rapid assessment studies on substance use were undertaken in 70 countries between 1993 and 2001 (Fitch, Stimson, Rhodes, & Poznyak, 2004). At least 12 different guidelines on the rapid assessment of substance use problems have been produced in various languages by WHO, UNAIDS, the United Nations Children's Fund (UNICEF), the United Nations Office on Drugs and Crime (UNODC), the U.S. Office of HIV/AIDS Policy, Médecins sans Frontières, the United Nations Development Programme (UNDP), and the HIV/AIDS Alliance (Fitch & Stimson, 2003; Greig, 2001; Stimson, Fitch, & Rhodes, 1998; United Nations International Drug Control Programme, 1993, 1998; U.S. Department of Health and Human Services, 1999; Wong, 2002).

Although some of these guides have sections dealing with alcohol, there appear to be no equivalent guideline documents focusing exclusively on alcohol. Rapid assessment in the alcohol field remains remarkably underdeveloped. Whereas in many public health domains some kind of assessment is a prerequisite, the alcohol field seems to have been rather neglectful of the merits of this approach. Consequently, there is a lack of expertise in assessing alcohol problems at a local level and lack of tradition of using this information to develop targeted interventions.

Multiple Methods and Multiple Sources

No single source of data or single research method can provide a comprehensive picture of drinking. Assessments, therefore, are characterized by the use of multiple methods and data sources. Where available, the approach uses existing data of the sort employed in conventional epidemiological assessments and from existing surveys. But rapid assessments also use a wider array of existing information, drawn, for example, from industry and market research and documentary sources (such as policy documents, newspapers, television and radio reports, and information from treatment and social services) (Stimson et al., 2003). Essentially, this style of work uses a multimethod approach to gathering evidence. Existing data are likely to be supplemented by key informant interviews, focus groups, observations and visual recording, and mapping of problems (Stimson, Fitch, Rhodes, & Ball, 1999). A rapid assessment study of alcohol use in the Island of Jersey employed such a mix of information. Many of the methods utilized by this approach are also used by anthropologists, but, in contrast to conventional anthropology, rapid assessment does not have the luxury of months in the field.

Methods Used in a Rapid Assessment of Alcohol-related Problems on the Island of Jersey, Channel Islands

The assessment was undertaken in order to provide an evidence base for implementing Jersey's alcohol, drugs, and crime strategies. The largest of the nine English Channel Islands, the 45-square-mile Island of Jersey has its own independent government, legal, and monetary systems. Although its official resident population comprises around 90,000 people (of whom 10,000 are of Portuguese origin), the island has large population flows with approximately 1 million tourists a year and temporary and seasonal workers employed in the core island industries of agriculture, tourism, and international finance; 653 establishments have licenses to sell alcohol.

Fieldwork for the alcohol assessment comprised the following:

Collection and analysis of existing data: Over 30 agencies were contacted, including the hospital, police, brewers, prisons, customs and excise, education and youth services, and treatment facilities. Most information sources focused on administrative or clinical objectives, rather than on being part of a broader surveillance framework. Data often had to be compiled from paper records and cross-checked with other sources.

Development of indicators of alcohol problems: This included a review of alcohol strategy documents; a stakeholder consultation meeting with members of the government Senior Officers Group; focus groups and interviews with law enforcement, public health, and commercial bodies; and a review of existing data sources in Jersey.

Jersey alcohol licensee survey: A structured survey was undertaken in 93 of the 159 establishments holding a public bar license. Interviewers were recruited from the social science course at a local college and were trained by research staff. The survey was developed in collaboration with the four major breweries and represents an area for potential future collaboration.

Interviews and focus groups: Thirty unstructured and structured interviews were held with people in law enforcement, public health, and commercial organizations, along with 10 focus groups with a total of 55 participants.

Alcohol consumption estimate: An estimate of the per capita alcohol consumption was based on customs and excise data (recording volume of alcohol imported or produced on the island and net of exports). Estimates took into account flows of tourists and seasonal workers, using statistics provided by the Department of Policy and Resources and Tourism, and were adjusted for the volume of spirits leaving the island as personal exports (estimated at 20% of all spirits sold in 1995).

Observation: Structured and unstructured observations were undertaken of the supply and consumption of alcohol in a range of drinking settings to cross-check existing information and interview/focus group data.

Source: Fitch, Stimson, Jones, and Hickman (2001).

The starting point and often the focus of an assessment may be a health or social issue (for example, fetal alcohol syndrome or alcohol and mental health), a particular at-risk population (such as young people, women of reproductive age, refugees, individuals employed in particular occupations, arrestees, and older adults), a specific setting (such as entertainment areas, prisons, refugee camps, and tourist resorts), or a risky behavior (such as alcohol-impaired driving, drinking and sports, alcohol and sex, and mixing alcohol with other psychoactive drugs).

This approach to data collection has an investigative orientation, which, in more technical terms, means using data triangulation and inductive modes of analysis. *Triangulation* is the continual process of collecting and cross-checking information throughout an assessment (Denzin, 1978). The investigator compares information collected by different methods and from different data sources until confident of the accuracy and representativeness of the information and of the validity of the conclusions that can be drawn. Because of this emphasis on cross-checking, such assessment methods are potentially more rigorous, reliable, and valid than investigations using a single research method or data source (Rhodes, Stimson, Fitch, Ball, & Renton, 1999). *Induction* is a method for drawing conclusions and developing hypotheses from the data collected and searching for information that confirms, denies, or modifies these conclusions and hypotheses (Denzin, 1978). This approach, of critically examining and responding to the data while they are being collected, differs from research that adopts a linear or preplanned approach.

Characteristics of Rapid Assessment Methods

Speed: Time is vital when tackling social and health problems.

Cost-effective data collection: a preference for data collection techniques that have a high output of information in relation to input of research effort.

Parsimony: focus on collection of relevant information (rather than data exploration).

Practical relevance: The utility of an assessment may be judged by its adequacy for decision-making.

Strengthening local responses: encouragement of partnership and community participation to increase the practical relevance and applicability of the assessment.

Involvement of stakeholders: encouragement of participation and ownership of the problem by key local stakeholders, including community representatives, in the initial consultation, planning, and implementation of the assessment.

Use of existing information: gathering of new data undertaken only where the existing sources of information are inadequate.

Multiple methods and data sources: A single method or source of data cannot encompass all aspects of complex social problems.

Triangulation: Findings and conclusions are established through cross-checking multiple sources of data.

Inductive approach: generates and tests hypotheses during data collection.

Multilevel analysis: The assessment addresses the problem in the social, cultural, religious, political, and historical contexts.

Source: Fitch and Stimson (2003).

Multilevel Assessment

As shown elsewhere in this book, there is a multiplicity of opportunities to intervene to reduce alcohol-related problems. Rapid assessment methods have been designed to look at the many factors and levels by which behavior is influenced. In turn, this may suggest different levels at which interventions might be developed. For example, the incidence of alcohol-impaired driving is influenced by individual awareness of the problems and individual responsibility, the location of drinking venues in relation to people's residences, the availability of public transport, norms about drinking and driving, and drink-driving legislation and its enforcement. In turn, this means that interventions to reduce alcohol-impaired driving can operate at the individual, community, and structural levels.

The structural level—sometimes called the *macro level*—includes factors that are generally beyond the direct influence of the community or the individual, such as licensing laws, the beverage alcohol industry, national alcohol policies, taxation, health care systems, educational systems, and religion. It includes not only factors that are specific to alcohol but also ones that might not be so obviously linked: for example, the interaction between population migration and mobility, places of entertainment, and risky sexual behavior. Encased within this broad context are the community-level factors that influence how individuals drink, such as social networks to which they belong; the norms, beliefs, and values about alcohol that are shared with friends and local groups; and the characteristics of the environments where individuals live, work, and drink.

The example of beerhalls in Zimbabwe illustrates the link between structural and community influences on individual drinking (see "Zimbabwe: Beerhalls, Drinking, and Unsafe Sex"). A second example, from Cambodia (in " Cambodia: Links Between Migration and Mobility, HIV/AIDS, and Entertainment Venues"), indicates how economic liberalization and new transport infrastructure have an impact on the lives of male truck drivers and female staff of bars, brothels, gambling places, hotels, guesthouses, and restaurants. Such analyses show that some individuals in the population are more vulnerable to health problems than others because of their social networks, and provide valuable insight into the position of certain groups by virtue of age, occupation, or other social conditions. In turn, such information is pertinent to the development of targeted interventions.

Zimbabwe: Beerhalls, Drinking, and Unsafe Sex

In their rapid assessment of substance use and sexual behavior in Zimbabwe, Woelk and colleagues (2001) reported on the social significance of the drinking venues, beerhalls in particular. Given the general lack of recreational outlets, drinking establishments often serve as community centers and an opportunity for male bonding. Importantly, drinking in beerhalls was found to be central in generating risky sexual behaviors: As male patrons "share their resources to enable one another to get drunk, so they support each other in having casual or commercial sex" (p. 49).

Woelk and colleagues (2001) concluded that future interventions need to take into account the following factors found in this and associated studies:

- Local drinking establishments play an important role in the social life of men in many parts of Africa. In Zimbabwe, neighborhood beerhalls remain the primary recreational venue, especially among men from low-income, urban areas.
- Important as community institutions, drinking establishments usually have a frequent, loyal clientele, mostly from the immediate neighborhood.
- Drinking is a social activity among Black Zimbabwean men; it is more likely to occur in public drinking establishments with friends than at home.
- Peer influence in drinking venues can be an important protective or risk factor for unsafe sexual practices: "The peers sometimes actively contribute to each others' risk, and sometimes tacitly condone the risky

activities of their friends. In some circumstances, however, peers provide
support for HIV risk reduction by discouraging risky sex" (p. 49).

- Beerhalls' clients are generally aware of the link between alcohol use
and engaging in risky sexual behavior, and are also "ready to participate
in a risk reduction strategy" (p. 49).
- Although the prevalence of HIV/AIDS among Zimbabwean men is
particularly high, they have not been adequately targeted with intervention activities.

Source: Woelk et al. (2001).

Cambodia: Links Between Migration and Mobility, HIV/AIDS, and Entertainment Venues

The United Nations Development Programme (UNDP) undertook a number
of assessments of the link between transport, population movement, and
vulnerability to HIV/AIDS. In Cambodia, the assessment focused on two of
the main highways that run through the country.

According to Stimson and colleagues (2003, chapter 8.4, sec. 2.3),

> The rate of HIV infection in Cambodia is the highest in Southeast Asia. Economic
> liberalization, intermittent political instability, improvement of major road systems
> and increased exposure of formerly isolated communities and persons to outside
> contacts have exacerbated the vulnerability to HIV of the Cambodian people. The
> reconstruction of two of Cambodia's major roadways, Highway One and Highway
> Five, poses a number of challenges in the battle against HIV/AIDS transmission.
> Cutting across the country, these two highways link Cambodia to its neighbors
> of Thailand and Vietnam. Increased population movement, including short-term
> movements between villages and cities, and the increase in economic activity
> surrounding large-scale construction projects along transit routes, is a catalyst
> for the spread of HIV/AIDS. Mobile populations such as long-distance truck
> drivers, commercial sex workers, sea-farers, and migrant workers, are increas-
> ingly coming into contact with local communities where services are provided at
> places such as brothels, gambling places, hotels, guest houses, restaurants, bars
> and car parks. Interaction among these diverse sectors provides fertile ground for
> the transmission of HIV/AIDS. Effective intervention to reduce HIV vulnerability
> with the collaboration of communities, construction contractors, and government
> authorities is vital in preventing the HIV pandemic.

Source: Stimson et al. (2003).

FROM ASSESSMENT TO DECISIONS AND ACTION

In general, an assessment of alcohol issues encompasses the evaluation of both
the problem and the resources necessary to address it (including the identification

of already existing assets—such as agencies, people, and money—that can be further developed or adapted, and resources that are needed but not yet available). Assessments also identify factors that may constrain or facilitate interventions. They are used to assist the development of interventions and are not ends in themselves. A newer terminology used by WHO emphasizes this link between undertaking assessments and developing projects: The term *rapid assessment and response* (RAR) is a reminder of this approach's relevance to the development of interventions.

Rapid assessment studies often point to quite simple changes that can be made locally and that do not require adjustments in legislation, the development of new services, or major health promotion campaigns. For this reason, they may be particularly relevant to interventions targeting drinking behaviors, specific groups, and specific drinking contexts. For example, a flashpoint for alcohol-related incidents is often the combination of bars and clubs closing at the same time and lack of suitable means for dispersing large crowds from the entertainment areas in cities—on foot or by transport. The rapid assessment study on the Island of Jersey outlined earlier in this chapter identified a number of simple, short-term solutions to this problem (see "Bar Closing Times, Congregation, and Dispersal on the Island of Jersey").

Bar Closing Times, Congregation, and Dispersal on the Island of Jersey

Interviews with law enforcement officers and youth workers identified difficulties with current approaches to managing the flow of people in town center area and also the limited means available for dealing with individuals drinking alcohol in public. A lack of late-night transport was considered to be a key factor underpinning a large number of episodes of alcohol-related disorder. Inadequate bus services presented individuals with three main options: hiring a taxi from a taxi stand or company telephone service, leaving the area on foot, or waiting until the area cleared. Taxi availability was reported as limited, with particularly long delays during weekends. This was due to unwillingness among authorized taxi drivers to work weekends, and because of the cap imposed on the total number of drivers operating. As there are only three taxi stands in the town center, large queues could quickly develop in these locations, with resulting disputes and conflict over vehicle hire. Telephone taxi services were also observed to be prone to long delays before cars became available. Moreover, those leaving downtown on foot would often use the same main routes (for example, from outlying streets toward the taxi stand in a neighboring area). This concentrated the flow of people and was thought to increase the likelihood of episodes of alcohol-related disorder.

To address these problems, three suggestions emerged from interviews with taxi drivers and law enforcement staff: issuing "weekend-only" taxi licenses, thus increasing the number of vehicles working on Friday,

Saturday, and Sunday evenings; providing additional public taxi stands, particularly outside popular public houses or nightclubs; and making alternative walking routes more safe and attractive (for example, by improving existing street lighting).

Source: Fitch et al. (2001).

An assessment of alcohol problems may uncover some seemingly intractable difficulties, but it may also reveal opportunities for change. In the Zimbabwe example described above, for instance, both drinking and risky sexual behavior were found to be part of beerhall sociability. As Woelk and colleagues (2001) demonstrated, the social dynamics among drinking partners could provide an opportunity to reduce risky sexual behavior by encouraging friends to look out for each other, introducing new social norms (such as the use of condoms), and building awareness of the risks associated with casual sex.

Drink, Sex, and the Zimbabwean Beerhall: Opportunities to Reduce Alcohol-related Sexual Risk

A number of interventions were proposed to reduce risky sexual behavior in Zimbabwean beerhalls. Condoms could be made more easily available and accessible in drinking places (for instance, from vending machines). In addition, behavioral interventions could be developed to increase knowledge, skills, and social support related to HIV prevention among beerhall patrons.

In addition, popular opinion leaders among the beerhall clientele could be involved to spearhead initiatives to change drinking norms, including recognition of the unacceptability of casual sex while intoxicated. This strategy has been successfully used in the United States to target men in gay bars, reducing the incidence of risky sexual behavior among that population. The rationale behind this approach is that prominent individuals can be used as role models to influence changes in the attitudes, values, and behaviors of enough individuals within the target group to bring about a general change in that group's norms.

In addition to initiatives targeted at male beerhall patrons, measures could be developed to engage commercial sex workers. Woelk and colleagues (2001) proposed the decriminalization of commercial sex work, which could lead to more secure facilities, enabling sex workers to demand condom use. It would also then be possible to require regular health checkups and screenings for sexually transmitted diseases among this population. However, such an initiative would require a change in the law, a process likely to take years, and would most likely meet with strong opposition from Zimbabwe's religious leaders. Taking these and other such factors into account is important in choosing interventions that are most likely to succeed on the ground.

Source: Woelk et al. (2001).

The process also encourages people to think creatively. In a multicity evaluation of rapid assessment (Stimson et al., 2006), local teams used the knowledge that they gained to recommend a whole range of interventions specific to their communities and countries, including advocacy with government, means to influence policy, providing health information, training professionals, and enhancing treatment and rehabilitation. The recommended interventions were not "formulaic," but specific to the local context.

ASSESSMENT AND PARTNERSHIP

There are, thus, many ways in which assessments of the positive and negative aspects of drinking behavior can be undertaken. A starting point may well be existing and available epidemiological data, but richness and depth of understanding will be added by using a variety of research methods, often in combination. The range of issues that could be exploited in an alcohol assessment is shown in the "Components of an Alcohol Assessment."

Components of an Alcohol Assessment

- An understanding of the particular cultural, economic, social, and political context, and appreciation of the role of alcohol within it
- Information on prevailing drinking patterns, trends in drinking behavior, and societal norms about drinking
- Identification of social, community, and individual benefits of drinking
- Identification of health and social problems associated with drinking
- Identification of particular groups at risk of drink-related problems
- Identification of high-risk drinking locations and settings
- Information on prevailing market forces and future economic trends
- Analysis of policy measures already in place and areas in which these may need further development
- Analysis of current interventions and their effectiveness and limitations, and allocation of resources to different interventions
- Assessment of existing levels of cooperation among key stakeholders
- Identification of opportunities for developing new interventions and/or modifying existing ones
- Development of a plan of action to create and implement new or modified interventions

The growing interest in "evidence-based policy-making" and "evidence-based practice" has highlighted the gaps between information providers and decision-makers and led to various suggestions about how to get better evidence (Ross, Lavis, Rodriguez, Woodside, & Denis, 2003; Walter, Davies, & Nutley, 2003) and better utilization of evidence (Bero et al., 1998). There are definite advantages in reorienting the assessment process to make it more clearly linked to the development of interventions.

Assessment can itself be an inclusive process. Rather than being a result of research conducted by outside experts working in isolation from communities, the assessment approach outlined here recognizes the importance of involving local stakeholders. A range of local key players can be consulted before the assessment begins and then remain involved by helping with data collection, evaluation, and interpretation. Encouraging stakeholders to be involved in assessment introduces a pragmatic and analytical approach to social and health problems, an approach that is often missing in countries that do not have a tradition of public health analysis. For example, one of the lessons in implementing rapid assessment in Russia was that in the former Soviet Union, there was little understanding of how to assess and respond to problems within the community (Burrows, Trautmann, Bijl, & Sarankov, 1999). The assessment process encouraged the development of novel ways to analyze health and social issues in that country. Stakeholders can contribute vital expert knowledge, and their involvement in the entire process could enhance the sense of community ownership of subsequent interventions. Being involved in the assessment of problems helps develop partnerships—a theme central to this book (see Chapters 9 and 10, in particular)—and is the first step to developing appropriate and acceptable interventions.

REFERENCES

Adams, W. R. (1995). Guatemala. In D. B. Heath (Ed.), *International handbook on alcohol and culture* (pp. 99–109). Westport, CT: Greenwood.

Almedon, A. M., Blumenthal, U., & Manderson, L. (1997). *Hygiene evaluation procedures.* Boston: International Nutrition Foundation for Developing Countries.

Bero, L. A., Grilli, R., Grimshaw, J. M., Harvey, E., Oxman, A. D., & Thomson, M. A. (1998). Getting research findings into practice. Closing the gap between research and practice: An overview of systematic reviews of interventions to promote the implementation of research findings. *British Medical Journal, 317,* 465–468.

Black, N. (2001). Evidence-based policy: Proceed with care. *British Medical Journal, 323,* 275–278.

Burrows, D., Trautmann, F., Bijl, M., & Sarankov, Y. (1999). Training in the Russian Federation on rapid assessment and response to HIV/AIDS among injecting drug users. *Journal of Drug Issues, 29,* 811–842.

Chaloupka, F. J., Grossman, M., & Saffer, H. (2002). The effects of price on alcohol consumption and alcohol-related problems. *Alcohol Research & Health, 26,* 22–34.

Chambers, R. (1980). *Rapid rural appraisal: Rationale and repertoire.* Discussion paper 155. Brighton, UK: Institute for Development Studies.

Chen, C. M., Yi, H., & Hilton, M. E. (2005). *Trends in alcohol-related morbidity among short-stay community hospital discharges, United States, 1979–2003.* Surveillance Report 72. Bethesda, MD: National Institute on Alcohol Abuse and Alcoholism.

Child and Adolescent Health Research Unit. (2005). *Scottish Schools Adolescent Lifestyle and Substance Use Survey (SALSUS): National report. Smoking, drinking and drug use among 13 and 15 year olds in Scotland in 2004.* Edinburgh, UK: Stationery Office.

Connor, J., Broad, J., Rehm, J., Hoorn, V., & Jackson, R. (2005). The burden of death, disease, and disability due to alcohol in New Zealand. *New Zealand Medical Journal, 118*, U1579.

Currie, C., Roberts, C., Morgan, A., Smith, R., Settertobulte, W., Samdal, O., et al. (Eds.). (2004). *Young people's health in context: International report from the HBSC 2001/2002 survey.* WHO Policy Series: Health policy for children and adolescents, Issue 4. Copenhagen, Denmark: WHO Regional Office for Europe.

DeJong, W., Tsagarelli, T., & Schouten, E. (1999). Rapid assessment of injection drug use and HIV in the Republic of Georgia. *Journal of Drug Issues, 29*, 843–860.

Denzin, N. K. (1978). *The research act: A theoretical introduction to sociological methods.* 2nd ed. New York: McGraw-Hill.

Dill, P. L., Wells-Parker, E., & Soderstrom, C. A. (2004). The emergency care setting for screening and intervention for alcohol use problems among injured and high-risk drivers: A review. *Traffic Injury Prevention, 5*, 278–291.

Dorabjee, J., & Samson, L. (2000). A multi-centre rapid assessment of injecting drug use in India. *International Journal of Drug Policy, 11*, 99–112.

Dorn, N. (1981). Youth culture in the UK: Independence and round drinking—implications for health education. *International Journal of Health Education, 24*, 77–82.

Eck, J. E. (2002). *Assessing responses to problems: An introductory guide for police problem solvers.* Washington, DC: U.S. Department of Justice.

English, D. R., Holman, C. D. J., Milne, E., Winter, M. G., Hulse, G. K., Codde, J. P., et al. (1995). *The quantification of drug caused morbidity and mortality in Australia.* Canberra, Australia: Commonwealth Department of Human Services and Health.

Fitch, C., & Stimson, G. V. (2003). *RAR Review: An international mapping and retrospective evaluation study of rapid assessments conducted on drug use.* Report from the WHO Drug Injection Study Phase II. Geneva, Switzerland: World Health Organization.

Fitch, C., Stimson, G. V., Jones, S., & Hickman, M. (2001). *Responding to drug and alcohol use in Jersey.* Unpublished report, Imperial College School of Medicine, London, U.K.

Fitch, C., Stimson, G. V., Rhodes, T., & Poznyak, V. (2004). Rapid assessment: An international review of diffusion, practice and outcomes in the substance use field. *Social Science and Medicine, 59*, 1819–1830.

Glass, R. I., & Noji, E. K. (1992). Epidemiologic surveillance following disasters. In W. E. Halperin, E. L. Baker, & R. R. Monson (Eds.), *Public health surveillance* (pp. 195–205). New York: Van Nostrand Reinhold.

Grant, B. F., Kaplan, K., Shepard, J., & Moore, T. (2003). *Source and accuracy statement for Wave 1 of the 2001–2002 National Epidemiologic Survey on Alcohol and Related Conditions.* Bethesda, MD: National Institute on Alcohol Abuse and Alcoholism.

Greig, A. (2001). *HIV and drug use: A toolkit on participatory assessment and response.* Unpublished guidelines, International HIV/AIDS Alliance, Brighton, U.K. Retrieved July 25, 2006, from http://www.aidsalliance.kiev.ua/ru/library/pdf/par_toolkit.pdf.

Gusfield, J. R. (1987). Passage to play: Rituals of drinking time in American society. In M. Douglas (Ed.), *Constructive drinking: Perspectives on drink from anthropology* (pp. 73–90). Cambridge: Cambridge University Press.

Hall, W., & Hunter, E. (1995). Australia. In D. B. Heath (Ed.), *International handbook on alcohol and culture* (pp. 7–19). Westport, CT: Greenwood.

Harford, T. C., Zobeck, T. S., Grant, B. F., Stinson, F. S., Aitken, S. S., Dufour, M., et al. (1988). Alcohol surveillance program of the Division of Biometry and Epidemiology: History, growth, and future directions. *Alcohol Health and Research World, 12,* 309–313.

Heath, D. B. (Ed). (1995). *International handbook on alcohol and culture.* Westport, CT: Greenwood.

Heath, D. B. (1999). Drinking and pleasure across cultures. In S. Peele & M. Grant (Eds.), *Alcohol and pleasure: A health perspective* (pp. 61–72). Philadelphia: Brunner/Mazel.

Heath, D. B. (2002). *Drinking occasions: Comparative perspectives on alcohol and culture.* Philadelphia: Brunner/Mazel.

Hibell, B., Andersson, B., Bjarnason, T., Ahlström, S., Balakireva, O., Kokkevi, A., et al. (2004). *The ESPAD Report 2003: Alcohol and other drug use among students in 35 European countries.* Stockholm: Swedish Council for Information on Alcohol and Other Drugs (CAN) and the Pompidou Group at the Council of Europe.

Holloway, K., & Bennett, T. (2004). *The results of the first two years of the NEW-ADAM programme.* Home Office Online Report 19/04. Retrieved March 3, 2006, from http://www.homeoffice.gov.uk/rds/pdfs04/rdsolr1904.pdf.

International Center for Alcohol Policies. (2002). *Alcohol policy development: Partnership in practice.* Washington, DC: Author.

Jacobson, N., Butterill, D., & Goering, P. (2003). Development of a framework for knowledge translation: Understanding user context. *Journal of Health Services Research and Policy, 8,* 94–99.

Johnston, L. D., O'Malley, P. M., Bachman, J. G., & Schulenberg, J. E. (2004). *Monitoring the Future national survey results on drug use, 1975–2003: Volume II, College students and adults ages 19–45.* Bethesda, MD: National Institute on Drug Abuse.

Kalichman, S. C., & Cain, D. (2004). A prospective study of sensation seeking and alcohol use as predictors of sexual risk behaviors among men and women receiving sexually transmitted infection clinic services. *Psychology of Addictive Behaviors, 18,* 367–373.

King, E., Ball, J., & Carroll, T. (2001). *Alcohol consumption patterns among Australian 15–17 year olds from February 2000 to February 2004.* Sydney, Australia: Department of Health and Ageing.

Kumar, M. S., Mudaliar, S., Thyagarajan, S. P., Kumar, S., Selvanayagam, A., & Daniels, D. (2000). Rapid assessment and response to injecting drug use in Madras, South India. *International Journal of Drug Policy, 11,* 83–98.

Larson, A., & Manderson, L. (1997). *Contextual assessment procedures for STDs and HIV/AIDS prevention programmes: A manual.* Brisbane: Australian Centre for International and Tropical Health and Nutrition.

Leacock, S. (1979). Ceremonial drinking in an Afro-Brazilian cult. *American Anthropologist, 66,* 1393–1394.

Lin, D., Li, X., Yang, H., Fang, X., Stanton, B., Chen, X., et al. (2005). Alcohol intoxication and sexual risk behaviors among rural-to-urban migrants in China. *Drug and Alcohol Dependence, 79,* 103–112.

Macpherson, S. (2002). *Domestic violence: Findings from the 2000 Scottish Crime Survey.* Edinburgh, UK: Scottish Executive Central Research Unit.

Madhivanan, P., Hernandez, A., Gogate, A., Stein, E., Gregorich, S., Setia, M., et al. (2005). Alcohol use by men is a risk factor for the acquisition of sexually transmitted infections and human immunodeficiency virus from female sex workers in Mumbai, India. *Sexually Transmitted Diseases, 32*, 685–690.

Mandelbaum, D. G. (1965). Alcohol and culture. *Current Anthropology, 6*, 281–293.

Manderson, L. (1996). *Population and reproductive health programmes: Applying rapid anthropological assessment procedures.* New York: United Nations Population Fund.

Martin, S. E., Bryant, K., & Fitzgerald, N. (2001). Self-reported alcohol use and abuse by arrestees in the 1998 Arrestee Drug Abuse Monitoring Program. *Alcohol Research and Health, 2*, 72–79.

Murray, C. J. L., & Lopez, A. D. (Eds.). (1996). *Global burden of disease and injury: A comprehensive assessment of mortality and disability from diseases, injuries, and risk factors in 1990 and projected to 2020.* Cambridge, MA: Harvard School of Public Health and World Health Organization.

Mwenesi, H. A. (1996). Rapid assessment of drug abuse in Kenya. *Bulletin on Narcotics, 48*, 65–78.

Nevitt, J. R., & Lundak, J. (2005). Accuracy of self-reports of alcohol offenders in a rural midwestern county. *Psychological Reports, 96*, 511–514.

Nolte, E., Britton, A., & McKee, M. (2003). Trends in mortality attributable to current alcohol consumption in east and west Germany. *Social Science and Medicine, 56*, 1385–1395.

Osaki, Y., Matsushita, S., Shirasaka, T., Hiro, H., & Higuchi, S. (2005). Nationwide survey of alcohol drinking and alcoholism among Japanese adults. *Japanese Journal of Alcohol & Drug Dependence, 40*, 455–470.

Parry, C. D. H., Plüddemann, A., Steyn, K., Bradshaw, D., Norman, R., & Laubscher, R. (2005). Alcohol use in South Africa: Findings from the first demographic and health survey (1998). *Journal of Studies on Alcohol, 66*, 91–97.

Rehm, J., Patra, J., & Popova, S. (2006). Alcohol-attributable mortality and potential years of life lost in Canada 2001: Implications for prevention and policy. *Addiction, 101*, 373–384.

Rehm, J., Rehn, N., Room, R., Monteiro, M., Gmel, G., Jernigan, D., et al. (2003). Global distribution of average volume of alcohol consumption and patterns of drinking. *European Addiction Research, 9*, 147–156.

Rhoades, E. (1992). The coming revolution in methods for rural development research. In N. S. Scrimshaw & G. R. Gleason (Eds.), *Rapid assessment procedures: Qualitative methodologies for planning and evaluation of health related programs* (pp. 60–78). Boston: International Nutrition Foundation for Developing Countries.

Rhodes, T., Stimson, G. V., Fitch, C., Ball, A., & Renton, A. (1999). Rapid assessment, injecting drug use, and public health. *Lancet, 354*, 65–68.

Ridolfo, B., & Stevenson, C. (2001). *The quantification of drug-caused mortality and morbidity in Australia, 1998.* Canberra: Australian Institute of Health and Welfare.

Ross, S., Lavis, J., Rodriguez, C., Woodside, J., & Denis, J. L. (2003). Partnership experiences: Involving decision-makers in the research process. *Journal of Health Services Research and Policy, 8*, 26–34.

Sargent, M. (1979). *Australian studies. Drinking and alcoholism in Australia: A power relations theory.* Sydney, Australia: Longman Cheshire.

Scott, M. S. (2002). *Assaults in and around bars.* Washington, DC: U.S. Department of Justice.

Scrimshaw, S. C. M., & Hurtado, E. (1987). *Rapid assessment procedures for nutrition and primary health care.* Tokyo: United Nations University.

Simbayi, L. C., Kalichman, S. C., Jooste, S., Mathiti, V., Cain, D., & Cherry, C. (2004). Alcohol use and sexual risks for HIV infection among men and women receiving sexually transmitted infection clinic services in Cape Town, South Africa. *Journal of Studies on Alcohol, 65*, 434–442.

Singh, G. K., & Hoyert, D. L. (2000). Social epidemiology of chronic liver disease and cirrhosis mortality in the United States, 1935–1997: Trends and differentials by ethnicity, socioeconomic status, and alcohol consumption. *Human Biology, 72*, 801–820.

Single, E., Robson, L., Xie, X., & Rehm, J. (1998). Economic costs of alcohol, tobacco and illicit drugs in Canada, 1992. *Addiction, 93*, 991–1066.

Sjögren, H., Eriksson, A., Broström, G., & Ahlm, K. (2000). Quantification of alcohol-related mortality in Sweden. *Alcohol and Alcoholism, 35*, 601–611.

Sloan, F. A., Reilly, B. A., & Schenzler, C. (1994). Effects of prices, civil and criminal sanctions, and law enforcement on alcohol-related mortality. *Journal of Studies on Alcohol, 55*, 454–465.

Stimson, G. V., Donoghoe, M. C., Fitch, C., Rhodes, T., Ball, A., & Weiler, G. (2003). *Rapid assessment and response: Technical guide, TG-RAR.* Geneva, Switzerland: WHO Department of HIV/AIDS, Department of Child and Adolescent Health and Development.

Stimson, G. V., Fitch, C., des Jarlais, D., Poznyak, V., Perlis, T., Oppenheimer, E., et al. (2006). Rapid assessment and response studies of injection drug use: Knowledge gain, capacity building, and intervention development in a multisite study. *American Journal of Public Health, 96*, 288–295.

Stimson, G.V., Fitch, C., & Rhodes, T. (Eds.). (1998). Руководство по использованию методологии проведения экспресс-оценки и реагированию на ситуацию с инъекционным потреблением наркотиков [*The Rapid assessment and response guide on injecting drug use (draft for field-testing)*]. (Médecins sans Frontières Holland, Trans.). Retrieved July 25, 2006, from http://www.rararchives.org/document_centre.html.

Stimson, G. V., Fitch, C., Rhodes, T., & Ball, A. (1999). Rapid assessment and response: Methods for developing public health responses to drug problems. *Drug and Alcohol Review, 18*, 317–325.

Sverdlov, L. S. (2001). Cultural aspects of the social attitudes toward alcohol in Russia: Alcohol in Russia. *Common Health, 9*, 14–18. Retrieved March 27, 2006, from http://www.aiha.com/english/pubs/spr01/sverdlov14.pdf.

Trenk, M. (2001). Religious uses of alcohol among the Woodland Indians of North America. *Anthropos, 96*, 73–86.

Uehata, T., Suzuki, K., Wada, K., Yamaguchi, N., Minowa, M., Oida, T., et al. (2002). *Report on the 2000 National Survey on Adolescent Drinking Behaviour.* Tokyo: Study Group for the 2000 National Survey on Adolescent Drinking Behaviour.

United Nations International Drug Control Programme. (1993). *Guidelines for conducting a rapid assessment study.* Geneva, Switzerland: Author.

United Nations International Drug Control Programme. (1998). *Guidelines for the development and implementation of drug abuse rapid situation assessments.* Vienna, Austria: Author.

Unwin, N., & Aspray, T. J. (2001). Quick decision? Fast track data for health policy. *Id21 Insights, 1*. Retrieved March 2, 2006, from http://www.id21.org/insights/insights-h01/index.html.

U.S. Department of Health and Human Services. (1999). *A guide for conducting community-based rapid assessment, rapid response, and evaluation (RARE)*. Unpublished guidelines. Office of HIV/AIDS Policy, Washington, DC, U.S.

U.S. National Highway Traffic Safety Administration. (2005). *Alcohol-related fatalities in 2004*. Washington, DC: Author.

Walter, I., Davies, H., & Nutley, S. (2003). Increasing research impact through partnerships: Evidence from outside healthcare. *Journal of Health Services Research and Policy, 8*(Suppl. 2), 58–61.

Weiss, C. H. (1979). The many meanings of research utilization. *Public Administration Review, 39*, 426–431.

White, A. M., Kraus, C. L., Flom, J., Kestenbaum, L., Mitchell, J., Burleson, A., et al. (2005). College students lack knowledge of standard drink volumes: Implications for definitions of risky drinking based on survey data. *Alcoholism: Clinical and Experimental Research, 29*, 631–638.

White, I. R., Altmann, D. R., & Nanchahal, K. (2004). Mortality in England and Wales attributable to any drinking, drinking above sensible limits and drinking above lowest-risk level. *Addiction, 99*, 661–662.

Woelk, G., Fritz, K., Bassett, M., Todd, C., & Chingono, A. (2001). *A rapid assessment in relation to alcohol and other substance use and sexual behavior in Zimbabwe*. Harare: University of Zimbabwe.

Wong, E. (2002). *Rapid assessment and response on HIV/AIDS among especially vulnerable young people in South Eastern Europe*. Belgrade: UNICEF Area Office for the Balkans. Retrieved August 1, 2006, from http://www.un.org.al/download/publications/unicef/rar.pdf.

World Health Organization (WHO). (1995). *Field guide on rapid nutritional assessment in emergencies*. Geneva, Switzerland: Author.

World Health Organization (WHO). (2000). *International guide for monitoring alcohol consumption and related harm*. Geneva, Switzerland: Author.

World Health Organization (WHO). (2004). *Global status report on alcohol 2004*. Geneva, Switzerland: Author.

Zureik, M., & Ducimetière, P. (1996). High alcohol-related premature mortality in France: Concordant estimates from a prospective cohort study and national mortality statistics. *Alcoholism: Clinical and Experimental Research, 20*, 428–433.

4

Opportunities for Targeted and Tailored Interventions

In the broadest terms, the purpose of alcohol policy in countries where alcohol beverages are permitted is to establish appropriate, realistic, and sustainable approaches that will help reduce alcohol-related harms, promote safer drinking behaviors, and enhance the positive function of alcohol consumption for individuals and society. The consumption of alcohol is linked to positive and negative health and social outcomes and, as such, needs to be viewed within the broad context of health care, education, and social policies. Alcohol is also a commodity like many others, subject to trade and fiscal considerations. Some aspects of alcohol consumption are relevant to overall quality of life and to leisure, entertainment, and tourism. Other aspects have particular relevance within the judicial system, ranging from the enforcement of legal drinking ages and blood alcohol content (BAC) limits, to crime and violence linked to the supply and consumption of alcohol. Thus, in addressing alcohol issues, policies need to balance a wide range of interests and considerations.

Beverage alcohol policies are closely related to an array of other measures with an impact on societies and populations. If the drinking of alcohol were all bad—for example, if there were no safe level of consumption—or if the drinking of alcohol were all good, then the policy options would be simpler. However, as with other commodities, the policy task is to maximize benefits to individuals and society, while minimizing the harms.

Some countries have explicit policies on alcohol, in the sense of a guiding statement of how a given country wishes to promote wise consumption and reduce harms. In others, "policy" is less clearly formulated, and actions to influence consumption and drinking behavior are often a mix of potentially conflicting aims of different government departments. Thus, some departments—for example, departments of trade and agriculture—may be charged with promoting production and sale of beverage alcohol. Meanwhile, departments of culture and tourism may aim to improve entertainment and leisure, in which the drinking of alcohol has a role. Others, such as the departments of roads and transport, may be concerned about alcohol-impaired driving. Departments of health may be focused on consumption figures, drinking behavior, and morbidity and mortality data. In some countries, the revenue-raising potential of taxing alcohol may be the primary government interest. In many developing and transitional countries, however, the idea of a planned alcohol policy may be absent or low on the list of priorities.

Much of the academic and public health debate about alcohol policies has focused on ameliorating and avoiding negative consequences of alcohol consumption and on the reduction of drinking-related harms. This chapter will, of necessity, focus on problematic drinking, because that is the conceptual framework of the bulk of the alcohol literature. Most of the interventions considered in this chapter follow this emphasis on problem drinking in that they are designed to reduce harms. The alcohol policy and research field has neglected the promotion of the positive aspects of alcohol consumption (see Annex). Endorsement of positive drinking behaviors might be a policy aim, as in the case of the English changes in licensing laws, which, it is argued by government, will promote a "café culture" with convivial drinking prevailing over intoxication and loutish behavior (Department for Culture, Media and Sport, 2001). But beyond this policy aspiration, it is hard to find in the literature concrete projects that promote positive aspects of drinking.

The starting point for many alcohol policies is the population-level regulation of consumption through control of price and access to alcohol (for example, by age and rules on when and where alcohol may be sold and consumed). In this book, we argue that population-level measures alone are inadequate: They are unresponsive to the needs of different cultures and contexts, and may lack relevance to the requirements of at-risk individuals and groups. Targeted interventions are a critical component. These may be aimed at particular populations, drinking behaviors, or drinking contexts. A successful design for alcohol policies that is both realistic and sustainable relies on balancing population-level measures with targeted interventions.

NATIONAL-LEVEL REGULATORY MEASURES

All countries in which the sale and supply of alcohol are permitted impose a range of regulatory measures affecting manufacturers, retailers, and consumers. In some cases, the primary motivation for such regulation has been economic: States have seen the taxation of alcohol as a significant source of revenue. Controls have also been introduced to protect or promote economic efficiency and to deal with social disorder and alcohol-related harms.

Because they are directed toward the population as a whole, regulations must be broad enough to meet the general needs of society. They include attention to whether, where, and to what extent alcohol should be made available. Controls over alcohol access and availability, drinking age legislation, and licensing laws fall in this category. Pricing of alcohol and revenue generation are also covered through regulation, as are the marketing and sale of beverage alcohol. The extent to which each of these is regulated and how such measures are implemented vary across countries, reflecting different cultures and experiences with alcohol.

Many alcohol policies implemented at a regulatory level have relied on the assumption that there is a fixed and predictable relationship between the level of average per capita consumption across a population and the incidence of some social and medical problems (Babor et al., 2003; Edwards et al., 1994; Ledermann, 1952; Ledermann & Tabah, 1951). With this in mind, policies have often aimed to reduce consumption across entire populations (usually at the national level) in an attempt to reduce harm. Pricing and taxation, standards to ensure the quality and purity of beverages, restricted licensing hours, limits on the density of retail and serving outlets, state-run monopolies, and even complete prohibition are all part of the spectrum of alcohol controls (Babor et al., 2003).

Some restrictions on access and availability have proven effective in addressing harm related to particular patterns of drinking. For example, there is evidence that certain limits on access to alcohol may contribute to reducing public disorder and incidence of violence. Natural experiments carried out in Finland, Norway, and Sweden in the 1980s (when days to sell alcohol were restricted) resulted in a lower incidence of drunkenness and related disorder (Room, 2002).

The development and implementation of population-level measures concerning alcohol require attention to a number of critical factors to ensure their effectiveness. These relate to the feasibility of implementing the initiatives: the *obstacles* that need to be overcome, the *procedural requirements* within a country, and the *resources* that are needed. For example, the success of population-level policies hinges upon there being few obstacles to their acceptance. Generally, it means that there must be support among the public, and measures must be compatible and consistent with the local drinking culture. Perhaps most crucially, effective regulations need to go hand in hand with specific procedural requirements—in particular, a country's ability to tax and to enforce regulations. In many parts of the world, it is very difficult to regulate alcohol production and sale. For example, noncommercial alcohol produced in the informal production sector predominates in a number of countries. The efficiency of tax measures depends, in part, on there being a commercial alcohol industry through which taxes may be collected. Likewise, the efficiency of controls over where alcohol may be sold and consumed assumes the existence of adequate resources to ensure compliance, including a functioning, noncorrupt means of enforcement. Without adequate enforcement, the impact of regulation is likely to be negligible or even nonexistent.

The lack of specificity of broad-based measures may also trigger certain *unintended consequences*, creating additional harm rather than reducing it. For instance, high taxes and curtailed availability of commercially produced alcohol may increase unregulated trade and consumption, leading to a variety of social and health problems (Härstedt, 2004; Haworth & Simpson, 2004; Leifman, 2001; Lyall, 2003; Nordlund & Österberg, 2000). Such negative outcomes often occur where there are disparities in measures between jurisdictions. Cross-border trade in legally obtained and commercially produced beverage alcohol has flourished in an era of increasingly open borders in many parts of the world. Scandinavian countries—including Sweden, Norway, and Finland, where well-entrenched mechanisms for controlling the availability of alcohol have long been in effect through state-run monopolies and high taxation rates—offer a case in point. Geographic proximity to countries with fewer restrictions and cheaper alcohol has resulted in a flow of beverage alcohol from jurisdictions with less control (for example, European Commission, 1999; Lyall, 2003).

Restrictions on availability and high prices of beverage alcohol have been also found to promote growth in the alcohol black market, encouraging trade in smuggled and counterfeit beverage alcohol. Trade in these commodities is thriving, largely in association with organized crime. In addition, the dubious provenance and quality of many such black market beverages, often adulterated to reduce the cost of production, have resulted in a range of health and social problems, including poisoning and accidental death (Leifman, 2001; Room et al., 2002).

Differences in pricing and other regulations affecting alcohol access in adjoining jurisdictions have unintended negative consequences that extend beyond trade issues and beverage choice. In parts of the United States, for example, a legal purchase age of 21 years, higher pricing, and stringent enforcement of sales regulations have provided an incentive for some (particularly) young people to seek easier access to alcohol across the border in Mexico, where the drinking age is 18 and the cost of alcohol is lower. Those seeking to circumvent restrictions cross the border to drink, often heavily, with resulting increases in traffic crashes and fatalities and violent incidents. The term *blood border* has been used to reflect the high toll and social cost (Baker, Johnson, Voas, & Lange, 2000; Lange, Lauer, & Voas, 1999; Voas, Lange, & Johnson, 2002). Strict laws on underage drinking have also led to reluctance to seek help for alcohol overdose among U.S. college students (Lewis & Marchell, 2006).

Finally, because taxation of beverage alcohol is an important source of revenue generation for governments, increases in pricing of alcohol as a means of curtailing problems may lead to a decline in revenue, as nontaxed beverages are substituted for those that are taxed (Popham, Schmidt, & de Lint, 1975; Single, 2004).

Controls and Consequences: The Example of Russia

Heavy consumption of beverage alcohol and a pattern of heavy episodic ("binge") drinking have long been described in Russia (McKee, 1999). Reports from the Soviet Union in the early 1980s attributed a third of deaths to alcohol abuse, half of them due to accidents, poisonings, and violence (Nemtsov, 2002). During that time, the country also saw a decline in the age at which individuals began drinking and an increase in heavy drinking among women and young people (White, 1996). A relationship has been observed between the persistent economic failures of this era and the lack of productivity caused by alcohol abuse (McKee, 1999; Nemtsov, 2002).

From the early twentieth century, repeated government-led efforts were made to reduce alcohol-related problems. The most notable of these efforts was the Gorbachev-era anti-alcohol campaign in the mid-1980s. The campaign was a direct application of the population-level control model for alcohol policy. It sought to reduce harm by reducing production and sales of alcohol and increasing the price (Loukomskaia, 1997). In addition, a legal ban was introduced on the consumption of alcohol in the workplace and at official functions, and sales of alcohol before 2 p.m. and at off-premise locations were restricted (McKee, 1999).

These measures were initially successful and well received, especially among women. After the initial implementation of the plan, the production of alcohol decreased by a third (McKee, 1999), and the price increased by 20% in 1985 and 25% in 1986 (Nemtsov, 1998). A sharp decline in alcohol consumption (McKee; Nemtsov, 2002), alcohol-related injuries, deaths, crime, and work absenteeism (Loukomskaia, 1997) followed.

However, promising as those results were, they were short-lived. Within a year of implementation, the Soviet Union witnessed a burgeoning black market in alcohol. There was a sharp rise in the smuggling of alcohol across borders, as well as the illegal production of *samogon*, a home-produced spirit (Loukamskaia, 1997; McKee, 1999; Partanen, 1993; Zaigraev, 2004). The inability of the government to control the illicit production of alcohol brought about a rise in a range of health and social problems (Partanen).

It has been argued that the ultimate demise of the campaign was prompted by both its successes and its failures. Effective limits on production and sales of alcohol led to a significant drop in government revenue. In addition, the inability to control the black market led to a new set of health and social problems (McKee, 1999). Within two years, limits on alcohol availability and production were again loosened, and the need for revenue resulted in resumed government production and sales of alcohol (Loukomskaia, 1997).

Apart from the possibility of unintended consequences and increased harm, there is little to suggest that population-level measures alone are able to change problematic drinking patterns and the general drinking culture of excess that prevail in many countries. Despite continuing implementation of high taxes, restrictions on the availability of alcohol, and other population-level measures, harmful drinking patterns remain highly prevalent in the countries of Northern and Eastern Europe (see, for example, Hibell et al., 2000, 2004; Österberg & Karlsson, 2003).

Broad-based measures do not differentiate between individuals whose drinking is associated with harmful outcomes and those whose drinking is not (Grant & Litvak, 1998; Midanik, 1994; Norström, 2000; Rehm et al., 1999; Single, Brewster, MacNeil, Hatcher, & Trainor, 1995). By their very nature, broad-level approaches address the lowest common denominator and lack the flexibility to respond to individual problem drinking patterns. They may be insufficiently sensitive to the important cultural role alcohol plays around the world. Drinking is an integral part of many societies and offers a colorful panorama of traditions, uses, myths, and practices (Heath, 1995, 2000; Marshall, 1979). Each region of the world is characterized by its own idiosyncratic array of beliefs, attitudes, and rituals around alcohol and views on its appropriate place within everyday life. To be generally acceptable, interventions must take account of these considerations. Consequently, assessment of drinking behaviors is a prerequisite to developing appropriate interventions, as outlined in Chapter 3.

Finally, an emphasis on population measures may have a stultifying effect on the process of policy development. If controls at national level are seen as the main vehicle for influencing drinking, it may absolve other agencies and organizations from responsibility for developing and implementing measures that encourage responsible consumption. Moreover, if governments rely solely on raising prices and limiting alcohol availability to reduce alcohol consumption across an entire population, certain high-risk drinking patterns or behaviors among specific groups may remain overlooked.

Because of the limitations of population-based controls, policy and prevention efforts related to alcohol are increasingly focusing on targeted harm minimization among specific population groups, certain drinking settings, and particular patterns of drinking (International Center for Alcohol Policies [ICAP], 2005). As we argue, there are many opportunities to "do something about drinking" that target these three aspects and that can be applied to complement national-level measures or be implemented in the absence of national measures and policies. The corollary of this approach to targeted and tailored interventions is that it brings into the arena a wide range of organizations that might otherwise be excluded from contributing to reducing alcohol-related harms and ensuring the individual and social benefits of drinking alcohol.

Targeted interventions to minimize risk are pragmatic. They acknowledge that risks are inherent in many human behaviors, including the consumption of alcohol. The aim of strategies to minimize alcohol-related risks is to shift behaviors and norms linked with drinking to ensure that when people consume alcohol, they do so in the safest possible manner.

TARGETING POPULATIONS AT HIGH RISK

Many people consume alcohol moderately, with few—if any—problems. Certain individuals, however, are at great risk for harm because of their excessive drinking patterns, consumption of harmful beverage types, or involvement in activities that significantly heighten risk for harm both to themselves and to others when associated with alcohol.

For some, all drinking may be associated with harm. Such people include alcohol-dependent individuals, those whose drinking is chronically excessive and harmful, or those who, for reasons of genetic predisposition, health issues, or social status, may be particularly susceptible to harm (see Chapter 2). Targeted interventions offer a means of identifying problem drinkers and implementing various interventions aimed at changing their drinking behavior, including treatment, education, brief intervention techniques, therapy, behavior modification, or the promotion of abstinence.

For the majority of people, drinking may be generally moderate and unproblematic but occasionally hazardous as, for example, in binge drinking and intoxication (Grant & Litvak, 1998; Stockwell, Hawks, Lang, & Rydon, 1996). Targeted interventions offer a means of addressing specifically these episodes of excess in an effort to reduce their occurrence and the severity of their outcomes. The provision of information on what constitutes "risk" in drinking through drinking guidelines, information on standard units or standard drinks, and education for the general public is a useful approach (ICAP, 2003b). Various efforts also exist to target particular population groups (Plant, Single, & Stockwell, 1997). For example, approaches tailored to the needs and behaviors of young people have received considerable attention, as has guidance on drinking during pregnancy and drinking by older adults, many of whom take medications that may modify the effects of alcohol. For further discussion on young people, see Chapter 7.

Drinking and Pregnancy

The various populations known to be at increased risk for harm from drinking alcohol include pregnant women. More accurately, it is their unborn children who are at risk from maternal drinking patterns. Although there is conclusive evidence that heavy patterns of alcohol consumption, whether chronic or episodic, may be particularly risky (Plant, Abel, & Guerri, 1999), there is less agreement on the implications of low to moderate drinking. From a public health perspective, whether a "safe" limit of consumption during pregnancy exists and where it should be defined are two important questions (Abel, 1998a; Faden & Graubard, 2000; Lorente et al., 2000; Plant et al., 1999).

Drinking Patterns and Outcomes

The relationship between patterns and outcomes applies as much to drinking during pregnancy as it does to other areas where potential for health or social harm exists. Fetal defects are linked to a harmful combination of heavy alcohol consumption and other factors, such as drug use, smoking, poor diet and general health, lower socioeconomic status, and social deprivation (Chandler, Richardson, Gallagher, & Day, 1996; Faden & Graubard, 2000; Fried, 1995; Kesmodel & Olsen, 2001; Lorente et al., 2000; May et al., 2005; Plant et al., 1999).

Frequent heavy episodic drinking—also referred to as *binge drinking*—during pregnancy appears to be related to the severity of fetal harm (Abel, 1998a; Coles, Russell, & Schuetze, 1997), especially during the early stages of pregnancy. However, because growth and, particularly, neural development occur during the second and third trimesters, discouraging harmful drinking patterns is advisable at all stages of pregnancy. As with other pregnancy risks, those associated with drinking increase among women over 30 years of age (Jacobson et al., 1993; Larroque & Kaminski, 1998), and problem drinkers are more likely than non-problem drinkers to experience spontaneous abortion (Henriksen et al., 2004). In women who are light or infrequent drinkers, there is little robust evidence of either increased risk of fetal harm or of spontaneous abortion (Abel, 1998a; Cavallo, Russo, Zotti, Camerlengo, & Ruggenini, 1995).

Paternal drinking also appears to play a role in contributing to problems in infants. Heavy drinking by fathers, for example, has been linked to an increased risk of cardiovascular defects, such as ventricular septal defect, in offspring (Savitz, Schwingl, & Keels, 1991). Differences in weight and immune system problems have also been found in children of fathers who drink excessively (Abel, 1990; Bielawski & Abel, 1997; Gottesfeld & Abel, 1991; Savitz et al., 1991).

Fetal Harm

Perhaps the best-known outcomes of heavy maternal drinking during pregnancy are the conditions known as fetal alcohol syndrome (FAS) and fetal alcohol effects (FAE), a spectrum of harm found at lower levels of consumption, also known as "partial FAS with confirmed maternal alcohol exposure" (Institute of Medicine, 1996). A number of traits characterize FAS: pre- and postnatal growth deficiencies; physical anomalies, particularly visible in facial features; learning difficulties; and cognitive, hearing, and visual disabilities (Streissguth & O'Malley, 2000; Warren et al., 2001).

In most countries where data are available, FAS is reported relatively rarely (Abel, 1998b; Testa, Quigley, & Das Eiden, 2003). In the United States, for example, FAS is diagnosed in 0.5 to 2 out of every 1,000 live births (May & Gossage, 2001), with an average of 0.97 cases per 1,000 live births in developed countries (Abel, 1995). However, research evidence shows that there are certain populations among whom fetal alcohol-related disorders are disproportionately prevalent. The highest rate of FAS in the world has been described among communities in South Africa's Western Cape Province (May et al., 2000; Viljoen et al., 2005; Warren et al., 2001). Among African American and Native American populations in the United States and among First Nations communities in Canada, the incidence of FAS is higher than in other populations in either country (Abel, 1995; Miller et al., 2002).

Overall, higher rates of harm have been reported in populations of low socioeconomic status and among socially marginalized groups (Abel, 1995; May et al., 2005). In many cases, inadequate access to prenatal care and medical care in general contributes to the problem. There is also evidence that other factors, such as maternal age, smoking, poor nutrition, and use of other psychoactive substances (such as illicit and prescribed drugs), may contribute to the outcomes, meaning that the overall picture is still unclear.

Implications for Policy and Intervention

Any harm resulting from drinking during pregnancy is preventable. Various policy and prevention measures have been developed to address drinking among pregnant women and to minimize the potential for harm to the unborn fetus.

Information

There is strong international consensus that women should either abstain from or only drink low amounts of alcohol during pregnancy, reflected in official drinking recommendations provided in several countries (ICAP, 2003b, 2004b). Among countries with policies on alcohol and pregnancy, those recommending abstinence include Canada, Sweden, and the United States. Countries whose recommendations allow for occasional drinking of low or moderate amounts include Australia, Denmark, and the United Kingdom.

Although government guidelines are a useful first step, information regarding drinking during pregnancy may be more effectively shared on an individual basis by health care providers, such as nurses and physicians. For women without easy access to health care, relevant information may be imparted through the intervention of other professionals, for example, social workers.

Assessment of Drinking

Alcohol consumption by young women is becoming both more frequent and heavier in many countries. This may, in part, be due to the changing role of women in society, their access to disposable income, and increasing acceptance of drinking by women. As a basis for prevention, therefore, careful monitoring is required to examine these new consumption patterns (especially among women who are already pregnant) with attention to other factors, such as illicit and prescribed drug and tobacco use within this population.

Screening and Intervention

Early screening of pregnant women to identify problem drinkers is a useful approach to prevention. Particularly when coupled with advice and interventions aimed at changing drinking patterns and the general provision of prenatal care, early screening is highly effective. In many cases, such interventions also apply to new mothers who are identified as having a drinking problem. Advice should be given within the context of relevant country guidelines, where these exist. However, in many countries, especially in the developing world, information, screening, and advice are simply not available.

Support and Treatment

It is important that professionals working in alcohol and drug treatment agencies are trained to provide advice to any female client of child-bearing age and to provide help and support as early as possible for problem-drinking women who become pregnant. A support system is an essential component of education and any attempt to change the drinking patterns of individuals. The involvement of family members and others who play an important role in the lives of expectant mothers can help ensure that harm to both mother and child is minimized.

Several protocols for the treatment of women who abuse alcohol or other substances exist, although reaching the pregnant problem drinker continues to be difficult. Early identification and brief intervention approaches have shown promise. In particular, where pregnant women belong to otherwise marginalized groups (for example, Native communities or the urban poor), any effective approach must be culturally appropriate and, in some cases, must rely on the support of the community as a whole. Here, approaches have been implemented that are responsive to local needs and to cultural sensitivities and that can be integrated into the lifestyle of different populations.

Source: Adapted from ICAP (2005).

Targeted interventions aimed at individuals take on a variety of forms. Some approaches may at first glance appear unconventional, as they are not directly targeted at alcohol consumption itself but at secondary effects of particularly harmful drinking patterns. However, they embody the essence of targeted interventions—pragmatic approaches to reduce the potential for harm, both direct and indirect. For example, the shelter-based Managed Alcohol Project (MAP) in Canada was established to deliver health care to chronically homeless people with severe alcohol problems. Aiming to minimize personal and social harm in this marginalized population, the project offers housing, on-site access to health professionals, counseling, and treatment from alcoholism that allows provision of small, regulated amounts of beverage alcohol of known quality. In a small-group evaluation, MAP was shown to reduce consumption of beverage and nonbeverage alcohol (such as mouthwash) and the use of crisis services (such as emergency department visits, hospital admissions, and police encounters), while improving health, nutrition, hygiene, and compliance with medication and medical treatment among the participants (Podymow, Turnbull, Coyle, Yetisir, & Wells, 2006; see also Hass, 2001).

Another intervention, directed at individuals outside the mainstream of society, is an effort in Australia targeted at heavy chronic drinkers. The malnutrition that often accompanies heavy and abusive alcohol consumption may contribute to the development of certain neurological deficits, including Wernicke-Korsakoff syndrome (Manzo, Locatelli, Candura, & Costa, 1994; Thomson & Cook, 2000). The discovery that these deficits can be prevented with thiamine (vitamin B_1) in the diet sparked an effort to enrich flour with this supplement in order to counteract potential harm in heavy drinkers while causing no harm to others. Research evidence suggests that this measure has been effective in reducing the prevalence of Wernicke-Korsakoff syndrome in Australia (Drew & Truswell, 1998; Harper et al., 1998; Ma & Truswell, 1995).

Counseling and treatment are further examples of how interventions can be applied in a targeted way, delivered through psychotherapy, behavior modification, abstinence-based programs, or pharmacotherapy. If individuals with problematic drinking patterns (who are not alcohol dependent) are identified early, interventions can help reduce the development of subsequent problems through modification of behaviors and drinking patterns (Bien, Miller, & Tonigan, 1993). Several screening instruments have been developed for this purpose, including the Alcohol Use Disorders Identification Test (AUDIT) and other question-naires (Babor, de la Fuente, Saunders, & Grant, 1989; Babor, Higgins-Biddle, Saunders, & Monteiro, 2001; Cherpitel, 1995; Degenhardt, Conigrave, Wutzke, & Saunders, 2001; Ewing, 1984; Knight et al., 1999; Kelly, Donovan, Chung, Cook, & Delbridge, 2004; Selzer, 1971; Seppä, Lepisto, & Sillanaukee, 1998; Seppä, Mäkelä, & Sillanaukee, 1995). Each of these screening tools differs in its specificity and sensitivity, and some are more appropriate for particular target groups than others, depending on gender, age, and other factors (for example, Clements, 1998; Fleming, Barry, & McDonald, 1991; O'Hare & Sherrer, 1999; Smith, McCarthy, & Anderson, 2000; Soderstrom et al., 1997).

Screening tools are relatively easy to use and can be implemented in various settings by trained personnel without imposing an undue burden on health care providers. Emergency rooms, for example, offer an appropriate venue for screening, as those who are admitted may have already suffered harm from their drinking and can be identified (Bérenger, Schwan, Fleury, & Rigaud, 2002; Cherpitel, 1995; Thom, Herring, & Judd, 1999). In some countries, particularly in the developing world, pharmacists, social workers, and others may be appropri-ate implementers of early identification techniques, because regular contact with primary health care providers might be rare (Saitz, Sullivan, & Samet, 2000; Zunino, Litvak, & Israel, 1998). Homeless shelters and other similar venues are also useful targets. Once at-risk individuals are identified, a brief intervention session is administered with the objective of modifying drinking behaviors. In many cases, a single brief counseling session may be sufficient, or the interven-tion may take several short sessions.

A particularly effective approach to reducing harm at the individual level is offered by brief interventions aimed at problem drinkers (Babor et al., 2001; Bien et al., 1993). Brief intervention techniques can be adapted to suit the needs and interests of specific target groups. For example, electronic and Internet-based assessments have been developed that appeal to and have shown promise for young people (Miller, 2001; Saitz et al., 2004). For older individuals, brief interventions can be modified for geriatric needs and integrated into services provided in long-term care facilities. Similarly, screening for pregnant women may help prevent problems for both mother and fetus if implemented early, for example, as part of prenatal care. Brief interventions also offer a means of targeting hard-to-reach populations that may otherwise not be accessible to the health care sector (for example, individuals who may be socially marginalized or of low socioeconomic status).

Programs that offer the option of controlled drinking in a nonjudgmental setting may appeal to some drinkers and provide early access to help (Kosok, 2006). Still controversial (see, for example, Glatt, 1995; Humphreys, 2003), controlled drinking is a viable treatment goal for some problem drinkers (Kosok; Rosenberg, 1993; Sanchez-Craig, Wilkinson, & Davila, 1995).

Moderating Drinking

Moderation Management (MM) is a support group for individuals concerned about their alcohol consumption (Kishline, 1994). This harm reduction program seeks to encourage problem drinkers to limit or stop their alcohol intake by providing information about alcohol, low-risk drinking levels, and self-management and problem-solving techniques, and helps clients achieve balance in all aspects of life. The program was originally designed to be delivered in the face-to-face group format, but has gained significant membership when implemented via the Internet.

MM is relatively new and not widely available; its effectiveness is still being evaluated. However, descriptive studies of the MM membership revealed that this program is filling an important niche by attracting individuals who have not previously sought help with their drinking and either are specifically looking to control their consumption or need guidance in deciding between moderation and abstinence. The majority of members are White, middle class, and college educated; most are heavy drinkers who may be mildly or moderately alcohol dependent. MM appears to be particularly attractive to women and individuals who prefer to participate online. Studies of MM membership indicate that the controlled drinking option would meet a significant demand if it were more widely available.

Source: Kosok (2006).

Minimum Purchasing and Drinking Age

Another area in which broad-based approaches have been used to target a large subset of the general population is the legislation that mandates the minimum allowable age for the purchase and consumption of beverage alcohol. Different countries set different age limits, often based on historical practice and cultural attitudes toward alcohol and the transition from childhood to adulthood. Most commonly, the age threshold ranges from 16 to 18 years, with some countries setting the bar at 21 years and others having no mandated age requirement at all (see Table 7.1 in Chapter 7; see also ICAP, 2002a; World Health Organization, 2004). Having a legally mandated drinking age provides a very important message regarding the status of alcohol as an adult product. A combination of legislation, enforcement, and implementation at the community and even the family levels has contributed to the effectiveness of age limits in reducing harm for young people (Grube, 1997; ICAP, 2002a; Wagenaar et al., 2000).

The success of a mandated drinking age relies on a combination of restricted access to alcohol (through the imposition of age restrictions), its enforcement, and the contribution of family, educators, the community, as well as retailers of beverage alcohol. For further discussion on young drinkers, see Chapter 7.

Targeting Specific Population Groups and Specific Risky Behaviors: Medical Amnesty Approach

Despite the fact that the minimum drinking age in the United States is 21 years, alcohol consumption among underage college students is widespread (see, for example, O'Malley & Johnston, 2002), with a significant number drinking in ways that put them at risk for alcohol-related harm, including alcohol poisoning (Wechsler, Dowdall, Maenner, Gledhill-Hoyt, & Lee, 1998; Wechsler, Nelson, & Weitzman, 2000). Although well-intended, universities' efforts to enforce minimum drinking age and other related policies may have negative consequences, deterring some students from calling for help in alcohol-related medical emergencies (Colby, Raymond, & Colby, 2000; Meilman, 1992).

In order to address this issue, some U.S. colleges and universities have adopted "Good Samaritan" or medical amnesty policies that reduce judicial consequences for students involved in certain alcohol-related incidents (Higher Education Center for Alcohol and Other Drug Prevention, 1996). For example, Cornell University (in rural New York State) implemented a Medical Amnesty Protocol in 2002, along with an awareness campaign on recognizing alcohol poisoning and responding effectively. The protocol had two main aims: (a) to increase the likelihood that students will call for help in alcohol-related medical emergencies, and (b) to increase the likelihood that students thus treated will receive follow-up psychoeducational interventions at the university health center (the Cornell Brief Alcohol and Screening Intervention for College Students—BASICS—program, consisting of screening and feedback administered in two sessions, with elements of motivational interviewing and cognitive-behavioral skills training).

An evaluation conducted two years after the implementation of the protocol revealed that the two chief aims of the initiative have been met. Over the two years, there has been a steady increase in alcohol-related calls for assistance to emergency medical services, with survey results indicating that, following the implementation of the protocol, students were less likely to cite fear of judicial consequences as a barrier to call. Moreover, the percentage of students who received brief psychoeducational follow-up after being treated for alcohol-related emergency at the university health center more than doubled—from 22% in the year before the protocol was implemented to 52% in its second year. Although the medical amnesty approach may not be deemed appropriate by some universities, in Cornell, the protocol and initiatives that surrounded it facilitated a positive dialogue and cooperation among students, staff, and faculty about the ways to reduce alcohol-related harm.

Source: Lewis and Marchell (2006).

TARGETING DRINKING BEHAVIORS

Separating Drinking From Other Risky Activities

Harm often results from activities and situations that may accompany alcohol consumption. As a result, attention to these activities and situations in the form of tailored measures, targeted policies, and specific prevention approaches can help reduce the potential for harm. Efforts aimed at alcohol-impaired driving provide a salient example of targeted interventions that have resulted in considerable reduction of harm but that also illustrate the range of possible approaches.

Drink-driving legislation and its enforcement, the setting of BAC limits for drivers, and the use of random breath testing have all proven useful (Davis, Quimby, Odero, Gururaj, & Hijar, 2003; ICAP, 2002b, 2005; Moynham et al., 2000; Peek-Asa, 1999; Stewart, 2000; Stewart & Sweedler, 1997). At the same time, initiatives such as designated driver programs and the provision of alternative transportation for those who have been drinking can be implemented alongside regulations and enforcement.

Enforcement of both mandated drinking age and driving age also has a clear impact on the reduction of harm (ICAP, 2002a). Graduated drivers' licenses or curfews for young drivers are options that have been tested in numerous settings (ICAP, 2002b; Rehn, Room, & Edwards, 2001). Particular regulations may also apply to repeat offenders. Measures targeting them specifically—such as loss of license, incarceration, interlock devices, or treatment—may be implemented to prevent the risk of future harm to self and others (Beirness, 2001; Bjerre, 2003; Voas, Blackman, Tippetts, & Marques, 2002). For further discussion on alcohol-impaired driving and interventions that address it, see Chapter 5.

Changing Behavior Through Information and Awareness Building

There is much debate surrounding the effectiveness of "alcohol education," and particularly of those measures that are applied in structured and formal settings such as schools (Babor et al., 2003; ICAP, 2004a). It is important to realize, however, that schools constitute only a portion of what is a much broader opportunity for aiding in responsible decision-making. Family, peers, cultural values and norms, and individuals' own experience are all important influences on a person's drinking behavior.

Examples of public alcohol education measures implemented outside school include official guidelines on consumption, campaigns against alcohol-impaired driving and designated driver initiatives, and information for particular groups— young people, older adults, pregnant women, or other "at-risk" populations (ICAP, 2005; Martinic & Leigh, 2004). Many governments, nongovernmental organizations, research organizations, and medical and other professional associations provide such information (ICAP, 2003b). Recommendations are given regarding "low/minimum risk" drinking levels for men and women, taking into account risk for both chronic and acute harm. There is variation in the recommendations provided by different countries both in the recommended limits for drinking and in the sizes of drinks used as a standard (see Table 4.1). In some countries, information includes limits for daily and weekly consumption and addresses drinking patterns (for example, ICAP, 2003b; National Health and Medical Research Council, 2001). Although most of the recommendations are provided for the general adult population, some guidelines include information tailored for pregnant women, young people, older adults, those who are alcohol dependent, or others deemed at increased risk for harm.

TARGETING DRINKING CONTEXTS

Drinking Venues

Creating a safer drinking environment also involves modifying the setting in which drinking occurs. Across cultures, drinking takes place in diverse venues, both public and private, that range from cafés, restaurants, bars, shebeens, and beer gardens to open public spaces at festivals or religious functions (Heath, 2000; Marshall, 1979).

Each of these settings can be modified in ways that are likely to reduce the potential for harm and injury (Plant et al., 1997). For example, the introduction of special glassware that crystallizes when shattered can reduce the risk for injury in drinking venues where fighting may break out. Modifying the physical space in which alcohol is consumed by changing lighting, creating partitions, and rearranging seating can also offer ways to reduce the potential for harm from violent confrontations. A powerful intervention approach includes the training of staff in serving and retail establishments to recognize signs of intoxication among patrons and to deal effectively with problematic situations, including managing crowd control.

Ensuring that the products served in drinking establishments are of good quality and do not contain toxic substances or contaminants is also an important part of responsible hospitality. Particularly in developing countries, the beverage alcohol consumed is largely noncommercial, especially among the poorer segments of society for whom commercial beverages are often unaffordable (Haworth & Simpson, 2004). As these traditional and often home-produced beverages are not subject to rigorous quality controls, ensuring their purity and safety is largely the responsibility of those who run establishments where non-commercial alcohol is served (such as shebeens and bodegas). Making drinking environments safer is discussed further in Chapter 6.

Public Order and Public Nuisance

Increasingly, there is recognition that communities are instrumental in developing responses and interventions aimed at improving the safety and wellbeing of their citizens. This is as true for alcohol as for other policy areas. The strength

Table 4.1 Sample Drinking Guidelines From Select Countries

Country	Men	Women	Standard Drink Unit, Grams (g) of Ethanol
Australia[a]	Not to exceed 4 units/day (40g/day); not to exceed 28 units/week (280g/week)	Not to exceed 2 units/day (20g/day); not to exceed 14 units/week (140g/week)	10g
Austria[b]	24g/day	16g/day	10g
France[c]	Not to exceed 20g/day	Not to exceed 20g/day	12g beer; 8g wine
Hong Kong[d]	Not to exceed 3–4 units/day; not to exceed 21 units/week	Not to exceed 2–3 units/ day; not to exceed 14 units/week	1 unit = glass of wine or pint of beer
Italy[e]	Not to exceed 2–3 units/day (24–36g/day)	Not to exceed 1–2 units/day (12–24g/day)	12g
Netherlands[f]	Not to exceed 3 units/day (29.7g/day)	Not to exceed 2 units/day (19.8g/day)	9.9g
New Zealand[g]	Not to exceed 3 units/day (30g/day); not to exceed 21 units/week (210g/week)	Not to exceed 2 units/day (20g/day); not to exceed 14 units/week (140g/week)	10g
Poland[h]	2 units/day (20g/day) up to 5 times/week (not to exceed 100g/week)	1 unit/day (10g/day) up to 5 times/week (not to exceed 50g/week)	10g
Portugal[i]	2–3 units/day (28–42g/day)	1–2 units/day (14–28g/day)	14g
South Africa[j]	Not to exceed 21 units/week (252g/week)	Not to exceed 14 units/week (168g/week)	12g
Spain[k]	Not to exceed 3 units/day (30g/day)	Not to exceed 3 units/day (30g/day)	10g
Sweden[l]	Not to exceed 20g/day	Not to exceed 20g/day	N/A
Switzerland[m]	Not to exceed 2 units/day (24g/day)	Not to exceed 2 units/day (24g/day)	10–12g
United Kingdom[n]	3–4 units/day (24–32g/day); not to exceed 21 units/ week (168g/week)	2–3 units/day (16–24g/day); not to exceed 14 units/ week (112g/week)	8g
United States[o]	1–2 units/day (14–28g/day); not to exceed 14 units/ week (196g/week)	1 unit/day (14g/day); not to exceed 7 units/week(98g/week)	14g

[a] National Health and Medical Research Council.
[b] Federal Ministry for Labour, Health and Social Affairs.
[c] Ministry of Health, Family and Persons with Disability.
[d] Department of Health and Social Security.
[e] Ministry for Agriculture and Forestry, and National Institute for Food and Nutrition.
[f] Stichting Verantwoord Alcoholgebruik.
[g] Alcohol Liquor Advisory Council (ALAC).
[h] State Agency for Prevention of Alcohol-Related Problems (PARPA).

Table 4.1 (continued) Sample Drinking Guidelines From Select Countries

[i] National Council on Food and Nutrition.

[j] South African National Council on Alcoholism and Drug Dependence.

[k] Ministry of Health and Spanish Institute for the Investigation of Beverage Alcohol.

[l] Swedish Research Council.

[m] Swiss Federal Commission for Alcohol Problems, and Swiss Institute for the Prevention of Alcohol and Drugs Problems.

[n] Department of Health and Social Security.

[o] U.S. Department of Agriculture, and U.S. Department of Health and Human Services.

Source: International Center for Alcohol Policies (2003b, 2004b).

of communities lies, among other things, in greater awareness about the reality of problems facing them, direct knowledge of the particular needs of those who live within them, and awareness of matters in need of change. The immediacy of problems for communities also means increased responsiveness and involvement that may often be diluted when issues are addressed at a national or even regional level. The likelihood of firsthand experience of community members with various problems and risks also ensures that a broader range of groups and sectors may become involved than where the responsibility for reducing problems is left to national-level government and law enforcement.

Influencing the Drinking Risk Environment: Community Prevention Approach

In addition to "traditional" alcohol harm reduction efforts that focus on particular groups within a community—including media campaigns, youth education programs, and treatment services—a systems approach may be applied to change local social, economic, or physical structures, or "the environment" (Holder, 2000, 2004). This approach targets local decision-makers and promotes community-level policy change that may include the following: "prioritizing alcohol-related problematic behavior (for example, by the police); enforcing laws to prevent alcohol sales to underage or intoxicated persons; controlling location and density of alcohol outlets; and ensuring server training for all licensed premises" (Mistral, Velleman, Templeton, & Mastache, 2006, p. 280). Central to the approach are partnerships among a wide range of community stakeholders (Holder, 2004). According to Holder (2000), "[T]here is much potential for more locally based strategies that do not depend upon national policy, and there is increased demand for local initiatives to prevent alcohol problems" (p. 845).

Particularly in urban areas around the world, there has been an increase over recent years in late-night entertainment activity in or near bars, pubs, and clubs. Although such venues contribute to the local economy for many communities, they are also the source of a range of social problems (Gruenewald, Millar, & Roeper, 1996; Single et al., 1997). Much late-night entertainment involves drinking, often geared toward young adults. Noise, rowdy behavior, littering, and public disorder are not uncommon in some areas, and crime and violence can be an undesirable side effect.

Public nuisance and disorder place a heavy burden on communities and high demand on services such as policing, street cleaning, emergency services, and public transport (Chisholm, Rehm, van Ommeren, & Monteiro, 2004; Reid, Hughey, & Peterson, 2003; Treno, Grube, & Martin, 2003; Weitzman, Folkman, Folkman, & Wechsler, 2003; Zhu, Gorman, & Horel, 2004). Access to areas where entertainment is concentrated also requires transportation, making alcohol-impaired driving, traffic crashes, and injuries subjects for concern (Wagenaar & Holder, 1991). Where an officially mandated purchase age for alcohol exists, attention should be given to preventing alcohol purchases by individuals under that age (Freisthler, Gruenewald, Treno, & Lee, 2003; Toomey et al., 1998; Wagenaar et al., 1996).

Various harm reduction approaches have been developed with regard to late-night entertainment (see Chapter 6). These measures complement efforts to restrict access to alcohol, such as limiting the hours of sale. Zoning restrictions relating to the service and sale of beverage alcohol for on- and off-premise consumption have also been used successfully to curtail public disorder. Limiting the number of outlets permitted within a given geographic area has been helpful in reducing the risk of violent crime (Laranjeira & Hinkley, 2002; Norström, 2000; Zhu et al., 2004). In particular, this appears to hold true where the concentration of bars rather than restaurants is high (Lipton & Gruenewald, 2002). At the same time, "hotspots" that might be created by restricting outlets to specific areas within a community have been countered by increased policing and enforcement. In these instances, active involvement at the community level (implemented in concert with controls) has been instrumental in ensuring success (Holder, 2000; Holder et al., 2000; Reynolds, Holder, & Gruenewald, 1997).

Local Alcohol Accords

Partnerships between the various stakeholders involved in the service of alcohol have shown considerable promise. Community intervention programs or "accords" have been tested in several countries in Western Europe, Australia, Canada, and the United States (Wallin, Norström, & Andreasson, 2003). Drink-driving campaigns are most successful when there is involvement of local police, government, media, and a variety of other stakeholders, which can ensure that information is disseminated and reaches its intended audiences. Local business owners, for example, may distribute informational materials to their employees and patrons; licensed premises can draw upon their staff to monitor drinking patterns and ensure safe transport home. Insurance companies have also begun to play a role in improving safety through increased premiums or even voiding of policies and coverage where alcohol-impaired driving is implicated in traffic crashes (California DUI, 2005; TD Canada Trust, 2005).

Where minimum legal purchase and drinking age limits exist for beverage alcohol, the community is also the main resource in determining whether and how these are enforced. Retailers, police, educators, and families play an important role in upholding regulations, identifying infractions, and promoting responsible behavior. Approaches include requesting identification from patrons and refusing service to those under the legal drinking age (Freisthler et al., 2003; Toomey et al., 1998; Wagenaar et al., 1996). The Cops in Shops program in the United States, for example, relies on the joint action of law enforcement and retailers at the community level to prevent sales of alcohol to underage young people (Century Council, 2005; for a brief discussion of this program, see Chapter 7).

TRUSTED SOURCES AND IMPLEMENTERS

It has been suggested that the source rather than the actual substance of information is the critical element in determining whether the message will be used and prove to be effective (Johnson & Slovic, 1994). When it comes to alcohol prevention and policy, the government and health sectors have traditionally been instrumental in both policy design and implementation. However, measures to reduce the risk for harm attached to specific patterns of drinking and to high-risk individuals, situations, or settings require broader involvement. It is particularly important to engage those groups and sectors that are familiar with the issues to be addressed, that are in tune with the culture in which efforts will be applied, and that enjoy the trust of given target populations (Martinic & Leigh, 2004).

Medical professionals are key players in delivering targeted interventions. They are the experts whose advice is sought when health problems arise, and they also have the ability to impart such advice before any harm has occurred. Familiar with their patients' drinking patterns, lifestyles, and health history, they are in a position to offer recommendations on drinking and other aspects of health-related behavior that can reduce the risk for harm. Health professionals have an obligation to provide their patients with balanced and accurate information on benefits and risks of drinking, and to help them identify the most appropriate course of action (Klatsky, 1999a, 1999b). A major prerequisite, therefore, is the adequate training of health professionals and social workers who fulfill the primary health care function in many countries (Aubrège, 2001; Bérenger et al., 2002; Chappel & Lewis, 1999; Klamen, 1999; Seppä, Pekuri, Kääriäinen, & Aalto, 2004).

The workplace is another venue for the implementation of targeted interventions (ICAP, 2003a). Workers can be provided with information about drinking and related health and social issues. Screening in the workplace may identify problematic patterns before harm has occurred and offer opportunities for further referral and interventions (Henderson, Hutcheson, & Davies, 1996; Hermansson et al., 2003; Raskin & Williams, 2003). Employers also have the means to enforce observance of responsible drinking practices while workers are on the job, and criminal charges related to accidents or other incidents involving alcohol may be grounds for dismissal (International Labour Organization, 2005; Müller, 1991).

Legal liability issues are often a strong incentive for licensed premises to implement prevention measures (Sloan, Stout, Whetten-Goldstein, & Liand, 2000).

In short, the broad range of possibilities offered by targeted interventions regarding alcohol involves an equally broad range of stakeholders in their implementation. Educators play a critical role in ensuring the effective delivery of information. The media can help to raise awareness of issues and to achieve solutions through its reporting and the provision of accurate and balanced information. Producers and retailers of beverage alcohol also have an important part to play, as do the social aspects organizations (SAOs), industry-sponsored organizations that have been established to deal with the reduction of harm and the promotion of responsible drinking practices.

Most important of all, however, efforts toward alcohol harm reduction must be meaningful to the intended audiences. As a result, often the most effective implementers of targeted interventions are family and peers, clergy, and others who are influential in shaping the lives of those around them (Milgram, 2001; Plant, 2001). Particularly when it comes to young people, there is evidence that highly structured interventions, such as school-based programs, are less effective than those relying on the involvement of peer groups or the family in their implementation (Centre for Addiction and Mental Health, 1999; Hanson, 1996; Hellandsjø Bu, Watten, Foxcroft, Ingebrigtsen, & Relling, 2002; Houghton & Roche, 2001; ICAP, 2004a; Paglia & Room, 1999).

Reaching certain marginalized groups is a challenge to harm reduction efforts. In developing countries, some communities may be generally inaccessible through conventional channels, health professionals may be few or ill-equipped to deal with their needs, and broad-based programs may be lacking. Illiteracy and the entrenchment of particular drinking patterns within different cultures often provide further hurdles. In addition, the concept of "health" may take on different meanings within different cultural contexts (Mussell, Nicholis, & Adler, 1991). In these cases, approaches may be developed that rely on the community as a whole to offer interventions and solutions in a culturally appropriate manner. Table 8.2 in Chapter 8 examines a range of different prevention measures that can be applied to reduce the potential harm associated with drinking.

First Nations and Inuit Initiative on FAE/FAS: It Takes a Community

Among the indigenous populations of Canada, the First Nations and Inuit, the prevalence of FAS and FAE is 1 in 5 live births, significantly higher than for the general population. Social marginalization and deprivation, cultural disruption, a lack of opportunities for education and employment, and a culture of paternalism and external control have contributed to high levels of substance abuse and alcohol dependence in these communities.

In 1997, the Canadian government launched an initiative, It Takes a Community, intended to provide a framework for addressing FAE/FAS that is responsive to the needs of indigenous populations, taking into account their values and principles (Health Canada, 1997/2001). The approach recognizes that the concept of health among these peoples focuses on wellness, balance, and harmony within the culturally accepted components of human nature—physical, mental, emotional, and spiritual. There is also emphasis on collective approaches to addressing individual problems that integrate the individual, the family, and the community.

It Takes a Community aims to prevent FAE/FAS births while at the same time increasing knowledge, skills, and quality of life among those already affected, be they children, parents, or families. A long-term objective is to promote capacity building within the communities to empower them to become self-sufficient in addressing similar issues in the future. The program relies on raising awareness through culturally relevant information and educational initiatives for all segments of the population. It is aimed particularly at pregnant women and women of child-bearing age, as well as at their partners, and trains community and health workers to deliver appropriate instruction, provide support, and facilitate access to prenatal care. Other elements include access to assistance programs—including mental health services and detoxification and treatment facilities—and interventions aimed at domestic violence, sexual abuse, and other factors.

At the heart of the program is the notion that causes and solutions are interrelated, and that interventions need to be implemented in synergy to avoid fragmentation among the involved groups and service providers or disconnects between the issues involved. The Native communities are themselves responsible for the implementation of the approach in a way that is responsive to the needs of their individual citizens affected by FAE/FAS.

Source: Health Canada (1997/2001).

CREATING BALANCED ALCOHOL POLICIES

Many factors affect why people drink, what they drink, when and where they drink, with whom they drink, and with what positive and negative outcomes. Because they focus on settings, situations, and at-risk individuals, targeted interventions are adaptable to the needs of diverse cultures and contexts. This flexibility allows them to be developed on the basis of the assessment of particular drinking patterns and practices. The research and evaluation literature gives some guidance as to which interventions are likely to be effective, but there are dangers in accepting "off-the-shelf" solutions. As argued in Chapter 3, the development of acceptable and appropriate interventions requires prior assessment of local drinking practices and the individual and social function of drinking, as well as identification of specific issues to be addressed. The choice of interventions also needs to consider the feasibility of their implementation, including obstacles to be overcome and the procedures and resources needed to get them into place (see Table 8.2 in Chapter 8).

Balance in alcohol policy requires implementation not only through top-down approaches that cast a wide net across the population as a whole, but also through efforts that both are aimed at and involve communities and their individual members. Measures that respond to the reality of how people drink can capture the many facets of drinking behaviors and related problems that exist around the world.

How this balance is created will vary from one country to another, reflecting prevailing attitudes, social and economic circumstances, and culture. Depending on specific needs and contexts, some initiatives may have more relevance than others or be of higher priority. How approaches are developed will depend on the culture in question, the role of alcohol within it, and the needs of a particular society. A balanced approach to alcohol policy does not view alcohol in isolation. Instead, it accepts that alcohol is a commodity with its own panoply of related risks and benefits. Like many other commodities—be they automobiles, medications, or foods—alcohol has positive effects and benefits, alongside negative ones. A sustainable alcohol policy must recognize this and strive to view issues surrounding alcohol as part of the broader panorama of human activity, risk, and responsibility.

REFERENCES

Abel, E. L. (1990). *Fetal alcohol syndrome*. Oradell, NJ: Medical Economics.

Abel, E. L. (1995). Update on incidence of FAS: FAS is not an equal opportunity birth defect. *Neurotoxicity and Teratology, 17*, 437–443.

Abel, E. L. (1998a). *Fetal alcohol abuse syndrome*. New York: Plenum.

Abel, E. L. (1998b). Fetal alcohol syndrome: The "American paradox." *Alcohol and Alcoholism, 33*, 195–201.

Aubrège, A. (2001). La place des médecins généralists [The role of private physicians]. *Alcoologie et Addictologie, 23*, 219–223.

Babor, T. F., Caetano, R., Caswell, S., Edwards, G., Giesbrecht, N., Graham, K., et al. (2003). *Alcohol: No ordinary commodity. Research and public policy*. Oxford: Oxford University Press.

Babor, T. F., de la Fuente, J. R., Saunders, J., & Grant, M. (1989). *AUDIT: The Alcohol Use Disorders Identification Test: Guidelines for use in primary health care*. Geneva, Switzerland: World Health Organization.

Babor, T. F., Higgins-Biddle, J., Saunders, J. B., & Monteiro, M. G. (2001). *AUDIT: The Alcohol Use Disorders Identification Test: Guidelines for use in primary care*, 2nd ed. Geneva, Switzerland: World Health Organization.

Baker, T. K., Johnson, M. B., Voas, R. B., & Lange, J. E. (2000). Reduce youthful binge drinking: Call an election in Mexico. *Journal of Safety Research, 31*, 61–69.

Beirness, D. J. (2001). *Best practices for alcohol interlock programs*. Ottawa, Canada: Traffic Injury Research Foundation.

Bérenger, P., Schwan, R., Fleury, B., & Rigaud, A. (2002). Propositions pour l'amélioration de la prise en charge des personnes en difficulté avec l'alcool à l'hôpital [A few suggestions for the improvement of alcoholics' treatment in hospital]. *Alcoologie et Addictologie*, *24*, 41–46.

Bielawski, D. M., & Abel, E. L. (1997). Acute treatment of paternal alcohol exposure produces malformations in offspring. *Alcohol: An International Biomedical Journal*, *14*, 397–401.

Bien, T. H., Miller, W. R., & Tonigan, S. (1993). Brief intervention for alcohol problems: A review. *Addiction*, *88*, 315–336.

Bjerre, B. (2003). Evaluation of the Swedish ignition interlock program. *Traffic Injury Prevention*, *4*, 98–104.

California DUI. (2005). *Car insurance after a DUI*. Retrieved August 29, 2005, from http://www.california-drunkdriving.org/car_insurance.html.

Cavallo, F., Russo, R., Zotti, C., Camerlengo, A., & Ruggenini, A. M. (1995). Moderate alcohol consumption and spontaneous abortion. *Alcohol and Alcoholism*, *30*, 195–201.

Centre for Addiction and Mental Health. (1999). *Alcohol and drug prevention programs for youth: What works?* Toronto, Canada: Author.

Century Council. (2005). *Cops in Shops*. Retrieved August 26, 2006, from http://www.centurycouncil.org/underage/cops.html.

Chandler, L. S., Richardson, G. A., Gallagher, J. D., & Day, N. L. (1996). Prenatal exposure to alcohol and marijuana: Effects on motor development of preschool children. *Alcoholism: Clinical and Experimental Research*, *20*, 455–461.

Chappel, J. N., & Lewis, D. C. (1999). Medical education. In M. Galanter & H. D. Kleber (Eds.), *Textbook of substance abuse treatment*, 2nd ed. (pp. 529–534). Washington, DC: American Psychiatric Press.

Cherpitel, C. J. (1995). Screening for alcohol problems in the emergency room: A rapid alcohol problems screen. *Drug and Alcohol Dependence*, *40*, 133–137.

Chisholm, D., Rehm, J., van Ommeren, M., & Monteiro, M. (2004). Reducing the global burden of hazardous alcohol use: A comparative cost-effectiveness study. *Journal of Studies on Alcohol*, *65*, 782–793.

Clements, R. (1998). Critical evaluation of several alcohol screening instruments using the CID-SAM as a criterion measure. *Alcoholism: Clinical and Experimental Research*, *22*, 985–993.

Colby, J., Raymond, G., & Colby, S. (2000). Evaluation of a college policy mandating treatment for students with substantiated drinking problems. *Journal of College Student Development*, *41*, 395–403.

Coles, C. D., Russell, C. L., & Schuetze, P. (1997). Maternal substance use: Epidemiology, treatment outcome, and developmental effects. An annotated bibliography, 1995. *Substance Use and Misuse*, *32*, 149–168.

Davis, A., Quimby, A., Odero, W., Gururaj, G., & Hijar, M. (2003, May). *Improving safety by reducing impaired driving in developing countries: A scoping study*. Crowthorne, UK: Transport Research Laboratory.

Degenhardt, L. J., Conigrave, K. M., Wutzke, S. E., & Saunders, J. B. (2001). The validity of an Australian modification of the AUDIT questionnaire. *Drug and Alcohol Review*, *20*, 143–154.

Department for Culture, Media and Sport (DCMS). (2001). *Time for reform: Proposals for the modernisation of our licensing laws*. London: Her Majesty's Stationery Office.

Drew, L. R., & Truswell, A. S. (1998). Wernicke's encephalopathy and thiamine fortification of food: Time for a new direction? *Medical Journal of Australia, 168*, 534–535.

Edwards, G., Andersen, P., Babor, T. F., Caswell, S., Ferrence, R., Giesbrecht, N., et al. (1994). *Alcohol policy and the public good.* New York: Oxford University Press.

European Commission. (1999, February 17). *Communication from the Commission to the Council concerning the employment aspects of the decision to abolish tax- and duty-free sales for intra-community travelers.* Brussels, Belgium: Author.

Ewing, J. A. (1984). Detecting alcoholism: The CAGE questionnaire. *Journal of the American Medical Association, 252*, 1905–1907.

Faden, V. B., & Graubard, B. I. (2000). Maternal substance use during pregnancy and developmental outcome at age three. *Journal of Substance Abuse, 12*, 329–340.

Fleming, M. F., Barry, K. L., & MacDonald, R. (1991). The Alcohol Use Disorders Identification Test (AUDIT) in a college sample. *International Journal of Addiction, 26*, 1173–1185.

Freisthler, B., Gruenewald, P. J., Treno, A. J., & Lee, J. (2003). Evaluating alcohol access and the alcohol environment in neighborhood areas. *Alcoholism: Clinical and Experimental Research, 27*, 477–484.

Fried, P. A. (1995). Prenatal exposure to marihuana and tobacco during infancy, early and middle childhood: Effects and an attempt at synthesis. *Archives of Toxicology*, (Suppl. 17), 233–260.

Glatt, M. M. (1995). Controlled drinking after a third of a century. *Addiction, 90*, 1157–1160.

Gottesfeld, Z., & Abel, E. L. (1991). Maternal and paternal alcohol use: Effects on the immune system of the offspring. *Life Sciences, 48*, 1–8.

Grant, M., & Litvak, J. (Eds.). (1998). *Drinking patterns and their consequences.* Washington, DC: Taylor & Francis.

Grube, J. W. (1997). Preventing sales of alcohol to minors: Results from a community trial. *Addiction, 92*(Suppl. 2), S251–S260.

Gruenewald, P. J., Millar, A. B., & Roeper, P. (1996). Access to alcohol: Geography and prevention for local communities. *Alcohol Health and Research World, 20*, 244–251.

Hanson, D. (1996). *Alcohol education: What must we do?* Westport, CT: Praeger.

Harper, C. G., Sheedy, D. L., Lara, A. I., Garrick, T. M., Hilton, J. M., & Raisanen, J. (1998). Prevalence of Wernicke-Korsakoff syndrome in Australia: Has thiamine fortification made a difference? *Medical Journal of Australia, 168*, 542–545.

Härstedt, K. (2004). *Vår gar gränsen?* [Where do we set the limit?] Stockholm: Statens Offentliga Utredningar.

Hass, J. (2001). Harm-reduction initiative provides alcohol to Ottawa's street alcoholics. *Canadian Medical Association Journal, 165*, 937.

Haworth, A., & Simpson, R. (Eds.). (2004). *Moonshine markets: Issues in unrecorded alcohol beverage production and consumption.* New York: Brunner-Routledge.

Health Canada. (2001). *It takes a community: Framework for the First Nations and Inuit Fetal Alcohol Syndrome and Fetal Alcohol Effects Initiative.* Ottawa, Canada: Author. (Originally published in 1997)

Heath, D. B. (Ed.). (1995). *International handbook on alcohol and culture.* Westport, CT: Greenwood.

Heath, D. B. (2000). *Drinking occasions: Comparative perspectives on alcohol and culture.* Philadelphia: Brunner/Mazel.

Hellandsjø Bu, E. T., Watten, R. G., Foxcroft, D. R., Ingebrigtsen, J. E., & Relling, G. (2002). Teenage alcohol and intoxication debut: The impact of family socialization factors, living area and participation in organized sports. *Alcohol and Alcoholism, 37*, 74–80.

Henderson, M., Hutcheson, G., & Davies, J. (1996). Alcohol and the workplace. *WHO Regional Publications, European Series No. 67.* Copenhagen, Denmark: WHO Regional Office for Europe.

Henriksen, T. B., Hjollund, N. H, Jensen, T. K., Bonde, J. P., Andersson, A. M., Kolstad, H., et al. (2004). Alcohol consumption at the time of conception and spontaneous abortion. *American Journal of Epidemiology, 160*, 661–667.

Hermansson, U., Knutsson, A., Brandt, L., Huss, A., Ronnberg, S., & Helander, A. (2003). Screening for high-risk and elevated alcohol consumption in day and shift workers by use of the AUDIT and CDT. *Occupational Medicine, 53*, 518–526.

Hibell, B., Andersson, B., Ahlström, S., Balakireva, O., Bjarnason, T., Kokkevi, A., et al. (2000). *The 1999 ESPAD Report: Alcohol and other drug use among students in 30 European countries.* Stockholm: Swedish Council for Information on Alcohol and Other Drugs (CAN) and the Pompidou Group at the Council of Europe.

Hibell, B., Andersson, B., Bjarnason, T., Ahlström, S., Balakireva, O., Kokkevi, A., et al. (2004). *The ESPAD Report 2003: Alcohol and other drug use among students in 35 European countries.* Stockholm: Swedish Council for Information on Alcohol and Other Drugs (CAN) and the Pompidou Group at the Council of Europe.

Higher Education Center for Alcohol and Other Drug Prevention. (1996). Under the influence: Dealing effectively with a drunken student. *The Catalyst, 2* [Electronic version]. Retrieved November 17, 2005, from http://www.edc.org/hec/pubs/catalst5.htm.

Holder, H. D. (2000). Community prevention of alcohol problems. *Addictive Behaviors, 25*, 843–859.

Holder, H. D. (2004). Community action from an international perspective. In R. Müller & H. Klingemann (Eds.), *From science to action? 100 years later—alcohol policies revisited* (pp. 101–112). Dordrecht, the Netherlands: Kluwer Academic.

Holder, H. D., Gruenewald, P. J., Ponicki, W. R., Treno, A. J., Grube, J. W., Saltz, R. F., et al. (2000). Effect of community-based interventions on high-risk drinking and alcohol-related injuries. *Journal of the American Medical Association, 284*, 2341–2347.

Houghton, E., & Roche, A. M. (Eds.) (2001). *Learning about drinking.* Philadelphia: Brunner-Routledge.

Humphreys, K. (2003). Research-based analysis of the moderation management controversy. *Psychiatric Services, 54*, 621–622.

Institute of Medicine. (1996). *Fetal alcohol syndrome: Diagnosis, epidemiology, prevention, and treatment.* Washington, DC: National Academy Press.

International Center for Alcohol Policies (ICAP). (2002a). *Drinking age limits*, rev. ed. ICAP Reports 4. Washington, DC: Author. (Originally published in 1998)

International Center for Alcohol Policies (ICAP). (2002b). *Blood alcohol concentration limits worldwide.* ICAP Reports 11. Washington, DC: Author.

International Center for Alcohol Policies (ICAP). (2003a). *Alcohol and the workplace.* ICAP Reports 13. Washington, DC: Author.

International Center for Alcohol Policies (ICAP). (2003b). *International drinking guidelines.* ICAP Reports 14. Washington, DC: Author.

International Center for Alcohol Policies (ICAP). (2004a). *Alcohol education and its effectiveness.* ICAP Reports 16. Washington, DC: Author.

International Center for Alcohol Policies (ICAP). (2004b). *Table: International drinking guidelines*. Retrieved May 5, 2006, from http://www.icap.org/PolicyIssues/DrinkingGuidelines/GuidelinesTable/.

International Center for Alcohol Policies (ICAP). (2005). *ICAP Blue Book: Practical guides to policy and prevention approaches*. Washington, DC: Author.

International Labour Organization. (2005). *Drug and alcohol abuse: An important workplace issue*. Retrieved August 29, 2005, from http://www.ilo.org/public/english/protection/safework/drug/impiss.htm.

Jacobson, J. L., Jacobson, S. W., Sokol, R. J., Martier, S. S., Ager, J. W., & Kaplan-Estrin, M. G. (1993). Teratogenic effects of alcohol on infant development. *Alcohol: Clinical and Experimental Research, 17*, 174–183.

Johnson, B. B., & Slovic, P. (1994). "Improving" risk communication and risk management: Legislated solutions or legislated disaster? *Risk Analysis, 14*, 905–906.

Kelly, T. M., Donovan, J. E., Chung, T., Cook, R. L., & Delbridge, T. R. (2004). Alcohol use disorders among emergency department treated older adolescents: A new brief screen (RUFT-Cut) using the AUDIT, CAGE, CRAFFT, and RAPS-QF. *Alcoholism: Clinical and Experimental Research, 28*, 746–753.

Kesmodel, U., & Olsen, S. F. (2001). Self-reported alcohol intake in pregnancy: Comparison between four methods. *Journal of Epidemiology and Community Health, 55*, 738–745.

Kishline, A. (1994). *Moderate drinking: A new option for problem drinkers*. Tucson, AZ: See Sharp Press.

Klamen, D. L. (1999). Education and training in addictive diseases. *Psychiatric Clinics of North America, 22*, 471–480.

Klatsky, A. L. (1999a). Is drinking healthy? In S. Peele & M. Grant, (Eds.), *Alcohol and pleasure: A health perspective* (pp. 141–156). Philadelphia: Brunner/Mazel.

Klatsky, A. L. (1999b). Is it the drink or the drinker? Circumstantial evidence only raises a probability. *American Journal of Clinical Nutrition, 69*, 2–3.

Knight, J. R., Shrier, L. A., Bravender, T. D., Farrell, M., Vander Bilt, J., & Shaffer, H. J. (1999). A new brief screen test among adolescent clinic patients. *Archives of Pediatric and Adolescent Medicine, 153*, 591–596.

Kosok, A. (2006). The Moderation Management programme in 2004: What type of drinker seeks controlled drinking? *International Journal of Drug Policy, 17*, 295–303.

Lange, J. E., Lauer, E. M., & Voas, R. B. (1999). Survey of the San Diego–Tijuana cross-border binging: Methods and analysis. *Evaluation Review, 23*, 378–398.

Laranjeira, R., & Hinkley, D. (2002). Evaluation of alcohol outlet density and its relation with violence. *Revista de Saúde Pública, 36*, 455–461.

Larroque, B., & Kaminski, M. (1998). Prenatal alcohol exposure and development at preschool age: Main results of a French study. *Alcoholism: Clinical and Experimental Research, 22*, 295–303.

Ledermann, S. (1952). Une mortalité d'origine économique en France: La mortalité d'origine ou d'appoint. *Semaine Médicale, 28*, 418–421.

Ledermann, S., & Tabah, F. (1951). Nouvelles données sur la mortalité d'origine alcoolique. *Population, G*, 41–56.

Leifman, H. (2001). Homogenisation in alcohol consumption in the European Union. *Nordisk Alkohol- & Narkotikatidskrift, 18*(English Suppl.), 15–30.

Lewis, D. K., & Marchell, T. C. (2006). Safety first: A medical amnesty approach to alcohol poisoning at a U.S. university. *International Journal of Drug Policy, 17,* 329–338.

Lipton, R., & Gruenewald, P. (2002). Spatial dynamics of violence and alcohol outlets. *Journal of Studies on Alcohol, 63,* 187–195.

Lorente, C., Cordier, S., Goujard, J., Ayme, S., Bianchi, F., Calzolari, E., et al. (2000). Tobacco and alcohol use during pregnancy and risk of oral clefts. *American Journal of Public Health, 90,* 415–419.

Loukomskaia, M. I. (1997). Recent alcohol policies in Russia. *Alcologia, 9,* 37–42.

Lyall, S. (2003, October 13). Something cheap in the state of Denmark: Liquor. *New York Times,* 4A.

Ma, J. J., & Truswell, A. S. (1995). Wernicke-Korsakoff syndrome in Sydney hospitals: Before and after thiamine enrichment of flour. *Medical Journal of Australia, 163,* 531–534.

Manzo, L., Locatelli, C., Candura, S. M., & Costa, L. G. (1994). Nutrition and alcohol neurotoxicity. *Neurotoxicology, 15,* 555–566.

Marshall, M. (Ed.). (1979). *Beliefs, behaviors and alcoholic beverages: A cross-cultural survey.* Ann Arbor: University of Michigan Press.

Martinic, M., & Leigh, B. (2004). *Reasonable risk: Alcohol in perspective.* New York: Brunner-Routledge.

May, P. A., Brooke, L., Gossage, J. P., Croxford, J., Adams, C., Jones, K. L., et al. (2000). Epidemiology of fetal alcohol syndrome in a South African community in the Western Cape Province. *American Journal of Public Health, 90,* 1905–1912.

May, P. A., & Gossage, J. P. (2001). Estimating the prevalence of fetal alcohol syndrome: A summary. *Alcohol Research and Health, 25,* 159–167.

May, P. A., Gossage, J. P., Brooke, L. E., Snell, C. L., Marais, A. S., Hendricks, L. S., et al. (2005). Maternal risk factors for fetal alcohol syndrome in the Western Cape Provide of South Africa: A population-based study. *American Journal of Public Health, 95,* 1190–1199.

McKee, M. (1999). Alcohol in Russia. *Alcohol and Alcoholism, 34,* 824–829.

Meilman, P. W. (1992). College health services should promote Good Samaritan rules as part of university alcohol policies. *Journal of American College Health, 40,* 299–301.

Midanik, L. T. (1994). Comparing usual quantity/frequency and graduated frequency scales to assess yearly alcohol consumption: Results from the 1990 U.S. National Alcohol Survey. *Addiction, 89,* 407–412.

Milgram, G. G. (2001). Alcohol influences: The role of family and peers. In E. Houghton & A. M. Roche (Eds.), *Learning about drinking* (pp. 85–105). Philadelphia: Brunner-Routledge.

Miller, E. T. (2001). Preventing alcohol abuse and alcohol-related negative consequences among freshmen college students: Using emerging computer technology to deliver and evaluate the effectiveness of brief intervention efforts. *Dissertation Abstracts International, 61,* 4417–B.

Miller, L., Tolliver, R., Druschel, C., Fox, D., Podvin, D., Mernick, S., et al. (2002). Fetal alcohol syndrome: Alaska, Arizona, Colorado, and New York, 1995–1997. *Journal of the American Medical Association, 288,* 38–40.

Mistral, M., Velleman, R., Templeton, L., & Mastache, C. (2006). Local action to prevent alcohol problems: Is the U.K. Community Alcohol Prevention Programme the best solution? *International Journal of Drug Policy, 17*, 278–284.

Moynham, A. F., Perl, J., Anderson, S. A., Jennings, S. R., Starmer, G. A., & Birch, J. (2000, September). *National standards, international standards and evidential breath analysis in Australia.* Paper presented at the 15th International Conference on Alcohol, Drugs and Traffic Safety, Stockholm, Sweden.

Müller, R. (1991). Alkoholprävention im Betrieb—soziale Kontroll oder Humanisierung der Arbeit? *Wiener Zeitschrift für Suchtforschung, 14*, 21–24.

Mussell, W. J., Nicholis, W. M., & Adler, M. T. (1991). *Making meaning of mental health challenges in First Nations: A Freirian perspective.* Chilliwack, Canada: Sal'i'shan Institute Society.

National Health and Medical Research Council (NHMRC). (2001). *Australian alcohol guidelines: Health risks and benefits.* Canberra, Australia: Author.

Nemtsov, A. V. (1998). Alcohol-related harm and alcohol consumption in Moscow before, during, and after a major anti-alcohol campaign. *Addiction, 93*, 1501–1510.

Nemtsov, A. V. (2002). Alcohol-related human losses in Russia in the 1980s and 1990s. *Addiction, 97*, 1413–1425.

Nordlund, S., & Österberg, E. (2000). Unrecorded alcohol consumption: Economics and its effects on alcohol control in the Nordic countries. *Addiction, 95*(Suppl. 4), S551–S564.

Norström, T. (2000). Outlet density and criminal violence in Norway, 1960–1995. *Journal of Studies on Alcohol, 61*, 907–911.

O'Hare, T., & Sherrer, M. V. (1999). Validating the alcohol use disorder identification test with college first-offenders. *Journal of Substance Abuse Treatment, 17*, 113–119.

O'Malley, P. M., & Johnston, L. D. (2002). Epidemiology of alcohol and other drug use among American college students. *Journal of Studies on Alcohol,* (Suppl. 14), 23–39.

Österberg, E., & Karlsson T. (Eds.). (2003). *Alcohol policies in EU Member States and Norway: A collection of country reports.* Helsinki, Finland: National Research and Development Centre for Welfare and Health (STAKES).

Paglia, A., & Room, R. (1999). Preventing substance use problems among youth: A literature review and recommendations. *Journal of Primary Prevention, 20*, 3–50.

Partanen, J. (1993). Failures in alcohol policy: Lessons from Russia, Kenya, Truk and history. *Addiction, 88*(Suppl.), 129S–134S.

Peek-Asa, C. (1999). Effect of random alcohol screening in reducing motor vehicle crash injuries. *American Journal of Preventive Medicine, 16*, 57–67.

Plant, M. (2001). Learning by experiment. In E. Houghton & A.M. Roche (Eds.), *Learning about drinking* (pp. 129–146). Philadelphia: Brunner-Routledge.

Plant, M., Abel, E. L., & Guerri, C. (1999). Alcohol and pregnancy. In I. McDonald (Ed.), *Health issues related to alcohol consumption*, 2nd ed. (pp. 182–213). Oxford: Blackwell Science.

Plant, M., Single, E., & Stockwell, T. (Eds.). (1997). *Alcohol: Minimizing the harm. What works?* London: Free Association Books.

Podymow, T., Turnbull, J., Coyle, D., Yetisir, E., & Wells, G. (2006). Shelter-based managed alcohol administration to chronically homeless people addicted to alcohol. *Canadian Medical Association Journal, 174*, 45–49.

Popham, R. E., Schmidt, W., & de Lint, J. (1975). Prevention of alcoholism: Epidemiological studies of the effects of government control measures. *British Journal of Addiction to Alcohol and Other Drugs, 70,* 125–144.

Raskin, E., & Williams, L. (2003). *Alcohol screening: A quick first step to reduce problem drinking.* Ensuring Solutions to Alcohol Problems Issue Brief 3. Washington, DC: George Washington University Medical Center.

Rehm, J., Greenfield, T. K., Walsh, G., Xie, X., Robson, L., & Single, E. (1999). Assessment methods for alcohol consumption, prevalence of high-risk drinking and harm: A sensitivity analysis. *International Journal of Epidemiology, 28,* 219–224.

Rehn, N., Room, R., & Edwards, G. (2001). *Alcohol in the European Region: Consumption, harm, and policies.* Copenhagen, Denmark: WHO Regional Office for Europe.

Reid, R. J., Hughey, J., & Peterson, N. A. (2003). Generalizing the alcohol outlet-assaultive violence link: Evidences from a U.S. Midwestern city. *Substance Abuse and Misuse, 38,* 1971–1982.

Reynolds, R. I., Holder, H. D., & Gruenewald, P. J. (1997). Community prevention and alcohol retail access. *Addiction, 92*(Suppl.), S261–S272.

Room, R. (Ed.) (2002). *Effects of Nordic alcohol policies: What happens to drinking and harm when alcohol controls change?* Helsinki, Finland: Nordic Council for Alcohol and Drug Research.

Room, R., Jernigan, D., Carlini-Marlatt, B., Gureje, O., Mäkelä, K., Marshall, M., et al. (2002). *Alcohol in developing societies: A public health approach.* Helsinki: Finnish Foundation for Alcohol Studies.

Rosenberg, H. (1993). Prediction of controlled drinking by alcoholics and problem drinkers. *Psychological Bulletin, 113,* 129–139.

Saitz, R., Helmuth, E. D., Aromaa, S. E., Guard, A., Belanger, M., & Rosenbloom, D. L. (2004). Web-based screening and brief intervention for the spectrum of alcohol problems. *Preventive Medicine, 39,* 969–975.

Saitz, R., Sullivan, L. M., & Samet, J. H. (2000). Training community-based clinicians in screening and brief intervention for substance abuse problems: Translating evidence into practice. *Substance Abuse, 21,* 21–31.

Sanchez-Craig, M., Wilkinson, D. A., & Davila, R. (1995). Empirically based guidelines for moderate drinking: One-year results from three studies with problem drinkers. *American Journal of Public Health, 85,* 823–828.

Savitz, D. A., Schwingl, P. J., & Keels, M. A. (1991). Influence of paternal age, smoking, and alcohol consumption on congenital anomalies. *Teratology, 44,* 429–440.

Selzer, M. L. (1971). The Michigan Alcoholism Screening Test: The quest for a new diagnostic instrument. *American Journal of Psychiatry, 127,* 1653–1658.

Seppä, K., Lepisto J., & Sillanaukee, P. (1998). Five shot questionnaire on heavy drinking. *Alcohol Clinical Experimental Research, 22,* 1788–1791.

Seppä, K., Mäkelä, R., & Sillanaukee, P. (1995). Effectiveness of the Alcohol Use Disorders Identification Test in occupational health screenings. *Alcoholism: Clinical and Experimental Research, 19,* 999–1003.

Seppä, K., Pekuri, P., Kääriäinen, J., & Aalto, M. (2004). Intervenciones breves en alcohol como rutina diaria. Proyecto de investigación acción de directrices para atención primaria [Brief alcohol intervention as a daily routine. Description of an action research project creating instructions for primary health care]. *Adicciones: Revista de Socidrogalcohol, 16,* 315–322.

Single, E. (2004). Key economic issues regarding unrecorded alcohol. In A. Haworth & R. Simpson (Eds.), *Moonshine markets: Issues in unrecorded alcohol beverage production and consumption* (pp. 167–175). New York: Brunner-Routledge.

Single, E., Beaubrun, M., Mauffret, M., Minoletti, A., Moskalewicz, J., Moukolo, A., et al. (1997). Public drinking, problems and prevention measures in twelve countries: Results of the WHO project on public drinking. *Contemporary Drug Problems, 24,* 425–448.

Single, E. W., Brewster, J. M., MacNeil, P., Hatcher, J., & Trainor, C. (1995). Nineteen ninety three (1993) General Social Survey II: Alcohol problems in Canada. *Canadian Journal of Public Health, 86,* 402–407.

Sloan, F. A., Stout, E. M., Whetten-Goldstein, K., & Liand, L. (2000). *Drinkers, drivers, and bartenders: Balancing private choices and public accountability.* Chicago: University of Chicago Press.

Smith, G. T., McCarthy, D. M., & Anderson, K. G. (2000). On the sins of short-form development. *Psychological Assessment, 12,* 102–111.

Soderstrom, C. A., Smith, G. S., Kufera, J. A., Dischinger, P. C., Hebel, J. R., Gorelick, D. A., et al. (1997). Psychoactive substance use disorders among seriously injured trauma center patients. *Journal of the American Medical Association, 277,* 1769–1774.

Stewart, K. (2000). *On DWI laws in other countries.* Washington, DC: National Highway Traffic Safety Administration.

Stewart, K., & Sweedler, B. M. (1997). Driving under the influence of alcohol. In M. Plant, E. Single, & T. Stockwell (Eds.), *Alcohol: Minimizing the harm. What works?* (pp. 126–142). New York: Free Association Books.

Stockwell, T., Hawks, D., Lang, E., & Rydon, P. (1996). Unraveling the preventive paradox for acute alcohol problems. *Drug and Alcohol Review, 15,* 7–15.

Streissguth, A. P., & O'Malley, K. (2000). Neuropsychiatric implications and long-term consequences of fetal alcohol spectrum disorders. *Seminars in Neuropsychiatry, 5,* 177–190.

TD Canada Trust. (2005). *Drinking, driving and your insurance.* Retrieved August 29, 2005, from http://www.tdcanadatrust.com/tdinsurance/auto/learningcentre/drink.jsp.

Testa, M., Quigley, B. M., & Das Eiden, R. (2003). Effects of prenatal alcohol exposure on infant mental development: A meta-analytical review. *Alcohol and Alcoholism, 38,* 295–304.

Thom, B., Herring, R., & Judd, A. (1999). Identifying alcohol-related harm in young drinkers: The role of accident and emergency departments. *Alcohol and Alcoholism, 34,* 910–919.

Thomson, A. D., & Cook, C. H. H. (2000). Putting thiamine in beer: Comments on Truswell's editorial. *Addiction, 95,* 1866–1868.

Toomey, T. L., Kilian, G. R., Gehan, J. P., Perry, C. L., Wagenaar, A. C., & Jones-Webb, R. (1998). Qualitative assessment of training programs for alcohol servers and establishment managers. *Public Health Reports, 113,* 162–169.

Treno, A. J., Grube, J. W., & Martin, S. E. (2003). Alcohol availability as a predictor of youth drinking and driving: A hierarchical analysis of survey and archival data. *Alcoholism: Clinical and Experimental Research, 27,* 835–840.

Viljoen, D. L., Gossage, J. P., Brooke, L., Adnams, C. M., Jones, K. L., Robinson, L. K., et al. (2005). Fetal alcohol syndrome epidemiology in a South African community: A second study of a very high prevalence area. *Journal of Studies on Alcohol, 66,* 593–604.

Voas, R. B., Blackman, K. O., Tippetts, A. S., & Marques, P. R. (2002). Evaluation of a program to motivate impaired driving offenders to install ignition interlocks. *Accident Analysis and Prevention, 34,* 449–455.

Voas, R. B., Lange, J. E., & Johnson, M. B. (2002). Reducing high-risk drinking by young Americans south of the border: The impact of a partial ban on sales of alcohol. *Journal of Studies on Alcohol, 63,* 286–292.

Wagenaar, A. C., & Holder, H. D. (1991). Effects of alcoholic beverage server liability on traffic crash injuries. *Alcoholism: Clinical and Experimental Research, 15,* 942–947.

Wagenaar, A. C., Murray, D. M., Gehan, J. P., Wolfson, M., Forster, J. L., Toomey, T. L., et al. (2000). Communities mobilizing for change on alcohol: Outcomes from a randomized community trial. *Journal of Studies on Alcohol, 61,* 85–94.

Wagenaar, A. C., Toomey, T., Murray, D. M., Short, B. J., Wolfson, M., & Jones-Webb, R. (1996). Sources of alcohol for underage drinkers. *Journal of Studies in Alcohol, 57,* 325–333.

Wallin, E., Norström, T., & Andreasson, S. (2003). Alcohol prevention targeting licensed premises: A study of effects on violence. *Journal of Studies on Alcohol, 64,* 270–277.

Warren, K. R., Calhoun, F. J., May, P. A., Viljoen, D. L., Li, T. K., Tanka, H., et al. (2001). Fetal alcohol syndrome: An international perspective. *Alcoholism: Clinical and Experimental Research, 25*(Suppl. 5), 202S–206S.

Wechsler, H., Dowdall, G. W., Maenner, G., Gledhill-Hoyt, J., & Lee, H. (1998). Changes in binge drinking and related problems among American college students between 1993 and 1997: Results of the Harvard School of Public Health College Alcohol Survey. *Journal of American College Health, 47,* 57–68.

Wechsler, H., Nelson, T., & Weitzman, E. (2000). From knowledge to action: How Harvard's College Alcohol Study can help your campus design a campaign against student alcohol abuse. *Change, 32,* 38–43.

Weitzman, E. R., Folkman, A., Folkman, K. L., & Wechsler, H. (2003). The relationship of alcohol outlet density to heavy and frequent drinking and drinking-related problems among college students at eight universities. *Health and Place, 9,* 1–6.

White, S. (1996). *Russia goes dry: Alcohol, state, and society.* Cambridge: Cambridge University Press.

World Health Organization. (2004). *Global status report: Alcohol policy.* Geneva, Switzerland: Author.

Zaigraev, G. (2004). The Russian model of noncommercial alcohol consumption. In A. Haworth & R. Simpson (Eds.), *Moonshine markets: Issues in unrecorded alcohol beverage production and consumption* (pp. 31–40). New York: Brunner-Routledge.

Zhu, L., Gorman, D. M., & Horel, S. (2004). Alcohol outlet density and violence: A geospatial analysis. *Alcohol and Alcoholism, 39,* 369–375.

Zunino, H., Litvak, J., & Israel, Y. (1998). Public and private partnerships in prevention and research: IV. The case of the College of Pharmacy, University of Chile. In M. Grant & J. Litvak (Eds.), *Drinking patterns and their consequences* (pp. 282–285). Washington, DC: Taylor & Francis.

5

Targeting Behavior: Alcohol-impaired Driving

In this chapter, we explore in more detail the measures targeted at alcohol-impaired driving. Most countries now set legal limits on blood alcohol content (BAC) for drivers. The prevention of alcohol-impaired driving is the prime example of a risk reduction approach, where the aim is not to eliminate alcohol consumption—or driving—but to separate the two activities, so that the risks of harm are lowered for both drinkers and their potential victims. The implementation of blood alcohol testing and its enforcement are the key components of this type of intervention, along with other strategies that separate drinkers from driving, such as designated driver campaigns and improvements in public transport.

ROAD TRAFFIC INJURIES AND ALCOHOL

Over 1 million fatalities occur each year on the world's roads, and many millions of additional injuries result from road crashes (Jacobs, Aeron-Thomas, & Astrop, 2000). Although estimates of death and injury caused by alcohol-impaired driving may vary from study to study, one point is clear: It is a leading contributor to motor vehicle crashes around the world. Researchers estimate that 30% of the disease burden attributable to alcohol is the result of unintentional injuries (Rehm et al., 2004), and motor vehicle crashes comprise a large portion of this burden. Estimates that between 30 and 50% of motor vehicle crash fatalities and injuries are alcohol-related are not uncommon (World Health Organization [WHO], 2004). For example, there were 42,636 road traffic fatalities in the United States in 2004 (U.S. National Highway Traffic Safety Administration [NHTSA], 2005). Of those fatalities, 16,694 (39%) were alcohol-related—defined as at least one driver or vehicle nonoccupant, such as a pedestrian or cyclist, having a blood alcohol concentration (BAC) of 0.1 milligrams per milliliter (mg/ml) or higher—and 14,409 (34%) fatalities involved a BAC of 0.8 mg/ml, the maximum legal BAC level in the United States. In the European Union, approximately 10,000 fatalities out of 40,000 annually are alcohol-related. Similarly, the economic impact of road traffic injuries is tremendous: The World Bank estimated that road crashes cost societies between 1 and 3% of gross national product (GNP) or US$500 billion annually worldwide (Ghee, Astrop, Silcock, & Jacobs, 1997; Global Road Safety Partnership [GRSP], 2005; WHO, 2004).

Such estimates demonstrate that alcohol-impaired driving provides a significant arena for reducing the burden of disease and the economic costs of alcohol abuse for society. There has been slow but regular improvement in road safety overall in the highly motorized countries of Asia and the Pacific (Australia, Japan, and New Zealand), North America, and Western Europe. Meanwhile, the number of road fatalities and injuries has been rising rapidly in less motorized but increasingly motorizing countries (primarily developing and transition economies), where the vehicle fleet and distance traveled annually have been doubling and trebling in recent years (Jacobs et al., 2000).

For example, a study on alcohol and drug use among individuals admitted to hospital for injuries in South Africa estimated that up to 50% of patients had elevated BAC levels (Peden, 2001). Two recent surveys in India found a similar level of alcohol-impaired driving in Indian urban centers. A report from Delhi concluded that 45% of drivers had consumed alcohol prior to driving, although BAC levels were not verified (Aggarwal, 2005). Similarly, in the State of Kerala, a study conducted by the Alcohol and Drug Information Centre (ADIC) found that approximately 40% of road traffic incidents had occurred as a result of alcohol-impaired driving (Edayaranmula, 2005).

The road environment includes not only motorized road users but also pedestrians and cyclists, who can also experience harm when using the roadway while intoxicated. The U.S. government estimated that 34% of all pedestrians and 20% of all cyclists killed in traffic crashes in 2004 had BAC levels of 0.8 mg/ml or higher (NHTSA, 2005). Developing and transition countries have higher alcohol-related fatality rates not only among drivers and passengers of motorized vehicles but also among pedestrians. A study in Cape Town, South Africa, showed that 62.1% of pedestrians admitted to hospital for road traffic injuries had measurable BAC levels, and 59.5% had levels above 0.8 mg/ml. The mean BAC for pedestrians testing positive for alcohol was 1.9 mg/ml. Most of the injured pedestrians had at least one lower limb injury, and nearly half had a head injury. Furthermore, the BAC-positive pedestrians sustained more severe injuries, more frequently required admission to intensive care units, had longer hospital stays, and were more likely to die as a result of their injuries than the pedestrians who had no alcohol in their system. Male pedestrians between the ages of 20 and 29 years who consumed alcohol on Saturday evening were at the highest risk for injuries (Peden et al., 1996).

Although the recent declines in alcohol-related road traffic injuries and fatalities in the United States and in several Western European countries highlight the feasibility of reducing the burden of alcohol-impaired driving, it remains one of the most complex issues facing road safety stakeholders. In spite of these complexities, decades of research have demonstrated that alcohol-impaired driving and alcohol impairment among pedestrians, motorcyclists, and cyclists represent areas for potential public health and socioeconomic gains. In order to continue to make improvements and reduce the incidence of alcohol-impaired driving, a vigorous commitment is needed to tackle particular high-risk patterns of alcohol consumption with targeted interventions and the engagement of all stakeholders through partnerships and complementary actions.

BLOOD ALCOHOL CONCENTRATION (BAC) LIMITS

Enforcement and deterrence have been the principal approaches for prevention of alcohol-impaired driving. A basic component of each government's road safety policies is the setting of a maximum legal BAC level for drivers of motor vehicles. Alcohol in blood is measured in terms of weight per volume. The most commonly used measurements are grams of ethanol per deciliter of blood (g/dl = g/100ml), used in the United States, and milligrams of ethanol per milliliter of blood (mg/ml), used in much of Europe. For example, 0.05 g/dl equals 0.5 mg/ml. Other metrics frequently used in policy and research are mg/dl (for example, 50 mg/dl) or g/l (for example, 0.5 g/l).

Maximum legal BAC levels vary from zero (in the case of novice drivers or commercial drivers in some countries) to 0.5 mg/ml (in much of Western Europe), 0.8 mg/ml (for example, in the United States and the United Kingdom), or 1.0 mg/ml (for example, in Albania) (International Center for Alcohol Policies [ICAP], 2005b). Establishment of BAC limits provides an objective and simple measurable standard when assessing alcohol impairment of drivers (see Table 5.1).

The impairment of normal driver behavior generally denotes a reduced ability to adequately perform the various elements of the driving task. Driver impairment may result from a number of factors, such as alcohol consumption, drug ingestion, injury, infirmity, fatigue, the natural aging process, or a combination of these factors. Alcohol consumption is known to impair reaction time and affect an individual's capacity to execute a range of motor tasks (Grant, Millar, & Kenny, 2000; Parks et al., 2002; Roldán, Frauca, & Dueñas, 2003). Driving is an activity that requires precision, relying heavily on motor skills, reflexes, and the ability to make quick decisions. Reaction time of an inebriated driver may be reduced by 10 to 30% as compared to a sober individual. Furthermore, vision is blurred and judgment of distance, speed, and hazards is impaired. Table 5.2 identifies degrees of impairment at different BAC levels.

A person's risk of being involved in a fatal crash increases with the amount of alcohol consumed (see, for example, Borkenstein, Crowther, Shumate, Ziel, & Zylman, 1964; Cherpitel, Tam, Midanik, Caetano, & Greenfield, 1995; Lucas, Kalow, McColl, Griffith, & Smith, 1955; Moskowitz, Blomberg, Burns, Fiorentino, & Peck, 2002; Moskowitz & Fiorentino, 2000; Mounce & Pendleton, 1992). These studies confirm that crash risk rises with increased BAC beginning at 0.4 mg/ml, and at an accelerated rate at BAC levels in excess of 1.0 mg/ml (see Figure 5.1).

Table 5.1 Blood Alcohol Concentration Limits

Country	Standard BAC (in mg/ml)	Country	Standard BAC (in mg/ml)
Albania	1.0	Japan	0.3
Algeria	0.1	Kenya	0.8
Argentina	0.5	Kyrgyzstan	0.5
Armenia	0.0	Lithuania	0.4
Australia	0.5	Luxembourg	0.8
Austria	0.5	Malaysia	0.8
Azerbaijan	0.0	Malta	0.8
Belarus	0.5	Mexico	0.8
Belgium	0.5	Moldova	0.3
Bolivia	0.7	Mongolia	0.2
Bosnia and Herzegovina	0.5	Nepal	0.0
Botswana	0.8	Netherlands	0.5
Brazil	0.6	New Zealand	0.8
Bulgaria	0.5	Nicaragua	0.8
Cambodia	0.5	Norway	0.2
Canada	0.8	Paraguay	0.8
China	0.3	Peru	0.5
Croatia, Republic of	0.0	Philippines	0.5
Czech Republic	0.0	Poland	0.2
Denmark	0.5	Portugal	0.5
Ecuador	0.7	Romania	0.0
El Salvador	0.5	Russia	0.2–0.5
Estonia	0.2	Singapore	0.8
Ethiopia	0.0	Slovak Republic	0.0
Finland	0.5	Slovenia	0.5
France	0.5	South Africa	0.5
Georgia	0.3	Spain	0.5
Germany	0.5	Sweden	0.2
Greece	0.5	Switzerland	0.5
Guatemala	0.8	Thailand	0.5
Honduras	0.7	Turkey	0.5
Hungary	0.0	Turkmenistan	0.3
Iceland	0.5	Uganda	0.8
India	0.3	United Kingdom	0.8
Ireland	0.8	United States	0.8
Israel	0.5	Venezuela	0.5
Italy	0.5	Zimbabwe	0.8

Source: ICAP (2005b); for the most up-to-date table on BAC levels, see ICAP (2005a).

Table 5.2 Impairment at Various Levels of Blood Alcohol Content

BAC Levels (mg/ml)	Degree of Impairment
0.2–0.3	Mental functions begin to be impaired.
0.3–0.5	Attention and visual field are reduced.
	Cerebral control relaxes, and there is a sensation of calm and wellbeing.
0.5–0.8	Reflexes become retarded.
	Difficulty of vision adaptation to luminosity differences.
	Overestimation of performance abilities.
	Aggressive tendency.
0.8–1.0	Difficulty in driving/controlling vehicles (for alcohol-impaired pedestrians, in walking along the road).
	Neuromuscular coordination impairment.
1.0–1.9	Lack of coordination.
	Inability to correctly interpret what is happening.
	Poor judgment.
	Difficulty in walking and standing steadily.
2.0–2.9	Nausea.
	Vomiting.
3.0–3.9	Serious intoxication.
	Lowered body temperature.
	Partial amnesia ("blackout") likely.
> 4.0	Alcohol poisoning.
	Coma.
	Risk of death (about 50% of people who have a BAC > 4.00 will die of alcohol poisoning).

Sources: ICAP (2005b), Lang (1992), and Melcop (2003).

Although Moskowitz and colleagues (2002) revealed that earlier research significantly underestimated true alcohol-related crash risk, their work showed that relative risk for BAC below 0.4 mg/ml was not significantly different from that at 0.0 mg/ml. Drivers with BAC between 0.2 and 0.4 mg/ml were only 1.4 times more likely to be involved in crashes than those who had not been drinking. This likelihood increased 11 times for drivers with BAC levels between 0.5 and 0.9 mg/ml, and 48 times for individuals with BAC between 1.0 and 1.4 mg/ml (Moskowitz et al., 2002; Zador, 1991; Zador, Krawchuk, & Voas, 2000). A comprehensive review of research on the biological impact of alcohol on psychomotor skills concluded that the threshold for negative effects is found generally at 0.4 to 0.5 mg/ml. Overall, 21% of the studies reported performance impairment by 0.4 mg/ml, 34% by 0.5 mg/ml, 66% by 0.8 mg/ml, and nearly all by 1.0 mg/ml (Moskowitz & Robinson, 1988).

Measuring BAC

There are various means of determining an individual's BAC level, the most common and inexpensive of which is by measuring the alcohol in an exhaled

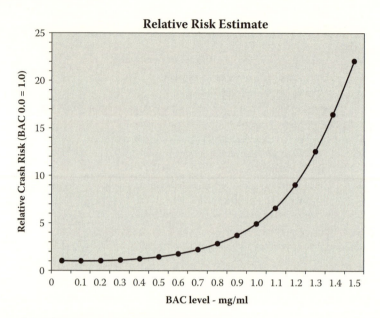

Figure 5.1 Relative Risk of Involvement in Crashes
Source: Global Road Safety Partnership (2004).

sample of breath (Jones, 1990). Law enforcement personnel can administer this test quickly on the scene where alcohol intoxication is suspected. Other tests measure alcohol content in bodily fluids and are generally carried out in clinics or laboratories. Although blood samples offer a more reliable measure of alcohol content than breath tests, both urine and blood samples are less practical from an enforcement point of view as they do not provide immediate results. In the time needed to reach a clinic or other testing site, an individual's BAC may drop, resulting in a lower reading.

How much alcohol an individual has consumed and over what period of time determine BAC levels as a function of absorption and metabolism rates. An individual's weight, gender, health, and food intake affect the levels of blood alcohol that are reached. In general, BAC increase is less rapid with greater body weight and with food intake, and is less rapid in men than in women.

In very broad terms, one standard drink of wine, beer, or spirits raises BAC to approximately 0.2 mg/ml. Official "drinks" or "units" generally contain between 8 and 14 grams of pure ethanol, although the measure varies among countries (see Table 5.3). To date, there is no common convention to define a standard drink among countries. Most countries do not use any standard definition for drinks, and, where serving sizes are defined, these measures depend to a great extent on local culture and customs. Where standard units are established, they may vary according to the type of beverage alcohol.

An average healthy person eliminates about 9 to 14 grams of pure alcohol per hour, roughly equivalent to the amount of pure alcohol contained in one standard

Table 5.3 Standard Alcohol Units

Standard Drink/Unit Size (grams of ethanol)	Country
8	United Kingdom
9.9	Netherlands
10	Australia, Austria, New Zealand, Poland, and Spain
11	Finland
12	Denmark, France, Italy, and South Africa
13.6	Canada
14	Portugal and United States

Source: ICAP (2005b).

drink (ICAP, 2005b). This rate of alcohol elimination is relatively constant, regardless of the number of drinks consumed. Therefore, the more alcohol an individual drinks, the longer it takes his or her body to get rid of it. The average metabolism rate for moderate drinkers results in a 0.17 mg/ml per hour decline in BAC level (NHTSA, 1994).

Without appropriate legal BAC levels, reducing alcohol-impaired driving is difficult. In jurisdictions where BAC limits have not been established or in contexts were BAC testing is not feasible, other standard field methods of sobriety testing may be used. These tests are designed to determine coordination and mental acuity. Similarly, in situations where a violation of BAC maximum limits cannot be reliably established—for example, because of lack of equipment, as is often the case in low- and middle-income countries—other charges, such as reckless driving, might be brought against an impaired driver instead.

Alcohol Limits in Other Fields of Activity

In addition to the road environment, there are other activities and professions in which misuse of alcohol can lead to increased risk of injury or death. In some cases, the law specifies maximum BAC limits for certain activities, such as piloting a plane, operating a boat or snowmobile, or functioning as a surgeon.

Aviation

In most countries, the use of alcohol and drugs by aircraft pilots is strictly regulated. For example, in the U.S., the Federal Aviation Administration's (FAA) regulations state that no person may operate or attempt to operate an aircraft within eight hours of having consumed alcohol, while under the influence of alcohol, with a BAC of 0.4 mg/ml or greater, or while using any drug that adversely affects safety (Federal Aviation Administration, 2006). The FAA regulations provide for both regular randomized testing and testing following an incident. This is carried out on aviation employees having safety-sensitive functions (pilots and other cockpit crew, cabin attendants, flight instructors, aircraft dispatchers, aircraft mechanical and maintenance crews, ground security, and air traffic controllers).

The FAA Civil Aerospace Medical Institute found that between 1999 and 2003, there were 1,629 fatal aviation accidents, and pilots were fatally injured in 1,587. Alcohol or drugs were found in 830 (52.3%) of the pilot fatalities (Chaturvedi, Craft, Canfield, & Whinnery, 2005).

Boating, Swimming, and Water Sports

Boating, swimming, water skiing, and scuba diving or snorkeling are activities that require special skills, training, and, in some cases, licensing. They have the potential to cause harm to those engaged in them and others. The risk of injury is increased when the individual is alcohol-impaired. The main hazards are drowning and impact injuries, particularly from hitting the head when diving. In adults and adolescents, drowning and impact injuries are frequently associated with alcohol consumption, as a result of impaired judgment and the inability to react effectively. Alcohol may also impair parental supervision of children near water, leading to drowning or injury. Figures for Australia showed that alcohol or drug use was implicated in 14% of unintentional drowning fatalities in that country in persons aged over 14 years, of whom 79% were male (WHO, 2005). The degree of increased risk of injury associated with alcohol in or around water is similar to that of alcohol-impaired driving. Persons engaging in recreational boating with a BAC of 1.0 mg/ml have a tenfold greater fatality risk compared to those who have not been drinking alcohol (Driscoll, Harrison, & Steenkamp, 2004). Because drowning and injuries affect swimmers as well as operators of recreational boats, education and prevention efforts are needed for broad segments of the population in order to reduce the risks of alcohol impairment around water. Strategies used to reduce alcohol-impaired driving may prove adaptable to preventing alcohol-impaired boating and swimming.

FREQUENT HEAVY DRINKERS

Although much attention with regard to alcohol-impaired driving focuses on BAC levels, enforcement, and deterrence, harmful drinking patterns are an equally important factor. A frequent heavy drinker, for example, has a higher risk of involvement in road crashes and a greater association with injury (Li, Smith, & Baker, 1994). The Century Council (2004) found that repeat drink-driving offenders tend to have higher rates of other alcohol-related problems as well. A study of convicted repeat drink-driving offenders revealed that 98% of them had histories of alcohol abuse and 75% were alcohol-dependent (Siegal et al., 2000). These findings point to the need to adopt targeted interventions and judicial solutions tailored to this high-risk group.

Hardcore Drunk Driving: A Judicial Guide

The Century Council (2004), an organization funded by leading U.S. distillers, has developed a guide for professionals involved in the prosecution, sentencing, monitoring, and treatment of alcohol-impaired driving offenders. The guide addresses the high-risk population of frequent heavy drinkers whose patterns of consumption and alcohol-impaired driving might be difficult to detect, sanction, and treat.

Hardcore drunk drivers, as the guide identifies them, are responsible for a disproportionate share of alcohol-related traffic fatalities. They drive with high BAC, exceeding the legal maximum limits, and, as their multiple arrests demonstrate, do so repeatedly. They are highly resistant to changing their behavior, despite previous sanctions, treatment, or education efforts. Such repeat offenders need special handling by the judicial and treatment systems. Research and the experience of judges suggest that certain and consistent sanctions coordinated with treatment and monitoring services are key components in reducing repeated alcohol-impaired driving. The guide points out that handling hardcore drunk drivers in this manner is more important than the severity of the penalty. Tailoring solutions and sanctions to the individual and his or her problem drinking patterns can have a profound effect on an offender's ability to avoid reoffending. Similarly, coordinated measures— such as suspension of driving license, imprisonment or confinement, supervision, treatment, or alcohol interlock device—can be instrumental in building effective solutions.

Source: Century Council (2004).

YOUNG PEOPLE AND ALCOHOL-IMPAIRED DRIVING

Young people are of particular concern because of their connection to alcohol-related motor vehicle crashes. In the United States, male drivers in the 21- to 34-year age group constitute the largest risk for alcohol-impaired driving, but U.S. data also reveal that the role of young women in the alcohol-crash problem appears to be slowly increasing from 12.5% of driver fatalities in 1982 to 15.6% in 1998 (Jones & Lacey, 1998, 2001).

The Insurance Institute for Highway Safety in the United States attributed 82% of crashes involving 16-year-old drivers to driver error caused by risk taking and lack of experience. Because of the underlying danger posed by inexperience and recklessness, governments in many parts of the world have implemented policies of zero tolerance (BAC limit of 0.0 mg/ml) for novice drivers and instituted graduated licensing laws that limit driving hours and/or the number of passengers a young driver may carry. Such measures are meant to provide the novice driver with experience and remove the likelihood of occasions in which they might harm themselves or others.

DEVELOPING COUNTRIES

As drinking patterns and mobility vary significantly around the world, most notably between highly motorized (the so-called developed) countries to less motorized (low- and middle-income) countries, so too does the profile of individuals at risk of impaired driving. In a review of studies examining alcohol-related road crashes in developing countries, the United Kingdom Transport Research Laboratory (TRL) identified several key groups at risk for alcohol-impaired driving (Davis, Quimby, Odero, Gururaj, & Hijar, 2003).

Although developed countries have much to offer in terms of their experience in addressing alcohol-impaired driving, it is not sensible to think that all countries share the same patterns, or that the same interventions or programs can be applied in developing countries without taking account of local circumstances. Any long-term effective strategy to reduce alcohol-impaired driving crashes in developing countries will need the support and encouragement of government and other stake-holders. A true picture of the scale and type of problem in a particular country or local area is indispensable in order to identify the appropriate interventions and what they can realistically achieve.

Alcohol-impaired Driving in Africa

Research conducted by the United Kingdom Transport Research Laboratory in five African countries (Ghana, Kenya, Nigeria, Tanzania, and Zambia) found the following:

- Men are predominantly more involved in alcohol- and drug-impaired driving than women. This reflects the existing gender differences in alcohol consumption patterns in the African societies examined and documented in several ethnographic studies (men, in general, are also more likely to drive than women in African societies).
- Men between the ages of 30 and 49 are more likely to drive while intoxicated than their younger or older counterparts.
- Operators of private vehicles are more likely to be under the influence of alcohol than drivers of commercial vehicles (such as buses, taxis, and trucks), but the risk caused by alcohol-impaired commercial drivers is greater because of the high passenger load of these vehicles and the large distances covered.
- Drivers with less education are more likely to drink and drive.
- Driving in the evenings, at night, and over weekends is associated with a high prevalence of alcohol impairment.

Source: Davis et al. (2003).

INTERVENTIONS TO REDUCE
ALCOHOL-IMPAIRED DRIVING

As Davis and colleagues (2003) indicated,

> There is a wide agreement in the international scientific literature that increasing drivers' perception of the risk of being detected for excess alcohol is a very important element in any package of measures to reduce alcohol-related crashes. Police powers, enforcement and judicial procedures, and the type of evidentiary equipment used to test breath and/or blood alcohol levels all play a large part in determining the extent to which this objective can be reached. (p. viii)

Publicity campaigns, backed up by enforcement, have been shown to reduce the incidence of crashes involving alcohol. Yet, without effective legislation, raising awareness through publicity campaigns and public information schemes remains a short-term action, of limited value in influencing people's driving behavior. Experience from highly motorized countries demonstrates that awareness, enforcement, and sanctions through the legal system are needed to make clear that alcohol-impaired driving is unacceptable. It is clear that campaigns must take account of local circumstances and culture, although the principle that legislation and enforcement are essential in order to make a major impact appears to be robust. Law enforcement and appropriate penalties for drivers that flout drink-driving laws are essential. Without enforcement by local authorities and police forces, legislation against drink-driving is virtually redundant. Unless potential offenders perceive that they will be detected and that there is an effective general deterrent, alcohol-impaired driving offenses will continue to rise.

A range of interventions has been introduced to target drink-driving. Examples include the following:

- **Roadside checkpoints**: Alcohol screening is an important tool within the arsenal of police actions to reduce alcohol-impaired driving. It can be either *specific* or *random*. Specific, targeted roadside alcohol screening focuses typically on specific locations, known patterns of drinking and driving, as well as routine patrols, observations, and responses to crashes. This approach provides a *specific* deterrence based on a *detection* strategy resulting in the interception of impaired drivers. Random interventions, on the other hand, provide a *general* deterrence based on a *preventative* strategy. With the effective use of random alcohol screenings, drivers perceive a high risk of detection were they to be impaired. In order to be effective, research suggests that random checkpoints must (a) be highly visible and known by drivers, (b) apply the law and sanctions rigorously to ensure credibility, (c) be a sustained activity over a long term, and (d) publicize the dangers of impaired driving, the high risk of detection, and the severity of the consequences/sanctions using education and media to ensure that the desired behavior becomes normative (Homel, 1988). In a review of research on the introduction of roadside alcohol testing, the weight of evidence suggests that random screening interventions are an effective tool in reducing the incidence of crashes involving fatalities and injuries (Peek-Asa, 1999). There is evidence, however, that certain populations (the so-called hard-core, habitual drunk drivers, and young males) are less influenced by the general deterrence of random screenings and therefore require more specific, targeted intervention approaches, using stiffer sanctions, alcohol-interlock devices, and lower or zero BAC limits (Mathijssen, 2005).

- **Designated driver programs**: These programs encourage a group of people who go out drinking together to assign one of them not to drink on a given occasion. The designated driver provides a safe ride for the group (he or she can also help the group avoid other risks as well).

European Union: The EuroBOB Campaigns

EuroBOB is an awareness campaign, originally launched in Belgium, to educate the public regarding the dangers of alcohol-impaired driving and to promote the concept of choosing a designated driver ("Bob") before a night out. Since its inception, young people were the particular focus of the campaign, but over the years other groups (men between 35 and 55 years, and male drivers aged over 55 years) were also targeted. Campaign elements include billboards and posters distributed to schools, police stations, public buildings, cafés, bars, and restaurants; TV and radio spots; the Internet (http://www.bob.be); and articles and advertisements in magazines of the Belgian Road and Safety Institute intended for road safety professionals and the police. Since 1998, the EuroBOB bus has been a permanent awareness-raising tool: The bus is available on demand and offers a driving simulator, informational folders, and breathalyzers. In addition, the police are asked to increase the number of alcohol checks and to organize random breath testing during the program's annual run. Today, variations of EuroBOB are active in Belgium, Greece ("Not Tonight"), the Netherlands ("Bob Jij of Bob ik?"), Portugal ("100% Cool"), Spain ("Programa un conductor cada noche"), and other European Union countries. According to the 2003 data, 97% of individuals surveyed in Belgium were familiar with the EuroBOB initiative and message and nearly 60% of respondents under 35 years old have already been driven home by a "Bob." EuroBOB campaigns are sponsored in large part by European alcohol producers, social aspects organizations active in individual countries, and, more recently, the European Commission. The programs are run in partnership with a variety of transport, safety, hospitality, and sports associations, agencies, and government departments.

Sources: Amsterdam Group: European Forum for Responsible Drinking (2003), and Arnoldus Group & Institut Belge pour la Sécurité Routière (2002).

- **Alternative transportation schemes:** Some programs provide free or subsidized transportation for people who have been drinking, making it easier for them to choose a safe way home. Such schemes include free (Operation Red Nose, 2005) or discounted regular taxis or volunteer drivers dedicated solely to transporting alcohol-impaired individuals home.
- **On-site education campaigns:** Such campaigns generally consist of interaction among drinking establishments' patrons and enforcement agencies, educators, and peers. Taking place in licensed premises or parking areas (or petrol stations), such campaigns offer a brief intervention on the risk of alcohol-impaired driving and provide patrons with an opportunity to use BAC-measuring equipment (breathalyzers).
- **Server training programs:** Well-managed drinking environments can enhance the pleasure derived from a drinking occasion and reduce the risks of harm associated with alcohol abuse. Such programs provide training for proprietors, managers, waiters, and bartenders on their legal and social responsibilities as providers of beverage alcohol (for example, not serving alcohol to already intoxicated individuals and those below the legal drinking age). Additionally, such programs educate servers about alcohol effects and about their role in intervening in the risk situations of clients. Ensuring adequate enforcement of regulations regarding on-premise consumption is vital not only to the enjoyment of patrons but also to their safety (Graham & Homel, 1997; Graham et al., 2004; Graham, Schmidt, & Gillis, 1995). Server training measures are most effective when coupled with enforcement and formal or informal agreements or partnerships between police, licensed premises, and local communities (see Chapter 2; see also ICAP, 2005b; Stockwell, 2001).
- **Education programs:** Many countries have established school-based curricula for young people in high schools and universities (and, in some jurisdictions, even before high school). Such programs focus on responsible drinking patterns and issues of road safety (using of seat belts and helmets, for example), means of avoiding drinking and driving (arranging for alternative transportation before going out), and increasing youths' intention not to ride with intoxicated drivers.
- **Holiday and "fiesta" campaigns:** These are mass media campaigns to remind drivers and other road users of the risks associated with alcohol-impaired driving and to alert the public to a period of increased enforcement of drink-driving laws. The objective is to deter and dissuade individuals from taking risks and to raise their perception about the risk of a crash and/or their apprehension about being caught. Such campaigns often use fear arousal as a deterring factor; for this to be effective, the level of fear may need to be moderated so as to be realistic. Such campaigns increase in effectiveness when they are backed up with real and visible enforcement, as well as viable coping strategies and

alternatives to driving while impaired (for example, available public transport, safe rides, or designated driver programs).

Brazil: More Life in Revelry

Mais Vida na Folia (More Life in Revelry) is an awareness campaign aired during one of Brazil's most popular festivals—the Carnival, a celebration traditionally accompanied by a lot of music, dancing, and drinking. Launched in 2003, the program is run by Centro de Prevenção às Dependências, the Municipality of Recife, the State of Pernambuco, and the federal government, and consists of several components. First, booklets providing advice on minimizing harm to self and others and stressing the importance of not driving while intoxicated are distributed to the population; a phone information service is advertised for those wishing to call in with immediate questions. Second, training programs are organized for individuals in a range of professions. Employees of bars and restaurants are trained to promote responsible hospitality practices, such as not serving alcohol to intoxicated customers and calling taxis for patrons who have had too much to drink. Emergency personnel are trained to deal with alcohol-related incidents and intoxicated victims. Taxi drivers are encouraged to enforce the use of seat belts among their passengers. To further reduce the incidence of alcohol-impaired driving, public transport is free during the time of the Carnival. The main objective of these initiatives is to enhance the enjoyment of the festival while minimizing harm for drivers, pedestrians, and the community.

The campaign has already brought some positive results. For example, the Expresso da Folia (Revelry Express, the public transport service) is growing in popularity, with a 35% increase in the number of customers from 2003 to 2004. The Municipality of Recife has been invited to train personnel in other cities wishing to replicate this annual program.

Source: Gorgulho and Da Ros (2006).

- **Alcohol ignition interlock device on vehicles**: This is a breath-testing device connected to the ignition system of a motor vehicle that prevents an operator from starting the vehicle if the breath alcohol concentration (BrAC) exceeds a predetermined threshold (usually set to zero, trace—for example, 0.1 to 0.2 mg/ml—or the legal maximum BAC in a given jurisdiction). As these devices are generally used with convicted alcohol-impaired drivers (typically, first offenders with very high BAC and multiple offenders), they are viewed as a sanction, a means of harm reduction, and a general road safety approach. The main behavior goal of the interlock device is for the user to learn to separate drinking from driving. Monitoring and review of the device's data recorder by the legal authority is generally recommended. This enables the legal or judicial authority to evaluate whether and how often the driver has attempted to start the vehicle with BAC above the established threshold. Recidivism rates once the device is removed are high in many studies (see, for example, Marques, Voas, Tippetts, & Beirness, 2000). Treatment for alcohol dependence and harm reduction approaches designed to help drivers reevaluate their vehicle use, including dissociating the drinking environment from driving and planning for transport needs before drinking, can augment the effectiveness of the alcohol interlock programs (Mathijssen, 2001).

PARTNERSHIPS AND COMPLEMENTARY ACTIONS

There is an acute need to focus the attention of governments, police, and road users on drink-driving issues. Resources, personnel, legal and institutional capacity, training, and equipment are needed in most jurisdictions to bring down the incidence of alcohol-impaired driving. Countermeasures—such as establishing BAC limits, random breath testing, campaigning, and education—are some of the measures that, if implemented in a consistent and lasting manner, can produce positive changes in drinking patterns and societies' views on alcohol-impaired driving. The responsibility for education and information about the risks of drinking and driving does not exclusively lie with government; the beverage alcohol industry can support and complement government and advocacy groups' efforts.

The World Report on Road Traffic Injury Prevention, issued jointly by WHO and the World Bank, calls for a new model to tackle road traffic fatalities and injuries:

> Road safety is a shared responsibility. . . . Reducing the risk in the world's road traffic systems requires commitment and informed decision-making by government, industry, nongovernmental organizations and international agencies and participation by people from many different disciplines. (WHO, 2004, p. 158)

This new model highlights road injury and death as serious public health threats and points to the need to create institutional capacity across a broad range of sectors and stakeholders, including the beverage alcohol industry. The Global Road Safety Partnership is one international road safety program that promotes a shared responsibility approach and aims to include all concerned stakeholders (GRSP, n.d.).

The issue of alcohol-impaired driving in developing countries may be of considerable interest to the transport sector and agencies dealing with poverty alleviation. There is, however, very little information from low- and middle-income countries on the extent of the problem, the feasibility of designing practical harm mitigation strategies and targeted interventions suitable for the local situation, and the capability of local enforcement efforts to provide a sufficient deterrent against alcohol-impaired driving.

If traffic crashes are to be reduced, an approach that is as multidimensional as the problem itself, excluding no one from the public discourse, needs to be adopted. That means seeking help from a wider variety of stakeholders and forming new public-private partnerships among health officials, law enforcement, transportation officials, the judicial system, community organizations, and the private sector.

Because the problem of drinking and driving affects society at large, it needs cooperation from a variety of sectors and disciplines to solve it. Government efforts through legislation, education, and enforcement can be pooled with efforts by the beverage alcohol industry, community-based organizations, and academic institutions to address the problem.

REFERENCES

Aggarwal, V. (2005). Drink driving in India. *The Globe, 2*, 20–21.

Amsterdam Group: European Forum for Responsible Drinking. (2003). *Designated driver campaigns against drink-driving in Europe 2003*. Brussels, Belgium: Author.

Arnoldus Group & Institut Belge pour la Sécurité Routière. (2002). "EuroBOB": European designated driver campaign against drinking and driving 2001–2002. Final Report. Retrieved May 9, 2002, from http://europa.eu.int/comm/transport/road/roadsafety/behaviour/campaigns/doc/eurobob_2001_2002.pdf.

Borkenstein, R. F., Crowther, R. F., Shumate, R. P., Ziel, W. B., & Zylman, R. (Eds.). (1964). *Role of the drinking driver in traffic accidents*. Bloomington: Indiana University, Department of Police Administration.

Century Council. (2004). *Hardcore drunk driving judicial guide*. Washington, DC: Author.

Chaturvedi, A. K., Craft, K. J., Canfield, D. V., & Whinnery, J. E. (2005). *Epidemiology of toxicological factors in civil aviation accident pilot fatalities, 1999–2003*. Oklahoma City, OK: FAA Civil Aerospace Medical Institute.

Cherpitel, C. J., Tam, T. W., Midanik, L. T., Caetano, R., & Greenfield, T. K. (1995). Alcohol and non-fatal injury in the U.S. general population: A risk function analysis. *Accident Analysis and Prevention, 27*, 651–661.

Davis, A., Quimby, A., Odero, W., Gururaj, G., & Hijar, M. (2003, May). *Improving road safety by reducing impaired driving in developing countries: A scoping study*. Crowthorne, UK: Transport Research Laboratory.

Driscoll, T. R., Harrison, J. A., & Steenkamp, M. (2004). Review of the role of alcohol in drowning associated with recreational aquatic activity. *Injury Prevention, 10*, 107–113.

Edayaranmula, J. J. (2005). Road accidents in Kerala. *The Globe, 2*, 22–23.

Federal Aviation Administration (FAA). (2006). *Code of federal regulations: Alcohol or drugs (91.17)*. Retrieved January 19, 2006, from http://www.faa.gov/regulations_policies/.

Ghee, C., Astrop, A., Silcock, D., & Jacobs, G. (1997). *Socio-economic aspects of road accidents in developing countries*. TRL Report 247. Crowthorne, UK: Transport Research Laboratory.

Global Road Safety Parternship (GRSP). (2004). *Impaired driving in developed countries*. Retrieved September 17, 2005, from http://www.grsproadsafety.org.

Global Road Safety Partnership (GRSP). (2005). *The problem worldwide*. Retrieved September 27, 2005, from http://www.grsproadsafety.org.

Global Road Safety Partnership (GRSP). (n.d.). *What is GRSP.* Retrieved January 19, 2004, from http://www.grsproadsafety.org.

Gorgulho, M., & Da Ros, V. (2006). Alcohol harm reduction in Brazil. *International Journal of Drug Policy, 17,* 350–357.

Graham, K., & Homel, R. (1997). Creating safer bars. In M. Plant, E. Single, & T. Stockwell (Eds.), *Alcohol: Minimizing the harm. What works?* (pp. 171–192). London: Free Association Books.

Graham, K., Osgood, D. W., Zibrowski, E., Purcell, J., Gliksman, L., Leonard, K., et al. (2004). The effect of the Safer Bars programme on physical aggression in bars: Results of a randomized controlled trial. *Drug and Alcohol Review, 23,* 31–41.

Graham, K., Schmidt, G., & Gillis, K. (1995). Circumstances when drinking leads to aggression: An overview of research findings. *Contemporary Drug Problems, 23,* 493–557.

Grant, S. A., Millar, K., & Kenny, G. N. C. (2000). Blood alcohol concentration and psychomotor effects. *British Journal of Anaesthesia, 85,* 401–406.

Homel, R. (1988). *Policing and punishing the drinking driver: A study of general and specific deterrence.* New York: Springer-Verlag.

International Center for Alcohol Policies (ICAP). (2005a). *Table: Blood alcohol concentration limits worldwide.* Retrieved April 18, 2006, from http://icap.org/PolicyIssues/DrinkingandDriving/BACTable/tabid/199/Default.aspx.

International Center for Alcohol Policies (ICAP). (2005b). *Blue Book: Practical guides for alcohol policy and targeted interventions.* Washington, DC: Author.

Jacobs, G., Aeron-Thomas, A., & Astrop, A. (2000). *Estimating global road fatalities.* TRL Report 445. Crowthorne, UK: Transport Research Laboratory.

Jones, A. W. (1990). Physiological aspects of breath-alcohol measurement. *Alcohol, Drugs and Driving, 6,* 1–25.

Jones, R. K., & Lacey, J. H. (1998). *Alcohol highway safety: Problem update.* Washington, DC: U.S. National Highway Traffic Safety Administration.

Jones, R. K., & Lacey, J. H. (2001). *Alcohol and highway safety 2001: A review of the state of knowledge.* Washington, DC: U.S. National Highway Traffic Safety Administration.

Lang, A. R. (1992). Alcohol: Teenage drinking. In S. Snyder (Ed.), *Encyclopedia of psychoactive drugs,* 2nd ed. (Vol. 3). New York: Chelsea House.

Li, G., Smith, G. S., & Baker, S. P. (1994). Drinking behavior in relation to cause of death among U.S. adults. *American Journal of Public Health, 84,* 1402–1406.

Lucas, G. H., Kalow, W., McColl, J. D., Griffith, B. A., & Smith, H. W. (1955). Quantitative studies of the relationship between alcohol levels and motor vehicle accidents. *Alcohol and road traffic: Proceedings of the Second International Conference on Alcohol and Road Traffic (1953)* (pp. 139–142). Toronto: Garden City Press Cooperative.

Marques, P., Voas, R. B., Tippetts, A. S., & Beirness, D. R. (2000). *Predictors of failed interlock BAC tests and using failed BAC test to predict post-interlock repeat DUIs* Paper presented at the 15th International Conference on Alcohol, Drugs and Traffic Safety, Stockholm, Sweden. Retrieved August 3, 2006, from http://www.icadts.org/proceedings/2000/icadts2000-181.pdf.

Mathijssen, M. P. (2005). Drink driving policy and road safety in the Netherlands: A retrospective analysis. *Transportation Research Part E-Logistics and Transportation Review, 41,* 395–408.

Mathijssen, R. (Ed.). (2001). *Feasibility of alcolock implementation in EU drink-driving policies: Presentation at the European Commission, 4 December 2001, Brussels.* Leidschendam, the Netherlands: Institute for Road Safety Research (SWOV).

Melcop, A. G. (2003). Stop here and now: The challenges of approaching harm reduction in traffic violence. In E. Buning, M. Gorgulho, A. G. Melcop, & P. O'Hare (Eds.), *Alcohol and harm reduction: An innovative approach for countries in transition* (pp. 87–105). Amsterdam, the Netherlands: International Coalition on Alcohol and Harm Reduction (ICAHR).

Moskowitz, H., Blomberg, R., Burns, M., Fiorentino, D., & Peck, R. (2002). Methodological issues in epidemiological studies of alcohol crash risk. In D. R. Mayhew & C. Dussault (Eds.), *Proceedings of the 16th International Conference on Alcohol, Drugs and Traffic Safety, Montreal, Canada, August 4–9, 2002* (pp. 45–50). Quebec, Canada: Société de l'assurance automobile du Québec.

Moskowitz, H., & Fiorentino, D. (2000). *A review of the literature on the effects of low doses of alcohol on driving-related skills.* Springfield, VA: U.S. Department of Transportation, National Highway Traffic Safety Administration.

Moskowitz, H., & Robinson, C. D. (1988). *Effects of low doses of alcohol on driving-related skills: A review of the evidence.* Washington, DC: U.S. National Highway Traffic Safety Administration.

Mounce, N. H., & Pendleton, O. J. (1992). Relationship between blood alcohol concentration and crash responsibility for fatally injured drivers. *Accident Analysis and Prevention, 24,* 201–210.

Operation Red Nose. (2005). *Opération Nez Rouge/Operation Red Nose.* Retrieved September 29, 2005, from http://www.operationnezrouge.com.

Parks, V., Leister, C., Palat, A., Troy, S., Vermeeren, A., Volkerts, E. R., et al. (2002). Effects of ethanol at a blood alcohol concentration of 0.4 g/L on actual driving and memory. *European Neuropsychopharmacology, 12*(Suppl. 3), S432–S433.

Peden, M. M. (Ed.) (2001). *The sentinel surveillance of substance abuse and trauma, 1999–2000.* Final Report. Tygerberg, South Africa: Medical Research Council.

Peden, M. M., Knottenbelt, J. D., van der Spuy, J., Oodit, R., Scholtz, H. J., & Stokol, J. M. (1996). Injured pedestrians in Cape Town: The role of alcohol. *South African Medical Journal, 86,* 1103–1105.

Peek-Asa, C. (1999). The effect of random alcohol screening in reducing motor vehicle crash injuries. *American Journal of Preventive Medicine, 16,* 57–67.

Rehm, J., Room, R., Monteiro, M., Gmel, G., Graham, K., Rehn, N., et al. (2004). Alcohol use. In M. Ezzati, A. D. Lopez, A. Rodgers, & C. J. Murray (Eds.), *Comparative quantification of health risks: Global and regional burden of disease attributable to selected major risk factors* (pp. 959–1108). Geneva, Switzerland: World Health Organization.

Roldán, J., Frauca, C., & Dueñas, A. (2003). Intoxicación por alcoholes [Alcohol intoxication]. *Anales del Sistema Sanitario de Navarra, 26*(Suppl.), 129–139.

Siegal, H. A., Falck, R. S., Carlson, R. G., Rapp, R. C., Wang, J., & Cole, P. A. (2000). The hardcore drunk driving offender. *Proceedings of the 15th International Conference on Alcohol, Drugs and Traffic Safety.* Stockholm: International Council on Alcohol, Drugs and Traffic Safety.

Stockwell, T. (2001). Responsible alcohol service: Lessons from evaluations of server training and policing initiatives. *Drug and Alcohol Review, 20,* 257–265.

U.S. National Highway Traffic Safety Administration (NHTSA). (1994). *Computing a BAC estimate.* Washington, DC: Author.

U.S. National Highway Traffic Safety Administration (NHTSA). (2005). *Traffic safety facts, 2004 data: Alcohol*. Retrieved August 3, 2006, from http://www-nrd.nhtsa. dot.gov/pdf/nrd-30/NCSA/TSF2004/809905.pdf.

World Health Organization (WHO). (2004). *World report on road traffic injury prevention*. Geneva, Switzerland: Author.

World Health Organization (WHO). (2005). *Drowning fact sheet*. Retrieved September 12, 2005, from http://www.who.int/violence_injury_prevention/publications/other_injury/en/drowning_factsheet.pdf.

Zador, P. L. (1991). Alcohol-related relative risk of fatal driver injuries in relation to driver age and sex. *Journal of Studies on Alcohol, 52*, 302–310.

Zador, P. L., Krawchuk, S. A., & Voas, R. B. (2000). Alcohol-related relative risk of driver fatalities and driver involvement in fatal crashes in relation to driver age and gender: An update using 1996 data. *Journal of Studies on Alcohol, 61*, 387–395.

6

Targeting Drinking Contexts: Public Disorder

The second example of targeted interventions explores the association between drinking and public disorder. The link between alcohol consumption and violence is a concern in many communities. Significantly, anthropological studies in developed and developing countries show that drinking is not associated with violence in all cultures; drinking outcomes are shaped by norms and expectations.

Communities may also be concerned about social nuisance (such as noise, litter, and vandalism) around some premises that serve alcohol. Bars and other public drinking venues are a prime opportunity for changing drinking behavior. Indeed, in many countries, licensing regulations include provisions that are designed to reduce or prevent intoxication—such as standard sizes for serving drinks, rules about who may buy drinks (in some countries, for instance, "round buying" is prohibited), and rules against serving intoxicated patrons. More recently, a range of interventions has focused on responsible server training programs, changes to the physical drinking environment, and the implementation of community "alcohol accords." As described in Chapter 4, accords are initiatives that bring together a range of stakeholders—the hospitality trade, local business, police, licensing authorities, transport authorities, and city planners. The collaborative effort is then directed at facilitating responsible alcohol consumption. Such accords have often developed in city center areas and tourist venues, where alcohol is a key part of local entertainment.

PUBLIC DISORDER AND ANTISOCIAL BEHAVIOR

The complete spectrum of human behavior occurs under the influence of alcohol, including disruptive, antisocial, and aggressive behavior. In a study in Thunder Bay, Ontario, Canada, over 40% of violent crime involved alcohol consumption by either the perpetrator or the victim (Pernanen, 1991). In Australia, research has shown that property damage and offensive verbal behavior are strongly predicted by the availability of alcohol (Stevenson, Lind, & Weatherburn, 1999). Even in nonindustrialized societies, alcohol is often associated with public disorder. The Abipone Indians of Paraguay, who are normally very austere and even-tempered, become uncontrolled, assertive, and violent during occasions of alcohol consumption (MacAndrew & Edgerton, 1969).

The seminal work by MacAndrew and Edgerton (1969) demonstrated that drinking occasions are characterized by violent outbursts in some cultures and by cheerful or tranquil behavior in others. The authors attributed these findings to the different meanings each culture ascribed to alcohol. Individual drinking behavior, however, is also influenced by many other factors, such as the type and amount of alcohol consumed, personal differences in temperament, alcohol expectancies, and impulsiveness—as well as the social context in which drinking takes place.

As noted by Fagan (1993), it is not easy to disentangle the effects of the different aspects of the drinking situation on intoxicated behavior. Alcohol's pharmacological effects interact with personality differences in the consumer, as well as with characteristics of the drinking environment, to guide a person's behavior during consumption. To understand how alcohol contributes to antisocial behavior and public disorder, it is important to recognize that the drinking context plays two important roles. The first role is the influence of the situation on alcohol consumption patterns (the decision whether, where, and how much to drink). Second, there is the influence of the situation directly—and in interaction with intoxication—on the decision to engage in unhealthy and antisocial behaviors (such as interpersonal violence, crime, and sexual assault).

Public venues in which alcohol is consumed may provide an environment where a myriad of otherwise antisocial behaviors are acceptable. Thus, heavy alcohol use is correlated with a range of antinormative behaviors in such places as bars and at sporting events and other public venues, because individuals interested in heavy drinking are also often interested in other deviant behaviors and congregate in places where both are accepted. In addition, drinking situations may set up a behavioral set in which other antisocial behaviors become expected. For example, in an analysis of Skinhead drinking culture in Australia, a night out for young men who had adopted the Skinhead subculture consisted of ritualized drinking of beer and was often accompanied by violence and casual sexual encounters. Heavy drinking, rowdy behavior, and casual sex were expected by the participants to be natural aspects of a night out with other Skinheads (Moore, 1990).

Public Drinking Venues

Bars are the most studied drinking venues in research on the links between alcohol consumption and public disorder. Although this does not apply to all bars, some are locations at which individuals frequently experience violence. According to U.S. surveys of 433 college students and 967 individuals aged 18 to 30 years in a general population sample, the two most frequent locations in which individuals reported experiencing violence were in the stands at sporting events and in or around bars, with the most severe violent incidents occurring in the latter (Leonard, Quigley, & Collins, 2002).

Venues that bring together young men tend to be more dangerous locations, because this group has a predilection toward engaging in aggressive behavior. Being younger and male are the two strongest demographic factors predicting frequency of bar attendance, according to an analysis of the responses of 5,828 individuals aged 18 or older to the U.S. General Social Survey (Parks & Quigley, 2001). In another U.S. survey of young adults, Felson (1997) found that young men who frequently engaged in nightlife activities were more likely to be targets of violence and more likely to experience violence outside the family. This was not true for young women, although their alcohol consumption was positively associated with being a target of violence.

Nightlife activities are often permeated by a culture of masculinity, as Campbell (2000) demonstrated in his analysis of rural nightlife in New Zealand. The study found that drinking itself was used to promote masculinity, with "real men" being able to hold their liquor and "one up" others in the pub in what Campbell termed "conversational cockfighting." Associated with this affirmation of masculinity in pubs is the occurrence of physical aggression during drinking. Tomsen's (1997) analysis of drinking occasions in Sydney, Australia, demonstrated physical aggression while drinking to be motivated by the need both to assert one's masculinity (if confronted at a pub, individuals would fight because not fighting would put their masculinity into greater question than fighting and losing) and to achieve personal pleasure. In addition, much violence is also motivated by the carnival atmosphere at some drinking establishments. It provides both a show for the clientele and a "pleasurable" diversion for those who wish to engage in the behavior. However, the emphasis on masculinity does not mean that only men experience violence in public drinking establishments. At least one U.S. study has shown that nearly half of female frequent bar drinkers reported experiencing physical aggression, and nearly a third reported experiencing some form of sexual assault associated with drinking in a bar (Parks & Miller, 1997).

Not everyone who drinks at bars, however, experiences violence. The Bar Violence Study in Buffalo, New York, United States, was designed to investigate the individual differences among patrons who experience bar violence and those who do not, the characteristics of bars where violence tends to occur, and the characteristics of the violent incidents themselves. Individuals who reported frequenting bars at which violence was known to occur were younger, more impulsive, heavier drinkers, more likely to have alcohol problems, and more likely to hold the belief that alcohol makes them aggressive than individuals who frequented bars where violence did not usually occur (Quigley, Leonard, & Collins, 2003).

Characteristics of the bar itself—independent of the clientele—also predict the likelihood of violence taking place. Quigley and colleagues (2003) found that bars in which violence is frequent tended to be smokier, higher in temperature, dirtier, darker, more crowded, more likely to have competitive games, and more likely to employ bouncers and male employees. These bars also tended to have a more permissive atmosphere with regard to antinormative behaviors, including sexual behaviors and illegal activities (for example, prostitution and drug use). When both client characteristics and characteristics of the bar were entered into a regression equation to predict the violence proneness of a given establishment, bar characteristics were stronger predictors than the characteristics of the clientele (Quigley et al., 2003). However, it was not possible to determine the true direction of the relationship. It may be that individuals with certain characteristics are attracted to certain types of bars, or that the characteristics of the bars are driven by the type of clientele that frequents the establishment. It is likely that both processes occur. However, it is clear from this study, as well as others (Buddie & Parks, 2003; Graham, La Rocque, Yetman, Ross, & Guistra, 1980), that a permissive atmosphere in a drinking venue is one of the strongest indicators that problems, such as violence, are likely to occur.

Barroom Behavior

The bar atmosphere provides a time-out from ordinary behavior, a time when actions not normally sanctioned, such as drunkenness and physical and sexual aggressiveness, may be accepted. Certain qualities of the bar and bar management and the symbolic qualities of alcohol lead some individuals to believe that they will be held less responsible for misdeeds performed while under the influence of alcohol (Critchlow, 1983). Bars in which aggression is frequent are also bars where overserving, serving minors, and other illegal activities are, if not condoned, at least not discouraged (Quigley et al., 2003).

On the other hand, strict controls inside the bar may engender violence outside the premises. Removing aggressive or disruptive clients from an establishment only moves them on to another location. In an Australian example, Tomsen (1997) found that bars with rigorous enforcement of rules inside the premises experienced excessive levels of violence and antisocial behavior outside their doors. This occurred as a part of a power play between clientele and the bar staff. Although the staff had power inside the bar, the rowdy patrons were able to demonstrate their autonomy by engaging in whatever activities they felt like outside the premises, including vandalism, public urination, and violence.

The interaction between alcohol consumption, deviant behavior, and the environment is illustrated in Figure 6.1, showing that there are two paths from environmental cues to antisocial behaviors that involve alcohol consumption. First are cues in the environment that promote such antisocial behaviors as heavy drinking. These cues can be of many types, including advertising and happy hour specials, the reference group an individual is with at a bar (for example, a Skinhead gathering), and the purpose of the gathering (a celebration or an excuse to get drunk). Some environments activate more alcohol-related thoughts than others (Wall, McKee, & Hinson, 2000) and, subsequently, lead to greater consumption

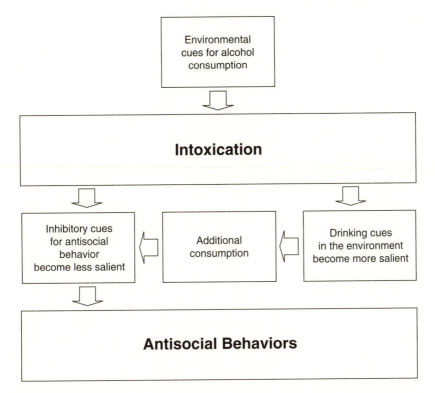

Figure 6.1 Influence of Drinking Environment Characteristics on Alcohol Consumption and Antisocial Behavior.

(Roehrich & Goldman, 1995). In addition, the presence of heavy-drinking others (Quigley & Collins, 1999), the motivation to prove that one can "hold one's liquor" (Campbell, 2000), or an expectation among certain drinking subcultures that a person cannot leave until he or she has bought a round of drinks for the group (Moore, 1990) can also have strong influences on individual consumption levels.

Second, the intoxication that results from alcohol consumption makes certain cues in the environment have more influence on behavior than others. Alcohol is proposed to have an effect primarily in situations of "inhibition conflict," when instigation and inhibitions are relatively equal. Intoxication is thought to constrain attention to and processing of these negative consequences, thereby enabling the instigating motivations to have a much greater influence on behavior (Steele & Josephs, 1990; Taylor & Leonard, 1983).

Some cues in a bar environment are cues for rowdy or antisocial behavior. For example, witnessing an aggressive incident may encourage aggression in another person who has no role in the conflict but is drawn in simply because it seems to be "the thing to do" at that time and place (Tomsen, 1997). Intoxication has an enhanced impact on the attention paid to facilitation cues and the dismissal of inhibitory cues in the environment. To the extent that a bar or public venue provides an environment that promotes public disorder, the more one consumes in that venue, the more effective will be the cues promoting antisocial behavior. Although antisocial behavior in public cannot entirely be attributed to the interaction of intoxication and aggressive cues in the environment, evidence from bar intervention programs has shown that changing the qualities of the bar environment can reduce the occurrence of violence.

Intervening to Reduce Alcohol-related Public Disorder

Several programs have been instituted to deal with public disorder related to drinking venues (Daly, Campbell, Wiggers, & Considine, 2002; Graham et al., 2004; Homel, Carvolth, Hauritz, McIlwain, & Teague, 2004; International Center for Alcohol Policies, 2002, 2005; Quigley et al., 2003; Single et al., 1997; Wallin, Norström, & Andreasson, 2003). They include modifying the environment, training servers and security personnel in how to handle drunken patrons, liability issues, and the importance of server judgment in reducing the likelihood of alcohol-impaired driving (Burns, Nusbaumer, & Reiling, 2003; Johnsson & Berglund, 2003; Sloan, Stout, Whetten-Goldstein, & Liand, 2000; Stockwell, 2001). The Safer Bars Program in Canada dealt only with bar interventions (Graham, Jelley, & Purcell, 2005), whereas Surfers Paradise Safety Action Project in Australia focused on both community and bar interventions to reduce problems in an entire district (Homel, Hauritz, Wortley, McIlwain, & Carvolth, 1997). In both cases, reductions in problems were observed. These interventions worked to affect two aspects of the model presented in Figure 6.1: They attempted to reduce those cues in the environment that lead to disruptive behavior, and they worked to discourage intoxication, which exacerbates reactions to such cues when they are present.

Physical Changes to the Environment. A number of environmental interventions have been suggested to create a bar atmosphere that would not encourage disruptive behavior or that would minimize harm should altercations occur (Graham & Homel, 1997). These interventions include having clean, attractive, and well-maintained premises and restrooms. Such conditions would signal to patrons that antinormative behavior will not be condoned in the establishment. Creating a physical space that allows easy access to the bar or that provides sitting areas without causing crowding or traffic jams reduces potential sources of conflict among patrons. To avoid conflict, it is also important to have clearly defined rules posted for any games offered in the venue.

In order to minimize injuries if aggression does occur, bars may reduce the use of conventional glassware and bottles and replace them with safety glass or plastic cups and cans (Plant, Single, & Stockwell, 1997). Serving food may fulfill two useful purposes. It can provide an expectancy that certain conduct (such as heavy drinking and behaviors associated with heavy drinking) is not encouraged; secondly, it will slow the absorption of alcohol, resulting in lower levels of intoxication. There is evidence that the presence of entertainment such as music, games, or dancing reduces the likelihood of violent incidents (Arnold & Laidler, 1994; Portman Group, 2000). Promotional materials (beer mats on the tables or posters in bathrooms, for example) can be used to impart advice about safety, particularly for women, or about testing for drugs that may have been added to drinks.

Server Practices. Many well-managed drinking establishments implement training of serving staff. In New Zealand, for example, server training is a requirement for obtaining a license to serve beverage alcohol under the Host Responsibility program (Wellington City Council, 2005). The need to ensure responsible practices and adequate enforcement of regulations regarding on-premise consumption is vital not only to the enjoyment of patrons but also to their safety (Graham & Homel, 1997; Graham et al., 2004; Graham, Schmidt, & Gillis, 1995). Responsible hospitality efforts have proven effective in a number of settings (Graham et al., 2005; Holder & Wagenaar, 1994; McKnight & Streff, 1994; Saltz, 1987).

Servers need to be trained about standard drink sizes, proper ID checking, recognizing inebriation, not overserving intoxicated individuals, and dealing (in nonconfrontational ways) with patrons who have consumed too much alcohol. In addition to training the serving staff, security staff should be trained to recognize potential conflicts before they occur and to deal with problems constructively rather than aggressively. Training of employees at 18 violent bars in the Safer Bars program demonstrated that, compared to control bars with similar characteristics, establishments receiving the training had fewer instances of severe aggression by patrons and fewer instances of severe violence by the staff (Graham et al., 2005).

Community Interventions. The owners of establishments holding liquor licenses must be motivated to create the types of changes described above. Often, the desire to reduce problems is in conflict with the desire to maintain financial success. Cutting down on the clientele's drinking has the potential to cut into profits. In the Surfers Paradise district of Australia, competition among bar owners frequently led to overserving patrons and, as a result, to public disorder. Interventions under the Surfers Paradise Safety Action Project (developed as one initiative within the Queensland Safety Action Projects, described below) were implemented at the level of individual establishments; however, they were only one part of that community-based effort, which also involved funding from the local government, a community-based steering committee, and community-based task groups that assessed safety in local venues. Bar owners were asked to create a code of practice that outlined regulations regarding serving, as well as other aspects of the business. Results indicated dramatic reductions in physical and nonphysical altercations following the interventions, according to both community monitoring and police records (Homel et al., 1997).

Community Contribution in the Queensland Safety Action Projects

Australia's Queensland Safety Action Projects were developed out of community frustration and pain: Local chambers of commerce were scathing in their reports of damage to their members' business premises and harassment of clients; nightclub patrons were suffering from the aggression and injuries being sustained; and emergency services (police, ambulance, and hospital services) were being unnecessarily overloaded, as were the courts. Griffith University researchers, with funds from Commonwealth and state governments, developed and coordinated the project to find what characteristics of venues and environs were most associated with violence and to lead a suite of interventions.

At the implementation level, the community role was as important as the role of regulators and industry. A Community Monitoring Committee was set up, including members from the chamber of commerce, state health department, women's crisis group, and local government. The committee would call a licensee to attend a meeting whenever a serious breach of the agreed code of practice was noted. Such breaches were usually signaled by the fact that police or ambulance services had been called to the venue. Interventions, other than by industry (in the venues), included action by local government to address the lack of visibility and lighting in the external environment and by transport providers to introduce the presence of security personnel near taxi stands and improved late bus services. The project was later replicated in three additional coastal communities. The rate of observed physical violence in nightclubs in the two trials across the four communities was reduced by between 52% for the Surfers Paradise nightclub precinct (Homel et al., 1997) and 88.3% for Cairns central business district venues (Hauritz, Homel, Townsley, Burrows, & McIlwain, 1998).

In addition, according to Queensland Health, the effectiveness of community contributions is enhanced when community representatives

- maintain current knowledge of best practice interventions in minimizing harm related to the licensed environment;
- ensure regular liaison with other licensed environment partners, including the local authority, liquor licensing, police, transport, licensed venues associations . . . health and other partner community agencies, such as sobering up centers, organizations, such as sexual assault centers, alcohol and drug action groups . . . and . . . service clubs;
- develop an informed position on key public health and safety issues related to the licensed environment;
- maintain an informed position on the proposals and initiatives of the main governmental bodies concerned;
- ensure [that] the views and recommendations of [community] organization and members are regularly communicated to the public and promoted to the other main organizations involved, i.e. to appropriate

local and regional forums and authorities, as well as to corporate offices within departments;

- participate, where appropriate, in activities to minimize harm related to the licensed environment [for example, local safety audits of public spaces]; [and]
- liaise with authorities involved in licensed environment projects to develop procedures for setting up and maintaining a register of incidents and issues to better assist the authorities in their work and in monitoring outcomes. (Alcohol, Tobacco and Other Drug Services, Queensland Health, 1998, p. 9)

As discussed in Chapter 5, providing alternative transportation has also been successfully applied as a risk reduction measure. Safe and convenient public transport not only has helped reduce the likelihood of alcohol-impaired driving but can also contribute to public order (see "The Manchester City Center Safe Scheme"). Schemes such as Operation Red Nose/Opération Nez Rouge, implemented in Canada, France, and Switzerland around the holiday season, ensure that patrons of drinking establishments reach their homes safely. This particular approach relies on volunteer drivers who escort intoxicated individuals home (see Operation Red Nose, n.d.). Other similar initiatives include providing free taxi rides home.

The Manchester City Centre Safe Scheme

Like many other metropolitan areas, the city of Manchester in the United Kingdom has seen its leisure and entertainment industry grow since the 1990s. The revitalization of the city's downtown area has given rise to an increase in drinking venues. More venues and options for entertainment and leisure have also meant an influx of people who wish to enjoy them. An accompanying rise in threats to public safety and issues of public disorder has prompted the development of a scheme to reduce the risk for harm around licensed premises and the general downtown area.

In 2002, the Greater Manchester Police developed a multi-stakeholder partnership to address these issues through the City Centre Safe program. The program involves law enforcement, city government, the alcohol service and retail industry, the transportation industry, city workers, social services and health professions, and others. The partnership has four major objectives: to partner with other agencies to decrease the number of serious assaults and glass-related injuries that involve alcohol; to partner with the licensed trade and others to better manage licensed establishments; "to promote the provision of safe drinking"; and to reduce the perception of public drunkenness, rowdiness, and public disorder in Manchester city center (Civic Trust, 2005, p. 2).

Implementation has occurred at a number of key levels:

Designated public places order. Police have been given the power to confiscate beverage alcohol and containers in areas that are particularly problematic, and to dispose of them in specially created "bottle banks."

High-profile targeted policing. Uniformed police presence is highly visible around late-night public transport and in known crime "hotspots."

Safe public transport. Bus companies and police have jointly implemented safety procedures, including "loaders" at bus stops to ensure minimum disorder among waiting passengers, closed-circuit TV on buses, crisis management training for bus operators, improved lighting, and the establishment of "safe transport corridors" and "safe havens" where individuals can seek help.

Campaigns and promotion. Marketing campaigns promoting coping strategies, an award for responsible practices in the sale and service of alcohol, and promotion of safe drinking on premises have been implemented by various stakeholders.

Other efforts include frequent and high-profile visits to sites within the city center to ensure that standards are being upheld and measures are being implemented. Training of bar, pub, and restaurant staff is also part of the effort, as are improvements to the design of licensed premises and efforts in crowd control. In addition, individuals whose drinking and behavior are particularly problematic are referred to counseling and treatment programs.

Since the implementation of the Manchester City Centre Safe scheme, crime, including violent crime, has dropped by 13%.

Source: Civic Trust (2005).

Although most of the interventions mentioned here are targeted at bars, they would be appropriate for any public locale where alcohol is served and that may provide the potential for public disorder. For example, a ban on serving alcohol during sporting events at one college stadium resulted in decreases in the number of assaults, arrests, and ejections from the stadium (Bormann & Stone, 2001). Permissive atmospheres in public venues increase the probability of antisocial behavior, and heavy alcohol consumption raises the likelihood that individuals will misbehave. Although it is likely that some individuals will cause trouble regardless of what precautions are taken, findings from such efforts as the Safer Bars Program and the Surfers Paradise Safety Action Project indicate that attention to the social and physical atmosphere in public venues such as bars, sporting events, and other public gatherings can reduce the likelihood of antisocial behavior and encourage greater public order.

REFERENCES

Alcohol, Tobacco and Other Drug Services, Queensland Health. (1998). *A guide for the health sector on partnerships to reduce intoxication, violence and injury in the licensed environment.* Brisbane, Australia: Queensland Health.

Arnold, M. J., & Laidler, T. J. (1994). *Alcohol misuse and violence: Situational and environmental factors in alcohol-related violence*. Canberra: Commonwealth of Australia.

Bormann, C. A., & Stone, M. H. (2001). The effects of eliminating alcohol in a college stadium: The Folsom Field beer ban. *Journal of American College Health, 50*, 81–88.

Buddie, A. M., & Parks, K. A. (2003). The role of the bar context and social behaviors on women's risk for aggression. *Journal of Interpersonal Violence, 18*, 1378–1393.

Burns, E. D., Nusbaumer, M. R., & Reiling, D. M. (2003). Think they're drunk? Alcohol servers and the identification of intoxication. *Journal of Drug Education, 33*, 177–186.

Campbell, H. (2000). The glass phallus: Pub(lic) masculinity and drinking in rural New Zealand. *Rural Sociology, 65*, 562–581.

Civic Trust. (2005). *Manchester: Manchester City Centre Safe*. Retrieved January 30, 2006, from http://www.civictrust.org.uk/evening/studies.shtml.

Critchlow, B. (1983). Blaming the booze: The attribution of responsibility for drunken behavior. *Personality & Social Psychology Bulletin, 9*, 451–473.

Daly, J. B., Campbell, E. M., Wiggers, J. H., & Considine, R. J. (2002). Prevalence of responsible hospitality policies in licensed premises that are associated with alcohol-related harm. *Drug and Alcohol Review, 20*, 113–120.

Fagan, J. (1993). Set and setting revisited: Influences of alcohol and illicit drugs on the social context of violent events. In S. E. Martin (Ed.), *Alcohol and interpersonal violence: Fostering interdisciplinary research* (pp. 161–191). NIAAA Research Monograph No. 24. Rockville, MD: National Institutes of Health.

Felson, R. B. (1997). Routine activities and involvement in violence as actor, witness, and target. *Violence and Victims, 12*, 209–221.

Graham, K., & Homel, R. (1997). Creating safer bars. In M. Plant, E. Single, & T. Stockwell (Eds.), *Alcohol: Minimizing the harm. What works?* (pp. 171–192). London: Free Association Books.

Graham, K., Jelley, J., & Purcell, J. (2005). Training bar staff in preventing and managing aggression in licensed premises. *Journal of Substance Use, 10*, 48–61.

Graham, K., La Rocque, L., Yetman, R., Ross, T. J., & Guistra, E. (1980). Aggression and barroom environments. *Journal of Studies on Alcohol, 41*, 277–292.

Graham, K., Osgood, D. W., Zibrowski, E., Purcell, J., Gliksman, L., Leonard, K., et al. (2004). The effect of the Safer Bars programme on physical aggression in bars: Results of a randomized controlled trial. *Drug and Alcohol Review, 23*, 31–41.

Graham, K., Schmidt, G., & Gillis, K. (1995). Circumstances when drinking leads to aggression: An overview of research findings. *Contemporary Drug Problems, 23*, 493–557.

Hauritz, M., Homel, R., Townsley, M., Burrows, T., & McIlwain, G. (1998). An evaluation of the local government safety action projects in Cairns, Townsville and Mackay. A report to the Queensland Department of Health, the Queensland Police Service and the Criminology Research Council. Brisbane, Australia: Centre for Crime Policy and Public Safety, Griffith University.

Holder, H. D., & Wagenaar, A. C. (1994). Mandated server training and reduced alcohol-involved traffic crashes: A time series analysis of the Oregon experience. *Accident Analysis and Prevention, 26*, 89–97.

Homel, R., Carvolth, R., Hauritz, M., McIlwain, G., & Teague, R. (2004). Making licensed venues safer for patrons: What environmental factors should be the focus of interventions? *Drug and Alcohol Review, 23,* 19–29.

Homel, R., Hauritz, M., Wortley, R., McIlwain, G., & Carvolth, R. (1997). Preventing alcohol-related crime through community action: The Surfers Paradise Safety Action Project. In R. Homel (Ed.), *Policing for prevention: Reducing crime, public intoxication, and injury* (Crime Prevention Studies Vol. 7) (pp. 35–90). Monsey, NY: Criminal Justice Press.

International Center for Alcohol Policies (ICAP). (2002). *Violence and licensed premises.* ICAP Reports 12. Washington, DC: Author.

International Center for Alcohol Policies (ICAP). (2005). *Blue Book: Practical guides for alcohol policy and targeted interventions.* Washington, DC: Author.

Johnsson, K. O., & Berglund, M. (2003). Education of key personnel in student pubs leads to a decrease in alcohol consumption among the patrons: A randomized controlled trial. *Addiction, 98,* 627–633.

Leonard, K. E., Quigley, B. M., & Collins, R. L. (2002). Physical aggression in the lives of young adults: Prevalence, location, and severity among college and community samples. *Journal of Interpersonal Violence, 17,* 533–550.

MacAndrew, C., & Edgerton, R. (1969). *Drunken comportment: A social explanation.* Chicago: Aldine.

McKnight, A. J., & Streff, F. M. (1994). The effect of enforcement upon service of alcohol to intoxicated patrons of bars and restaurants. *Accident Analysis and Prevention, 26,* 79–88.

Moore, D. (1990). Drinking, the construction of ethnic identity and social process in Western Australian youth subculture. *British Journal of Addiction, 85,* 1265–1278.

Operation Red Nose. (n.d.). *Opération Nez Rouge/Operation Red Nose.* Retrieved July 17, 2006, from http://www.operationnezrouge.com.

Parks, K. A., & Miller, B. A. (1997). Bar victimization of women. *Psychology of Women Quarterly, 21,* 509–525.

Parks, K. A., & Quigley, B. M. (2001). Riskier lifestyle, aggression, and public drinking: Findings from a general population of adults in the United States. In M. Martinez (Ed.), *Prevention and control of aggression and the impact on its victims* (pp. 267–274). New York: Kluwer Academic/Plenum.

Pernanen, K. (1991). *Alcohol in human violence.* New York: Guilford.

Plant, M. A., Single, E., & Stockwell, T. (Eds.). (1997). *Alcohol: Minimizing the harm. What works?* London: Free Association Books.

Portman Group. (2000, April). *Keeping the peace: A guide to the prevention of alcohol-related disorder.* Retrieved April 5, 2005, from http://www.portman-group.org.uk/uploaded_files/documents/35_49_KeepingthePeace.pdf.

Quigley, B. M., & Collins, R. L. (1999). Modeling of alcohol consumption: A meta-analytic review. *Journal of Studies on Alcohol, 60,* 90–98.

Quigley, B. M., Leonard, K. E., & Collins, R. L. (2003). Characteristics of violent bars and the patrons who frequent them. *Journal of Studies on Alcohol, 64,* 765–772.

Roehrich, L., & Goldman, M. S. (1995). Implicit priming of alcohol expectancy memory processes and subsequent drinking behavior. *Experimental and Clinical Psychopharmacology, 3,* 402–410.

Saltz, R. F. (1987). The roles of bars and restaurants in preventing alcohol-impaired driving: An evaluation of server intervention. *Evaluation and the Health Professions, 10,* 5–27.

Single, E., Beaubrun, M., Mauffret, M., Minoletti, A., Moskalewicz, J., Moukolo, A., et al. (1997). Public drinking, problems, and prevention measures in twelve countries: Results of the WHO project on public drinking. *Contemporary Drug Problems, 24,* 425–448.

Sloan, F. A., Stout, E. M., Whetten-Goldstein, K., & Liand, L. (2000). *Drinkers, drivers, and bartenders: Balancing private choices and public accountability.* Chicago: University of Chicago Press.

Steele, C. M., & Josephs, R. A. (1990). Alcohol myopia: Its prized and dangerous effects. *American Psychologist, 45,* 921–933.

Stevenson, R. J., Lind, B., & Weatherburn, D. (1999). Property damage and public disorder: Their relationship with sales of alcohol in New South Wales, Australia. *Drug and Alcohol Dependence, 54,* 163–170.

Stockwell, T. (2001). Responsible alcohol service: Lessons from evaluations of server training and policing initiatives. *Drug and Alcohol Review, 20,* 257–265.

Taylor, S. P., & Leonard, K. E. (1983). Alcohol and human physical aggression. In R. G. Geen & E. I. Donnerstein (Eds.), *Aggression: Theoretical and empirical reviews* (pp. 77–101). New York: Academic Press.

Tomsen, S. (1997). A top night: Social protest, masculinity and the culture of drinking violence. *British Journal of Criminology, 37,* 90–102.

Wall, A., McKee, S. A., & Hinson, R. E. (2000). Assessing variation in alcohol outcome expectancies across environmental context: An examination of the situational-specificity hypothesis. *Psychology of Addictive Behaviors, 14,* 367–375.

Wallin, E., Norström, T., & Andreasson, S. (2003). Alcohol prevention targeting licensed premises: A study of effects on violence. *Journal of Studies on Alcohol, 64,* 270–277.

Wellington City Council. (2005). *Host responsibility: Programme requirements.* Retrieved November 15, 2005, from http://www.wellington.govt.nz/services/liquor/host/host.html.

7

Targeting Groups:
Young People

Interventions aimed at reducing the possible harm related to drinking may be targeted and tailored to particular behaviors, drinking contexts, or groups sharing common traits or drinking practices. Whereas the application of targeted interventions to specific behaviors and contexts has been discussed in Chapters 5 and 6, respectively, the focus of this chapter is on the third of these elements: individuals and groups at particular risk for harm, more specifically young people.

DRINKING AND YOUNG PEOPLE

There is no consensus regarding the age threshold at which a "young person" becomes an adult. According to the World Health Organization (WHO), a young person is someone between the ages of 10 and 24 years (World Health Organization [WHO], 1986, pp. 11–12). Most countries set a minimum age limit at which drinking and/or the purchase of alcohol becomes legally permitted (see Table 7.1). This may or may not coincide with the age of majority for other activities, such as voting, entering the military, driving, or getting married. Where such limits are set, they range from the ages of 16 to 25 years, although many countries have no such legislation in place (International Center for Alcohol Policies [ICAP], 2005; WHO, 2004; see also ICAP, 2002). These legal differences reflect cultural views on when young people reach adulthood and, in turn, have an impact on their drinking.

Whatever legal age is set as the threshold for drinking, young people are "at risk" for a variety of reasons. Changes in physiological development occurring in adolescence, particularly neurological changes, are likely to increase sensitivity to the effects of alcohol (for example, Brown & Tapert, 2004; Brown, Tapert, Granholm, & Delis, 2000; Monti et al., 2005; Spear, 2004). Young people's inexperience with alcohol and inability to gauge and stick to their own limits increase the potential risk for harm, especially where drinking is paired with other activities, such as driving. Finally, much has been written about adolescence

Table 7.1 International Levels, in Years, for Minimum Legal Drinking Age (MDA) and Minimum Legal Purchase Age (MPA)

Country	Minimum Drinking Age (MDA)	Minimum Purchasing Age (MPA)	Notes
Argentina	18	—	
Armenia	No MDA	No MPA	
Australia	18	18	State and territory laws prohibit sale or serving of alcohol to individuals under 18 years of age.
Austria	16, 18 *	16, 18	On-premise consumption of alcohol is subject to provincial regulation. In general, the MDA is 16. Some provinces prohibit consumption of spirits by individuals under 18 years. * In one Bundesland, MDA is 16 for spirits and 15 for wine and beer.
Azerbaijan	—	18	
Belarus	—	18	
Belgium	16	16, 18	The MPA in bars is 18 for spirits and 16 for beer and wine. No specific restrictions apply to purchase of beer and wine in shops. The law prohibits anyone under the age of 16 (unless married or accompanied by parent or guardian) from entering a "dance hall" where fermented beverages are sold.
Bolivia	—	18	
Bosnia and Herzegovina	—	16	The MPA of 16 applies to buying alcohol for on-premise consumption (e.g., in bars). No age limit is set for buying alcohol in shops.
Brazil	18	—	
Bulgaria	18	18	
Cambodia	—	No MPA	
Cameroon	18	—	
Canada	18, 19	18, 19	The MDA and MPA are 18 in Alberta, Manitoba, and Quebec; in all other provinces, the MDA and MPA are set at 19. Drinking by minors under adult supervision is permitted in licensed premises in the provinces of Manitoba and New Brunswick and at home in Prince Edward Island, Alberta, British Columbia, Ontario, and Saskatchewan.
Chile	18	18	

Table 7.1 (continued) International Levels, in Years, for Minimum Legal Drinking Age (MDA) and Minimum Legal Purchase Age (MPA)

Country	Minimum Drinking Age (MDA)	Minimum Purchasing Age (MPA)	Notes
China	No MDA	18	
Colombia	18	18	
Costa Rica	—	18	
Croatia	—	18	
Czech Republic	18	18	
Denmark	16	16	Beverages with an alcohol content of 1.2% or more by volume must not be sold to persons under 16 years of age at shops where retail sale takes place. Such beverages (1.2% ABV or more) cannot be brought into Denmark from other EU countries by persons under 16 years of age. This regulation does not apply to beer.
Ecuador	—	18	
Eritrea	—	18	
Estonia	18	18	
Ethiopia	—	18	
Finland	18	18, 20	The MPA is 20 for purchasing spirits in shops and 18 for all other alcohol purchases.
France	16	16	Individuals under 16 years of age cannot enter bars unless accompanied by parent or guardian.
Georgia	No MDA	16	
Germany	16, 18	16, 18	The MDA and MPA are 16 for beer and wine, and 18 for spirits. Beer and wine may be served to individuals under 16 only if accompanied by parent or guardian.
Greece	18	17	The MDA and MPA apply to drinking in bars. No age limit is set for buying alcohol in shops or for off-premise consumption.
Guatemala	—	18	
Guyana	—	18	
Honduras	21	18	
Hungary	—	18	
Iceland	20	20	
India	18–25	18–25	Drinking ages are legislated by individual states.

continued

Table 7.1 (continued) International Levels, in Years, for Minimum Legal Drinking Age (MDA) and Minimum Legal Purchase Age (MPA)

Country	Minimum Drinking Age (MDA)	Minimum Purchasing Age (MPA)	Notes
Indonesia	—	21	
Ireland	18	18	Individuals under 18 are allowed in bars, but those under 15 must be accompanied by parent or guardian.
Israel	—	18	According to the 2004 regulations, the MPA applies to purchases from kiosks and convenience stores (previously, only applied to on-premise purchase).
Italy	16	16	
Japan	20	20	
Kazakhstan	—	18	
Kenya	18	18	
Korea (South)	19	19	
Kyrgyzstan	No MDA	No MPA	
Latvia	—	18	
Liechtenstein	17	—	
Lithuania	No MDA	18	
Macedonia	—	18	
Malaysia	No MDA	18	
Malta	No MDA	16	
Mexico	18	18	
Moldova	18	18	MDA and MPA of 18 apply to wine and spirits. No age specifications are made for buying or consuming beer.
Mongolia	—	18	
Namibia	—	18	
Netherlands	—	16, 18	The MPA is 18 for spirits. The MPA is 16 for beer, wine, and distilled beverages with an alcohol percentage under 15%.
New Zealand	18	18	
Nicaragua	—	19	
Niger	—	18	
Nigeria	—	18	
Norway	18, 20	18, 20	The MDA and MPA for spirits are 20. For beer and wine, the MDA and MPA are 18.
Palau	18	21	

Table 7.1 (continued) International Levels, in Years, for Minimum Legal Drinking Age (MDA) and Minimum Legal Purchase Age (MPA)

Country	Minimum Drinking Age (MDA)	Minimum Purchasing Age (MPA)	Notes
Panama	18	18	
Papua New Guinea	18	18	MDA for consumption in private or with meals on licensed premises is not specified. MPA for on-licensed premises is 18; MPA is not specified for off-licensed premises and supermarkets.
Paraguay	—	18	
Peru	18	18	
Philippines	18	18	
Poland	—	18	
Portugal	16	16	
Romania	18	18	
Russia	18	18	
Samoa	21	—	
Seychelles	—	18	
Singapore	18	18	
Slovakia	18	18	
Slovenia	18	18	
Solomon Islands	21	—	
South Africa	18	18	
South Korea	19	19	Consumption in private is at the discretion of parents or accompanying adults.
Spain	16, 18	16, 18	The MDA and MPA vary by region: Some autonomous communities set the MDA and MPA at 18, and others at 16. The Spanish government is currently considering a proposal to set the national MDA and MPA at 18.
Sri Lanka	18	18	
Suriname	—	16	
Sweden	18	18, 20	Purchase for off-premise consumption: the MPA varies. Generally, for beer and cider with an alcohol content of 3.5% or less, the MPA is 18, and it is 20 for all beverage alcohol with alcohol content over 3.5%. The MPA for buying any alcohol beverage in the Swedish monopoly stores is 20 years of age. For on-premise purchases, the MPA is 18.

continued

Table 7.1 (continued) International Levels, in Years, for Minimum Legal Drinking Age (MDA) and Minimum Legal Purchase Age (MPA)

Country	Minimum Drinking Age (MDA)	Minimum Purchasing Age (MPA)	Notes
Switzerland	18*	18*	*Federal law prohibits supplying spirits to individuals under 18. The MDA and MPA for beer and wine are controlled by the cantons and vary between 14 and 16.
Thailand	No MDA	18	
Turkey	—	18	
Turkmenistan	—	18	
Uganda	18	18	
Ukraine	No MDA	18	
United Kingdom	18	18, 16	In bars and off-licensed premises, the MDA and MPA are 18. The MPA for certain drinks, however, is 16 when purchased for consumption with meals in restaurants or pubs with separate eating areas. These drinks are beer, perry, cider, and, in Scotland, wine. MDA at home is 5, given parental consent.
United States	21*	21**	* In 19 states, alcohol consumption by youths under 21 is not specifically illegal. ** Exceptions to the 21 law in some states include possession for religious purposes when accompanied by a parent, spouse, or legal guardian; in private clubs or establishments; or in the course of lawful employment by a duly licensed manufacturer.
Uruguay	—	18	
Uzbekistan	—	18	
Vanuatu	18	18	The MDA of 18 applies not only to consumption in public but also to drinking in private and with meals.
Venezuela	—	18	
Zambia	—	18	
Zimbabwe	18	—	

Source: ICAP (2005).

as a period for experimentation, when young people take risks, test their own limits, and respond to the pressures around them (see, for example, Plant & Plant, 1992). A combination of these factors contributes to the outcomes young people are likely to experience from alcohol consumption.

Patterns and Trends

Considerable research has been conducted on young people's drinking in various parts of the world. The body of evidence from developed countries—notably, North America and Western Europe, as well as Australia and New Zealand—is more extensive than that from other regions, particularly developing countries, where information may be difficult to gather, resources are scarce, but patterns of drinking may be changing at a rapid pace in step with social and economic transformations.

Available research points to several trends in young people's drinking that hold true across countries. Almost universally, there is concern that the age at which young people begin to drink is becoming lower. In particular, attention has been focused on instances where such drinking is regular or heavy and linked with adverse outcomes. Related to this is the issue of *binge drinking*, the rapid intake of alcohol to intoxication, more accurately termed *heavy episodic drinking* or *extreme drinking*. Such consumption is linked to other social issues that affect communities and societies, primarily public nuisance and safety (addressed in Chapter 6). Finally, the social cost of alcohol misuse by young people in the form of injuries and other outcomes is a major public health concern.

Young people's drinking patterns are changing around the world. These changes are a reflection of moves away from traditional drinking patterns and, more broadly, traditional lifestyles. They are a reflection of social transformations, increased purchasing power, the changing role of young people, and, in some instances, their growing social disenfranchisement. The sections that follow provide a broad overview of drinking among young people in several regions for which data are available. More research is needed to link the ongoing changes in drinking to broader social and cultural phenomena.

Australia and New Zealand. In Australia, the consumption of alcohol before the legal age of 18 years is the norm rather than the exception. The 2001 National Drug Strategy Household Survey (NDSHS) indicated that, among young people aged 14 to 17, 44% of boys and 52% of girls drink occasionally, whereas 20% and 17%, respectively, drink weekly (Hayes, Smart, Toumbourou, & Sanson, 2004). In addition, when they do drink, young people drink more per occasion than the general population (Chikritzhs et al., 2003). Young adults in their 20s drink more heavily than any other age group, and those aged from 18 to 25 years are at the highest risk of drink-related injury and harm (Lindsay, 2005; National Health and Medical Research Council, 2001).

Research from New Zealand suggests similar drinking patterns. Among 14- to 17-year-olds, 66% currently drink (Kalafatelis, McMillen, & Palmer, 2003), and 20% do so at least once a week. Moreover, 20% indicated at least one risky drinking occasion in the last 2 weeks, and 59% claimed to have really started drinking before the age of 15. There is a variation in drinking patterns among New Zealand's ethnic groups. Thus, although Maoris are less likely to be regular drinkers, their alcohol consumption, when it does occur, tends to be heavy among both adults and young people. Among youth, 48% of Maori and 45% of Pacific Islanders reported binge drinking, compared with 30% for other ethnic groups (Kalafatelis et al., 2003).

However, data also show that both heavier and lighter drinking have decreased among New Zealand youth since 2001, and that the proportion of nondrinkers has grown from 16% in 2000 to 34% in 2003. Despite this trend, risky drinking remains prevalent, reported by 23% of all 14- to 17-year-olds (Kalafatelis et al., 2003).

Europe. Within the European region, two large-scale international youth surveys relating to alcohol consumption dominate the field. These are the European School Survey Project on Alcohol and Other Drugs (ESPAD) and the Health Behaviour in School-aged Children study (HBSC). The two studies cover somewhat different age groups: ESPAD surveys 15- to 16-year-olds in 35 European countries (Hibell et al., 2004), whereas HBSC focuses on ages 11, 13, and 15 in 30 European countries, Canada, Israel, and the United States (Currie et al., 2004). Despite these differences, commonalities in the methodologies used in the surveys allow interesting comparisons to be made across countries regarding drinking patterns.

According to ESPAD data, 90% or more of 15- to 16-year-olds have consumed alcohol at least once in their lifetime in two thirds of the surveyed countries (Hibell et al., 2004). Heavy drinking patterns (including heavy episodic drinking) vary significantly across Europe. According to the ESPAD study, the lowest percentages of binge drinkers—from 5 to 13%—were found in southern European countries (for example, Cyprus, France, Greece, and Italy), some eastern European countries (Hungary and Romania), and Turkey. The percentages were generally higher in northern Europe (for example, Ireland, the Netherlands, and the United Kingdom). Drunkenness was more prevalent in countries from northern and eastern Europe than in southern European countries (Currie et al., 2004; Hibell et al., 2004).

Data from both ESPAD and HBSC reveal that the rate of heavy episodic drinking among young people is not necessarily related to population-level measures of alcohol consumption. So, for instance, in France and Italy, where per capita consumption levels are generally high, patterns of excessive drinking were relatively infrequent. There also appears to be little correlation between how often young people drink and whether they become intoxicated. For example, HBSC found relatively high rates of drunkenness and low rates of weekly drinking among Finnish teenagers. Meanwhile, Italian respondents—although more regular drinkers—reported lower rates of intoxication (Currie et al., 2004).

Shifts in alcohol consumption by young people have been reported across Europe. For example, although levels of drunkenness in Spain are low and similar to those in the other southern European countries, there seems to be a growing trend toward patterns of binge drinking, which was previously rare (Gamela, 1995). Youthful drinking in Spain appears to have moved out of the traditional context of meals with the family to other social contexts, particularly public venues, such as the street and parks; and the phenomenon of the *botellón*, discussed later in this chapter, is common. In some countries (for example, Denmark, Ireland, Norway, Poland, Slovenia, and the United Kingdom), earlier increases in the frequency of binge drinking among young people seem to have largely stabilized. In others, however, binge drinking appears to be on the rise. These include, for example, the Baltic States (Estonia, Latvia, and Lithuania), as well as Portugal, Slovakia, Sweden, and Ukraine (Hibell et al., 2004).

The sociopolitical and economic transformations in Eastern Europe may have influenced the observed increases in alcohol consumption among young people (Hibell et al., 2004). Here, the trends seen in earlier years in Western Europe are now being reproduced. Changes in Portugal, however, may reflect social changes of a different nature, because an increase in extreme drinking behavior has been accompanied by a rise in school dropout rates among Portugal's young people, as well as a rise in unemployment (Organization for Economic Co-operation and Development, 2006).

United States. What sets the United States apart from most other developed countries is its minimum legal alcohol purchase age of 21. As a result, issues related to young people's drinking are somewhat different from those in other countries. There is concern not only about various drinking patterns and related risk for harm, but also about underage drinking as an illegal behavior and the need to prevent it and effectively enforce relevant laws.

Despite the high minimum age limit, most young people in the United States have tried alcohol well before reaching the age of 21. However, according to the University of Michigan's Monitoring the Future (MTF) study, trends over the past three decades show declines in underage drinking (Johnston, O'Malley, Bachman, & Schulenberg, 2005). A majority of young people surveyed indicated that they were not regular drinkers. Similarly, according to the 2004 National Survey on Drug Abuse and Health, 82% of U.S. adolescents (aged between 12 and 17 years) and 71% of minors (aged between 12 and 20 years) do not drink. In addition, 94% of minors indicated that they were not heavy drinkers (U.S. Substance Abuse and Mental Health Services Administration [SAMHSA], 2004).

MTF data show that heavy episodic drinking or binge drinking is in decline. There is an increasing disapproval of such consumption patterns by young people. However, binge drinking remains a high-profile issue in the United States, particularly on college and university campuses. Among young people under the age of 21 but old enough to attend tertiary educational institutions, a high percentage is enrolled in colleges and universities, and many live away from home. Close to 7 million Americans between the ages of 14 and 21 years are enrolled at a college full-time (U.S. Bureau of Census, 2004). According to some estimates, 44% of all college students (regardless of age) are binge drinkers (Wechsler et al., 2002).

As in other multicultural societies, ethnic and cultural differences can be seen in drinking patterns and in a range of other behaviors in the United States. Analysis of young people's drinking by race and ethnicity in the 2004 National Survey on Drug Use and Health shows that among respondents aged 12 years and older, Whites were most likely to report drinking: 55.2%, compared with 40.2% of Hispanics, 37.4% of Asians, 37.1% of Blacks, and 36.2% of American Indian or Alaskan Native youths (SAMHSA, 2004). Asians reported the lowest levels of binge drinking (12.4%), with 18.3% for Blacks, 23.8% for Whites, 24.0% for Hispanics, and the highest prevalence of 25.8% for American Indians or Alaska Natives (SAMHSA).

Drinking Venues

Drinking within the home has long been viewed as part of a healthy and integrated approach to alcohol consumption and to learning about responsible drinking. Young people's exposure to moderate drinking within the home and in the context of the family is viewed as a positive influence later in life.

Over recent years, however, youth drinking has increasingly moved into public spaces, raising concerns among communities and policy-makers regarding social and health issues, including public nuisance, noise, safety, road traffic crashes, and injuries for young people. In Australia, drinking in public places and cars is on the rise (Australian Institute of Health and Welfare, 2002). European data also indicate that drinking among young people is shifting into public spaces, and that binge drinking in particular may be increasing in these venues (Currie et al., 2004).

Research into the relationships between alcohol consumption in public venues and adverse outcomes suggests an increased likelihood of violent incidents among both young men and women (Wells, Graham, Speechley, & Koval, 2005). However, there is also evidence that violence may be more related to the venue than to drinking itself. Research from Norway found that it is the public drinking venue and not intoxication, for example, that was strongly correlated with the likelihood of violence (Rossow, 1996). People in a gathering are more likely to fight, and some venues are more risky than others.

Public drinking venues can have a positive function. Research in the Netherlands examined young people's drinking contexts from a developmental perspective, focusing on public drinking places such as pubs (Engels, Knibbe, & Drop, 1999). Seventeen- and 18-year-olds who frequented pubs and discos had more friends and more positive social and personal interactions, including romantic relationships.

El Botellón

The *botellón* is a phenomenon of Spanish nightlife that has increasingly received both national and international attention (for example, Calafat et al., 2005). Large groups of young people (sometimes in the thousands) gather in city squares and plazas, parks, and other public places to socialize, talk, and drink. It is often a "pre-party," followed by socializing at nightclubs, bars, or discos. The *botellón*, literally meaning "big bottle," attracts both those who are there to drink and those who are not.

Although the origin of the *botellón* is unclear, public drinking has always been permitted in Spain. As a youth event, the *botellón* began gaining momentum in the 1990s and now seems to be a common and regular occurrence in many Spanish cities—schedules are even listed on travel guides for those wishing to visit and participate. Some *botellones* mark special events, such as the beginning of spring or the traditional Spanish fiestas. In 2004, a *botellón* held in Seville attracted some 70,000 participants ("Unos 70.000 jóvenes sevillanos," 2004).

The phenomenon of the *botellón* is viewed by many as a problem, and efforts are under way to address it, including by limiting drinking in public spaces (see, for example, Nahoum-Grappe, 2002). Health risks and the involvement of young people are among the main reasons for concern, but most attention appears to be directed at public order issues, including noise, public disturbance, and public safety.

It has been suggested that events such as the *botellón* are linked to the high cost of alcohol in serving establishments. Purchasing alcohol in supermarkets and other retail outlets is significantly cheaper, particularly given the generally restricted budgets of young people.

WHY DO YOUNG PEOPLE DRINK?

Young people drink for a wide variety of reasons. There is evidence that the heavier the drinking, the more reasons are cited for it (for example, Choquet, 2004; Kuntsche, Rehm, & Gmel, 2004; Plant, Bagnall, & Foster, 1990). However, most young people drink for social reasons, and because they enjoy it. They drink to have fun, to facilitate social interaction, to build confidence, or to build and maintain friendships. Similar results have been obtained from research in various countries across Europe, North and South America, Asia, and Africa (for example, Currie et al., 2004; Feldman, Harvey, Holowaty, & Shortt, 1999; Jerez & Coviello, 1998; Kairouz, Gliksman, Demers, & Adlaf, 2002; Lo & Globetti, 2000; Plant et al., 1990; Richardson & Budd, 2003; Rocha-Silva, 1998; Stewart & Power, 2002).

Youth is a period of experimentation with a range of behaviors that are considered the domain of adults. Drinking is no exception. Experimentation with alcohol is common in early adolescence, but only a minority of young people drinks regularly. Among younger groups, curiosity, a desire to experience the adult world, and limit testing are important reasons for drinking. Older groups are more likely to drink as a means of exploring increased freedoms and independence. In addition, drinking may be seen as a way to establish and maintain social cohesion and the sense of belonging to a particular group, with accompanying social support (see, for example, Coleman & Cater, 2005).

For most young people, experimentation with alcohol is part of normal psychosocial development and exploration of behaviors that are permissible for adults but not for them (Shedler & Block, 1990). Testing limits is part of the process of maturation into adulthood. However, there are risk factors in a young person's life that may propel experimentation into the development of serious problems. These risk factors include depression, low self-esteem, lack of connectedness, and a family history of alcohol or substance abuse.

Alcohol is well-known for its properties as a social lubricant and is used as such by young people as much as by adults. Drinking may facilitate social interactions and build the confidence to pursue them (Abrahamson, 2004). For some young people, as for adults, drinking is a way to deal with problems, depression, stress, and various other states (see, for example, Cooper, Frone, Russell, & Mudar, 1995). It is interesting to note that, although drinking in order to cope has been conceptualized as the opposite of social drinking, it may often involve social interactions and group support among young adults (Coleman & Cater, 2005).

Experimental Drinking Among Young People: European Survey Data

- In the European countries included in the ESPAD survey, 45 to 98% of 15- to 16-year-olds had consumed alcohol at least once in their lifetime (Hibell et al., 2004).
- The HBSC study found that first experimentation with alcohol occurs on average around the age of 12.3 years for boys and 12.9 years for girls. Young people were found to start drinking the earliest in Austria, the Czech Republic, and Lithuania, and the latest in Finland, Greenland, Israel, Italy, and Russia (Currie et al., 2004).
- By the age of 13 years, at least half of all young people surveyed had consumed a glass of wine or beer at least once in the majority of ESPAD countries. It was less likely for them to have tasted spirits at this age (Hibell et al., 2004).
- Generally, the adoption of regular drinking patterns lags behind the age of first drink. Indeed, weekly alcohol consumption (drinking at least once a week) is rare among most 11-year-olds (5%) and 13-year-olds (12%) across the HBSC countries. At the age of 15, however, the behavior becomes more prevalent (29%) (Currie et al., 2004).

Calculated Hedonism

Part of the experimentation with alcohol includes goal-directed behavior that involves determined drunkenness. For many young people, alcohol consumption is largely a planned activity (Brain, 2000; Brain, Parker, & Carnwath, 2000; Coleman & Cater, 2005; Engineer, Phillips, Thompson, & Nicholls, 2003; MacAskill, Cooke, Eadie, & Hastings, 2001; Sheehan & Ridge, 2001). Their goal is to get drunk, and consumption is tailored to meet this goal (Richardson & Budd, 2003).

Interviews with young binge drinkers in the United Kingdom revealed that they perceived their drinking as an "enjoyable" and "socially acceptable" experience (Coleman & Cater, 2005; Engineer et al., 2003). Occasions of heavy drinking were largely planned in advance, and not accidental or unintended (Coleman & Cater; Engineer et al.). To reach their goal of getting drunk on a "big night out," respondents used a number of strategies: mixing drinks to accelerate or intensify intoxication, having a "pre-party" with drinking before going out, or choosing stronger drinks (Engineer et al.).

Extreme Drinking across Cultures

Extreme drinking is often regarded as a rite of passage by those who engage in it and is a cause for concern within the context of public health and public order.[1] Among young people, extreme drinking is strongly correlated with other risk taking, may influence the development of antisocial or violent behaviors, and is driven largely by thrill seeking and the process of getting drunk.

The results of a recent international comparison of focus groups on extreme drinking suggest that, regardless of culture, alcohol consumption (whether moderate or excessive) appears to be uniformly regarded by young respondents as a social activity, particularly associated with celebrations, holidays, and parties. Although occasions of extreme drinking are viewed as part of the drinking experience, excess does not seem to be a necessary component, and moderate drinking equally can be part of normative behavior.

Although extreme drinking is recognized as part of the overall drinking experience, the degree to which it is considered "typical" varies across cultures. In the United Kingdom, for example, excessive alcohol consumption is part of the typical drinking situation, whereas in Italy it is rare and not thought of as normative behavior. An important influence identified across the cultures studied is *alcohol maturity*, the process of getting to know one's limits and developing the ability to control one's drinking and its outcomes. Age and experience determine alcohol maturity, as well as the definition of what constitutes excess and an extreme drinking occasion.

Extreme drinking has been described as goal-directed behavior, with the specific intention of getting drunk and losing control. At the same time, many respondents reported that extreme drinking is often an unintended turn of events, encouraged by the environment and the moment. Goal-directed drunkenness seems least likely to occur where drunkenness is socially stigmatized and generally considered an undesirable outcome (for example, in Italy).

In other countries, regular extreme drinking on weekends is typical. Among young people surveyed in the United Kingdom, especially among males, competitive drinking among peers is common, usually continuing until the money runs out to pay for another round. Having no money left makes a drinking occasion "a success."

Despite the differences that exist in drinking patterns and the acceptance of extreme drinking across societies, these results show that extreme drinking among young people is marked by a considerable number of similarities. It is a social behavior, closely linked to interaction with peers and friends. Extreme drinking is a rite of passage for many on the road to alcohol maturity. Although its saliency is largely influenced by culture and views on alcohol and drinking in general, extreme drinking appears to be both motivated and constrained by factors that transcend cultural boundaries. It seems likely, therefore, that extreme drinking is closely related to being young, to the absence of responsibilities, and to testing the world and one's own limits within it.

Source: Martinic & Measham (in print).

Parents, Family, and Peers

Young people's attitudes toward drinking, their drinking patterns, and the likely outcomes are most influenced by parents, family, and peers. Parents have been identified as the leading factor in decisions young people make about alcohol (Bjarnason et al., 2003; Kuntsche & Kuendig, 2006), and parental drinking habits provide the model and help shape behavior in youths. Parents' acceptance of drinking and whether they consider it a normative behavior also play a role (Donovan et al., 2004; Hellandsjø Bu, Watten, Foxcroft, Ingebrigtsen, & Relling, 2002; Milgram, 2001; Wood, Read, Mitchell, & Brand, 2004). Moreover, they are effective at modifying other influences on their children's drinking (Nash, McQueen, & Bray, 2005).

Family structure and functioning are important factors in the development of a range of social behaviors among young people, including alcohol consumption. Young people who have a close relationship with their parents and are surrounded by strong family support are less likely to experience problems than those whose families are not intact or who lack adult support and supervision (Bjarnason et al., 2003; Hellandsjø Bu et al., 2002; Milgram, 2001; Sanchez-Sosa & Poldrugo, 2001; Turrisi, Wiersma, & Hughes, 2000; Vakalahi, 2001; Wood et al., 2004).

There is no doubt that peers and friends also play an important role (Borsari & Carey, 2001; Geckova & Van Dijk, 2001; Milgram, 2001; Miller & Plant, 2003; Wood et al., 2004). Peer approval has a significant part in shaping youth drinking habits, particularly in the adolescent years (Milgram, 2001; Wood et al.), and peer influence emerges as the most consistent predictor of adolescent drinking (Gaughan, 2006).

Alcohol Expectancies

People learn how to react to alcohol from their social environments, forming so-called alcohol expectancies. These are generally positive and may be defined as the culturally determined anticipation of the likely, desirable, or undesirable outcomes of drinking and learned associations with alcohol. Thus, there are alcohol expectancies about social interaction, relaxation, enjoyment, and sexual enhancement. People who expect drinking to result in violence may be more likely to become aggressive when they drink; those who view it as relaxing—or inhibiting—are likely to act accordingly.

Beliefs about alcohol consumption develop before drinking begins. Children have well-formed beliefs and stereotypes about alcohol and drinking from an early age (reviewed in Leigh, 1999). These are largely negative and shift to more positive ones as experimentation with alcohol begins (Aitken, 1978; Johnson & Johnson, 1995). It has been suggested that this shift accompanies the change from acceptance of parental guidance to rebellion against them (Lang & Michalec, 1990).

Expectancies are especially relevant for young people's initiation into drinking and whether or not they continue to drink. Generally, it is the immediacy of the positive effects ("feeling good") and the anticipation of them that drive drinking behaviors. Even where negative outcomes are known—from personal experience as well as from observation—they will generally be overshadowed by positive expectancies. The expectation of positive social consequences and social enhancement seems to play a stronger role for young people than their actual experience with alcohol (see, for example, Aas, Leigh, Anderssen, & Jakobsen, 1998).

DRINKING OUTCOMES

Chronic Outcomes

Young people are affected by drinking in many of the same ways as adults. However, there is evidence that heavy and abusive drinking patterns may take a particularly high toll on young people (see, for example, Brown & Tapert, 2004; Jennison, 2004). This risk is largely due to a heightened sensitivity to alcohol as a result of developmental changes that occur during childhood and adolescence, potentially resulting in greater risk of physiological damage (Spear, 2004). The developing brain is particularly sensitive to disruption by heavy drinking (Brown & Tapert, 2004; Spear), which affects various regions of the brain, including those involved in learning and memory (Brown et al., 2000; DeBellis et al., 2000; Tapert et al., 2001). Animal and human studies suggest that early heavy alcohol use may have a number of deleterious effects on bone (Klein, 1997; Sampson, Gallager, Lange, Chondra, & Hogan, 1999), as well as growth and endocrine development (Dees, Dissen, Hiney, Lara, & Ojeda, 2000; Dees, Srivastava, & Hiney, 2001; Frias, Rodriguez, Torres, Ruiz, & Ortega, 2000).

There has been considerable concern regarding drinking by young people and potential to develop later alcohol dependence and related problems. Early drinking may be a risk factor for alcohol-related problems in adulthood, and drinking prior to age 14 is associated with a significantly increased risk of developing alcohol dependence later in life (Grant & Dawson, 1997; Hawkins et al., 1997). Other studies have supported the notion that beginning to drink at a young age is likely to progress to regular drinking in adolescence (Fergusson, Lynskey, & Horwood, 1996) and represents a risk factor in later abusive and risky drinking patterns (Toumbourou et al., 2004), as well as alcohol dependence (Bonomo et al., 2001), particularly if early drinking was related to stress and tension (Poikolainen, Yuulio-Henriksson, Aalto Setala, Marttunen, & Lonnqvist, 2001). Once the stressors are removed, however, early drinking is no longer predictive of harmful patterns later in life.

Whether early initiation of alcohol consumption is a causal factor leading to later problems remains controversial, and other research has found the association to be weak (Kuntsche et al., 2004). A number of studies have found that early age of drinking and later problems were both predicted by certain personality characteristics (for example, strong tendencies to act impulsively and to seek out new experiences and sensations) and genetic factors. Early drinking appears to serve as an indicator of an existing vulnerability to behavioral problems, including substance use, psychiatric, and conduct disorders (Dawson, 2000; Donovan, Jessor, & Jessor, 1983; Kono et al., 1997; McGue, Iacono, Legrand, & Elkins, 2001; Prescott & Kendler, 1999; Rose, 1998; Virkkunen & Linnoila, 1997). In general, factors that predict regular drinking in adolescents are similar to those that predict other forms of adolescent problem behavior. These include high levels of stressors, the inability to cope, alcohol and illicit drug use among parents and peers, little parental support, a low level of academic competence, and poor behavioral control.

Acute Outcomes

Perhaps the greatest risk for harm for young people lies in the acute outcomes related to injuries. These may be the result of single, isolated episodes of heavy drinking or intoxication or of repeated harmful drinking patterns. Young people make up a significant proportion of those injured or killed in road traffic crashes, often involving alcohol (for example, Hingson, Heeren, Zakocs, Kopstein, & Wechsler, 2002; U.S. National Highway Traffic Safety Administration [NHTSA], 2005). This includes both drivers and passengers. In the United States, for example, 49% of drivers with high blood alcohol content (0.8 mg/ml or higher) killed in traffic crashes in 2004 were under the age of 24 (NHTSA, 2005).

Intoxication has also been linked with risky sexual behavior, unwanted pregnancy, sexually transmitted diseases, sexual assault, and date rape (see, for example, Grunbaum et al., 2002; Harrington & Leitenberg, 1994; Mohler-Kuo, Dowdall, Koss, & Wechsler, 2004; Traeen & Kvalem, 1996). Risk of violence is also increased, as discussed in Chapter 6, particularly where drinking—and especially heavy drinking—occurs in public venues. Moreover, data show that the immediate effects of heavy drinking episodes not only may affect those engaged in them, but also have indirect effects on others in the community (see, for example, Wechsler, Moeykens, Davenport, Castillo, & Hansen, 1995).

OPPORTUNITIES FOR INTERVENTION

Various measures have been implemented around the world to address harmful drinking among young people, and yet how best to reduce risks among this population remains at best uncertain. No single strategy has been shown to be successful in all settings, and combined initiatives targeting particular behaviors or aspects of drinking may be a more useful approach. The broad principles that underlie targeted interventions are discussed in Chapter 4. Here, we discuss those opportunities and approaches that may be best suited to dealing with drinking among young people.

The context within which young people drink can be divided into a number of components. Among them are the prevailing norms and regulations related to drinking in a given society. They also include the physical venues in which young people drink, and those they frequent, whether for entertainment, education, or health care—all of these provide possible entry points for the purposes of prevention. Finally, the general culture around young people's drinking, that is, whether it is tolerated or sanctioned, also makes up part of the drinking context.

Drinking Age

Most countries have some regulation regarding the legal age at which drinking becomes allowed (see Table 7.1). However, there is no consistency regarding the level of this threshold among countries, nor is there consistency in whether or to what extent minimum age limits are enforced and upheld. Although alcohol consumption may be legally prohibited before a certain age, custom and practice may make drinking among the young a commonplace and accepted behavior, particularly within the context of the family.

It is also important to consider the feasibility of enforcing the legally mandated drinking and purchase age with regard to the procedural requirements and resources needed to uphold it: This includes police enforcement, community support, and the compliance of retailers, servers, and other adults who make alcohol available. According to data from the National Research Council and National Institute of Medicine in the United States (2004), depending on their location, between 30 and 70% of retail outlets are likely to sell to individuals below the 21-year minimum drinking age. The same study shows that adults—older siblings, friends, acquaintances, or others engaging in third-party transactions— are the primary sources for alcohol for young people under the legal drinking age (National Research Council & National Institute of Medicine, 2004).

"Cops in Shops"

A partnership between retailers and law enforcement in the United States aims to prevent the purchase of beverage alcohol by youths under the legal drinking age, as well as by adults making the purchase for young people. The Century Council (2006), a social aspects organization (SAO) operating in the United States, developed the "Cops in Shops" program, which involves plainclothes police officers posing as either employees or customers in retail outlets to apprehend underage buyers. Sellers caught breaking the law may lose their liquor sales licenses and be subject to fines and jail sentences.

Posters, billboards, and education campaigns aimed at young people and the community in general support the effort, together with training of police and retailers about the law and compliance with the law. The program is currently used by police in over 40 states, and has been implemented by police departments on college and university campuses.

"Cops in Shops" has been evaluated by the Governors Highway Safety Association in 15 states in the United States and found effective in increasing public awareness about underage purchases and drinking and the perception that those breaking the law will be identified and punished (Century Council, 2006; Governors Highway Safety Association, 2001).

Enforcement of compliance may be effective, especially if licensing is made contingent upon responsible sales and service. In some jurisdictions, proof-of-age cards or other identification is required to determine who may be permitted access to establishments or served beverage alcohol. Staff can be trained to request age identification and refuse service or access to individuals under the legal drinking age.

Drinking Venues

The importance of optimizing the drinking environment is described in Chapter 6. Young people's drinking, partly because of financial concerns and partly because of age constraints on obtaining alcohol and finding a place to drink it, has moved out of traditional contexts and into a more visible and public arena. Many of the prevention measures outlined in Chapter 6 that address crowd control, reduce noise level, and keep disturbance to a minimum will have an impact on young drinkers. The visibility of police and other authority figures in such venues can be particularly useful.

Other initiatives to reduce the potential for harm among young drinkers include the provision of additional transportation to venues and sites, especially around large-scale gatherings and raves. Not being able to park in the vicinity of the event is an effective deterrent to drinking and driving. In an effort to address potential problems related to the *botellón*, for example, some Spanish cities have moved these events to designated areas, such as unpopulated or industrial sites, which may be cordoned off and patrolled by police.

In some jurisdictions, young people below a certain age may not be permitted to drive during specified hours, thereby cutting down on the risk for drink-driving accidents (see Chapter 5). As discussed in Chapter 6, making alternative, nonalcoholic beverages and food available and linking events with entertainment are also measures likely to affect the volume and pattern of alcohol consumption. Dancing and music provide an alternative to drinking at an event, something that young people can focus on instead of drinking.

When carried out in conjunction with the enforcement of existing laws, these modifications of the drinking environment can reduce the potential risk for harm for young drinkers and those around them. Community involvement and willingness to show flexibility in the implementation of interventions are crucial. Many interventions that offer viable approaches are reasonably simple to implement, do not require structural changes or special procedural requirements, and do not hinge upon the availability of additional resources (see Table 8.2 in Chapter 8).

Alcohol Education

Alcohol education is heavily targeted at young people. It has been implemented in a variety of settings from schools and university campuses to less formal channels, and involves a range of key individuals and influences that shape young people's behavior.

An obvious point for the delivery of alcohol education to young people is in schools. Curricula and lesson plans may include information on alcohol and a range of related health and social issues. Most programs are intended to change young people's drinking beliefs, attitudes, and behaviors. Depending on the country, the approach used may be to recommend abstinence until the legal drinking age or may focus on attempts to minimize any potential harm by acknowledging that some drinking occurs despite existing laws.

Generally, school-based programs do not receive favorable reviews for their effectiveness, but there is also a lack of resources to carry out programs effectively, and program goals are sometimes unrealistic. The goal of abstinence, for example, is often criticized, because it does not reflect the actual behavior of young people. Despite these shortcomings, there is evidence that some school-based measures can be effective in raising awareness and even bringing about behavior change, at least in the short term (Caulkins, Pacula, Paddock, & Chiesa, 2004; Donohue, Allen, Maurer, Ozols, & DeStefano, 2004; McBride et al., 2000, 2004).

Other venues where young people gather also create opportunities for education about alcohol. These include religious and community centers, as well as clubs and discos. The home and family setting is important for conveying information about alcohol and drinking, as are physicians' practices and emergency rooms. Integrative education that includes the family and the community has been found to be particularly effective (Ashery, Robertson, & Kumpfer, 1998; Foxcroft, Ireland, Lister-Sharp, Lowe, & Breen, 2003; Holder et al., 2000; Kumpfer, Alvarado, & Whiteside, 2003; Spoth, Redmond, & Lepper, 1999; Wagenaar, Murray, & Toomey, 2000).

Among the promising approaches is *social norms marketing*, which tries to change young people's perceptions about how much their peers actually do (and do not) drink (Mattern & Neighbors, 2004; Perkins, 2003; Perkins & Craig, 2002). There is also evidence that life skills, when incorporated into a general approach to teaching about health and lifestyle issues, can be useful in changing behavior (Botvin, Baker, Dusenbury, Botvin, & Diaz, 1995; Botvin, Griffin, Paul, & Macaulay, 2003; ICAP, 2000, 2004).

Social Norms Marketing and Life Skills

Social Norms Marketing

Social norms are the perceived standards of acceptable attitudes and behavior that are prevalent within a community. The objective of social norms marketing is to influence these attitudes and behaviors in a positive way through the application of commercial marketing techniques to change awareness (Mattern & Neighbors, 2004; Perkins, 2003; Perkins & Craig, 2002).

Most social norms marketing has been targeted at young people, particularly on university and college campuses in the United States (Haines, Perkins, Rice, & Barker, 2004; Perkins, 2002; Perkins & Wechsler, 1996). The approach is based on the finding that most students on college campuses tend to overestimate their peers' drinking, in both quantity and frequency (Perkins, 1997; Perkins & Berkowitz, 1986; Perkins, Meilman, Leichliter, Cashin, & Presley, 1999). As a result, young people are likely to drink in a way that they wrongly believe emulates that of their peers, generally through increased consumption. Correcting these misperceptions can help reduce heavy drinking and harmful outcomes (see, for example, Fabiano, 2003; Haines, 1996; Haines & Barker, 2003; Haines et al., 2004; Jeffrey, Negro, Miller, & Frisone, 2003; Johanssen, Collins, Mills-Novoa, & Glider, 1999; Perkins & Craig, 2002).

Social norms marketing has also been adapted for use with students at the secondary school level, who have similar misperceptions about their peers' behavior (Beck & Treitman, 1996; Botvin, Griffin, Diaz, & Ifill-Williams, 2001; D'Amico et al., 2001; Perkins & Craig, 2003). Although it has shown positive results in a number of settings, the social norms marketing approach also has its shortcomings. It may have limited applicability where the primary message is abstinence. Where resources are scarce, it may also be expensive to implement in terms of program development, monitoring, and evaluation.

Life Skills

Life skills programs primarily target young people and are based on promoting healthy lifestyles through health education. Thanks to the involvement of WHO, life skills programs have come to play an important role in health, particularly mental health, in both developing and developed countries. With regard to alcohol, the life skills approach relies on encouraging responsible consumption and preventing misuse. However, opinions are divided on the interpretation of the term *life skills*, the concepts underlying it, and the content and effectiveness of individual initiatives developed within this framework.

The life skills approach lends itself well to implementation across cultures and has been integrated into curricula in various countries (for example, Bejarano, Ugalde, & Morales, 2005; Bils, 1999; Godfrey, Toumbourou, Rowland, Hemphill, & Munro, 2002; ICAP, 2000; Lloyd, Joyce, Hurry,

& Ashton, 2000). South Africa's Curriculum 2005, for instance, includes "life orientation" and skills for decision-making, critical and creative thinking, and effective communication. Also included are skills for developing healthy relationships and a positive self-concept (National Department of Education, 1997). Other initiatives that are not curriculum-based have been implemented (Godfrey et al., 2002; Spoth, Guyll, & Day, 2002). Life skills education has been used to help parents support their children and assess their own drinking behavior (Ashery et al., 1998; Foxcroft et al., 2003; Kumpfer et al., 2003; Spoth et al., 2002).

Although the impact of life skills education has been debated (Foxcroft et al., 2003; Gorman, 2002; Palinkas, Atkins, Miller, & Ferreira, 1996; Plant & Plant, 1999), certain "factors of success" have been identified (WHO, 1999, 2003): long-term programs, trained educators or providers, a focus on both generic and specific skills, active student involvement, user-friendly materials, and peer leadership components. Where these and other components have been implemented, life skills programs have contributed to a decrease in alcohol misuse and other problematic behaviors (see, for example, Botvin & Kantor, 2000; Perry, 1987).

Focusing on Groups at Risk

For some youths, the potential for harm is higher than it is for young people in general. Certain young people are at elevated risk for adverse outcomes from drinking by virtue of their familial and genetic predisposition to alcohol dependence, personality traits that make them more likely to engage in high-risk behaviors (including heavy drinking), or circumstances that make them more vulnerable to harm. Early identification of problem drinking has been successfully applied to young people, as it has to adults. Screening instruments that are simple to use, such as the Alcohol Use Disorders Identification Test (AUDIT), can be appropriately utilized for young people and offer a convenient tool for identifying high-risk youth (Babor, de la Fuente, Saunders, & Grant, 1992; Babor, Higgins-Biddle, Saunders, & Monteiro, 2001; Landry, Guyon, Bergeron, & Provost, 2002; Werner, Joffe, & Graham, 1999).

These screening instruments can be applied in a range of settings and use existing resources. School health workers, counselors, social workers, and others regularly in touch with young people can be trained to identify signs of potential alcohol abuse, particularly by using screening instruments. Those identified can be offered brief interventions and counseling to help reduce problems before they become severe. Physicians' offices, health centers, and emergency rooms also offer venues for screening and counseling. Online interactive tools that allow assessment of drinking and potential problems have proven useful among this population, and some have been tailored to provide individualized feedback (Miller, 2001; Saitz et al., 2004).

Alcohol Skills Training Program for High-risk College Students

Developed at the University of Washington in the United States, the Alcohol Skills Training Program (ASTP) is a brief intervention designed specifically for heavy-drinking college students (Fromme, Marlatt, Baer, & Kivlahan, 1994; Kivlahan, Marlatt, Fromme, Coppel, & Williams, 1990). Using a harm reduction approach, ASTP incorporates a range of techniques that challenge misperceptions of peer drinking, common drinking myths, and risky alcohol expectancies and encourage participants to monitor their own alcohol intake. ASTP uses motivational interviewing to overcome students' ambivalence about changing behavior (Miller & Rollnick, 2002) and provides personalized feedback based on self-reported alcohol consumption.

Generally offered in an adjustable number of 90-minute sessions, ASTP consists of several components designed to assess the participants' current drinking, educate them about the effects of alcohol and alcohol abuse, and help them develop skills to minimize drink-related harm (for example, students are taught how to estimate blood alcohol concentration levels and how to avoid or limit risky alcohol intake) (Blume & Marlatt, 2004; Fromme et al., 1994). The program has been implemented on a number of university campuses across the United States and can be delivered in classroom, small-group, and individual formats.

Participating in ASTP has been found to lower alcohol use and drink-related consequences among college students (Miller, Kilmer, Kim, Weingardt, & Marlatt, 2001), both at the end of the program and at 1- and 2-year follow-ups (Baer et al., 1992; Kivlahan et al., 1990). Recently, a culturally enhanced ASTP has shown promise in reducing alcohol consumption and problems among Mexican American students at a U.S. university (Hernandez et al., 2006).

Source: Hernandez et al. (2006).

As discussed above, the family has been shown to be an important factor in shaping young people's attitudes about drinking. Programs have been developed to strengthen parental influence and the role of the family. Such initiatives integrate behavioral training for parents, family skills training, education, support, and brief therapy, and appear to be cross-culturally applicable (Ashery et al, 1998; Foxcroft et al., 2003; Kumpfer, Alvarado, Tait, & Turner, 2002; Kumpfer et al., 2003). One example of such an initiative is the Strengthening the Families Program for 10- to 14-year-olds and their parents (SFP 10–14). Formerly called the Iowa Strengthening Families Program (ISFP) and developed at the University of Iowa in the United States, SFP 10–14 aims, in the long term, to reduce alcohol and drug use and behavior problems during adolescence. It is achieved through improved skills in nurturing and child management by parents, and improved interpersonal and personal competencies among young people.

This suggests a need in alcohol education to equip the "educators"—parents, teachers, youth workers, and religious and community leaders—with knowledge and skills to assess problems, recognize problematic behaviors and situations, and offer counseling to young people. Where high-risk youth are difficult to reach, medical personnel in emergency rooms, for example, can be valuable resources, as can social workers.

CONCLUSIONS

Alcohol consumption is a fact of life for young people in many parts of the world. As with adults, the drinking of alcohol in the company of others is an important part of social interaction, relaxation, and entertainment. For many young people, alcohol consumption is a part of normal psychosocial development and exploration of behaviors in the transition from youth to adulthood. Even extreme drinking, which might be perceived as an aberration by adults, may be seen by some young people as part of a socially accepted "calculated hedonism," something that is aimed for on certain occasions and with certain friends, and a passage on the way to "alcohol maturity."

As evidenced by the data presented in this chapter, substantial shifts in patterns of drinking are taking place among young people in many countries. However, despite trends in the globalization of youth culture, there are still substantial differences between countries in the ways this group drinks. Young people approach alcohol differently, depending on the culture in which they live and the influences around them. The changing trends in drinking patterns and the emergence of new issues emphasize the need for creative solutions.

The predominant approaches to youth drinking in most countries have abstinence as their goal, through both drinking and purchase age limits and alcohol education programs that seek to delay the age at which alcohol consumption begins. Evidence that either approach can effectively discourage drinking is disappointing: In many countries, many young people drink before the legal age. One might conclude that abstinence-based approaches are unrealistic and that a more sensible approach is to ensure that drinking, if it does occur, causes the least possible harm.

A variety of interventions to reduce drink-related harms discussed elsewhere in this book also apply to young people—for example, measures to reduce alcohol-impaired driving (see Chapter 5) and efforts to control public spaces and drinking venues (see Chapter 6). However, public concern about youth drinking has not yet been matched by a range of tailored and targeted interventions. There is much work to be done to develop interventions that are based on an assessment of the positive and negative aspects of alcohol consumption by this population, the reality of youth drinking, and an understanding of the role of alcohol for young people. It is important to address harm minimization through strategies aimed at this group's drinking contexts, particular behaviors that may increase their risk for harm, and those youths who are more likely than others to be adversely affected. There is much merit in an approach that is flexible rather than strictly wedded to enforcement and punitive measures, and that takes into account the changing face of drinking by young people.

NOTE

1. To examine extreme drinking across disparate cultures, the International Center for Alcohol Policies conducted a series of focus groups among young people during 2005. These were held in Brazil, Italy, Japan, Nigeria, Russia, South Africa, and the United Kingdom and surveyed young people over the legally mandated drinking age in each country. The data were collected using a uniform set of questions, and focus groups included a cross-section of gender, socioeconomic and educational levels, and, where appropriate, ethnic composition in each country. The data offer a flavor of prevailing drinking patterns and attitudes (Martinic & Measham, in press).

REFERENCES

Aas, H., Leigh, B. C., Anderssen, N., & Jakobsen, R. (1998). Two-year longitudinal study of alcohol expectancies and drinking among Norwegian adolescents. *Addiction, 93,* 373–384.

Abrahamson, M. (2004). When I drank too much: Young people in their 20s tell their stories. *Nordisk Alkohol- & Narkotikatidskrift, 21,* 63–78.

Aitken, P. (1978). *Ten- to fourteen-year-olds and alcohol: A developmental study in the Central Region of Scotland.* Edinburgh, UK: Her Majesty's Stationery Office.

Ashery, R. S., Robertson, E. B., & Kumpfer, K. L. (Eds.). (1998). *Drug abuse prevention through family interventions.* NIDA Research Monograph 177. Rockville, MD: National Institute on Drug Abuse.

Australian Institute of Health and Welfare. (2002). *2001 National Drug Strategy Household Survey: Detailed findings.* Drug Statistic Series No. 11. Canberra: Author.

Babor, T. F., de la Fuente, J. R., Saunders, J., & Grant, M. (1992). *AUDIT: The Alcohol Use Disorder Identification Test: Guidelines for use in primary health care.* WHO/PSA/92.4. Geneva, Switzerland: Substance Abuse Department, World Health Organization.

Babor, T. F., Higgins-Biddle, J., Saunders, J. B., & Monteiro, M. G. (2001). *AUDIT: The Alcohol Use Disorders Identification Test: Guidelines for use in primary care,* 2nd ed. Geneva, Switzerland: World Health Organization.

Baer, J. S., Marlatt, G. A., Kivlahan, D. R., Fromme, K., Larimer, M. E., & Williams, E. (1992). An experimental test of three methods of alcohol risk reduction with young adults. *Journal of Consulting and Clinical Psychology, 64,* 974–979.

Beck, K., & Treitman, K. A. (1996). The relationship of social context of drinking, perceived social norms, and parental influence to various drinking patterns of adolescents. *Addictive Behaviors, 21,* 633–644.

Bejarano, J., Ugalde, F., & Morales, D. (2005). Evaluación de un programa escolar en Costa Rica basado en habilidades para vivir [A life skills training program evaluation in Costa Rica]. *Adicciones: Revista de Socidrogalcohol, 17,* 61–70.

Bils, L. (1999). Prevention primaire en Belgique francophone [Primary prevention in French-speaking Belgium]. *Alcoologie, 21,* 187–192.

Bjarnason, T., Andersson, B., Choquet, B., Elekes, Z., Morgan, Z., & Rapinett, G. (2003). Alcohol culture, family structure and adolescent alcohol use: Multilevel modeling of frequency of heavy drinking among 15–16 year old students in 11 European countries. *Journal of Studies on Alcohol, 64*, 200–208.

Blume, A. W., & Marlatt, G. A. (2004). Motivational enhancement as a brief intervention for college student drinkers. In W. M. Cox & E. Klinger (Eds.), *Handbook of motivational counselling: Concepts, approaches, and assessment* (pp. 409–420). Chichester, UK: John Wiley & Sons.

Bonomo, Y., Coffey, C., Wolfe, R., Lynskey, M., Bowes, G., & Patton, G. (2001). Adverse outcomes of alcohol use in adolescents. *Addiction, 96*, 1485–1496.

Borsari, B., & Carey, K. B. (2001). Peer influences on college drinking: A review of the research. *Journal of Substance Abuse, 13*, 391–424.

Botvin, G. J., Baker, E., Dusenbury, L., Botvin, E. M., & Diaz, T. (1995). Long-term follow-up results of a randomized drug abuse prevention trial in a white middle-class population. *Journal of the American Medical Association, 273*, 1106–1112.

Botvin, G. J., Griffin, K. W., Diaz, T., & Ifill-Williams, M. (2001). Preventing binge drinking during early adolescence: One- and two-year follow-up of a school-based prevention intervention. *Psychology of Addictive Behaviors, 15*, 360–365.

Botvin, G. J., Griffin, K. W., Paul, E., & Macaulay, A. P. (2003). Preventing tobacco and alcohol use among elementary school students through life skills training. *Journal of Child and Adolescent Substance Abuse, 12*, 1–17.

Botvin, G. J., & Kantor, L. W. (2000). Preventing alcohol and tobacco use through life skills training. *Alcohol Research and Health, 24*, 250–257.

Brain, K. (2000). *Youth, alcohol, and the emergence of the post-modern alcohol order.* London: Institute of Alcohol Studies.

Brain, K., Parker, H., & Carnwath, T. (2000). Drinking with design: Young drinkers as psychoactive consumers. *Drugs: Education, Prevention and Policy, 7*, 5–20.

Brown, S. A., & Tapert, S. F. (2004). Health consequences of adolescent alcohol use. In National Research Council and Institute of Medicine, *Reducing underage drinking: A collective responsibility, background papers.* [CD-ROM]. Committee on Developing a Strategy to Reduce and Prevent Underage Drinking, Division of Behavioral and Social Sciences and Education. Washington, DC: National Academies Press.

Brown, S. A., Tapert, S. F., Granholm, E., & Delis, D. C. (2000). Neurocognitive functioning of adolescents: Effects of protracted alcohol use. *Alcoholism: Clinical and Experimental Research, 24*, 164–171.

Calafat, A., Juan, M., Becoña, E., Castillo, A., Fernández, C., Franco, M., et al. (2005). El consumo de alcohol en la lógica del botellón [Alcohol consumption and the logic behind the *botellón*]. *Adicciones: Revista de Socidragalcohol, 17*, 193–202.

Caulkins, J. P., Pacula, R. L., Paddock, S., & Chiesa, J. (2004). What we can—and cannot—expect from school-based drug prevention. *Drug and Alcohol Review, 23*, 79–87.

Century Council. (2006). *Cops in Shops.* Retrieved April 18, 2004, from http://www.centurycouncil.org/underage/cops.html.

Chikritzhs, T., Catalano, P., Stockwell, T., Donath, S., Ngo, H., Young, D., et al. (2003). *Australian alcohol indicators, 1990–2001: Patterns of alcohol use and related harms for Australian states and territories.* Perth, Australia: National Drug Research Institute.

Choquet, M. (2004). Underage drinking: The epidemiological data. In *What drives underage drinking? An international analysis* (pp. 14–24). Washington, DC: International Center for Alcohol Policies.

Coleman, L., & Cater, S. (2005). *Underage "risky" drinking: Motivations and outcomes.* York, UK: Joseph Rowntree Foundation.

Cooper, M. L., Frone, M. R., Russell, M., & Mudar, P. (1995). Drinking to regulate positive and negative emotions: A motivational model of alcohol use. *Journal of Personality and Social Psychology, 69,* 990–1005.

Currie, C., Roberts, C., Morgan, A., Smith, R., Settertobulte, W., Samdal, O., et al. (Eds.). (2004). *Young people's health in context. Health Behaviour in School-aged Children (HBSC) study: International report from the 2001/2002 survey.* Health Policy for Children and Adolescents No. 4. Copenhagen, Denmark: WHO Regional Office for Europe.

D'Amico, E. J., Metrik, J., McCarthy, D. M., Frissell, K. C., Appelbaum, M., & Brown, S. A. (2001). Progression into and out of binge drinking among high school students. *Psychology of Addictive Behaviors, 15,* 341–349.

Dawson, D. A. (2000). The link between family history and early onset alcoholism: Earlier initiation of drinking or more rapid development of dependence? *Journal of Studies on Alcohol, 61,* 637–646.

DeBellis, M. D., Clark, D. B., Beers, S. R., Soloff, P. H., Boring, A. M., Hall, J., et al. (2000). Hippocampal volume in adolescent-onset alcohol use disorders. *American Journal of Psychiatry, 157,* 737–744.

Dees, W. L., Dissen, G. A., Hiney, J. K., Lara, F., & Ojeda, S. R. (2000). Alcohol ingestion inhibits the increased secretion of puberty-related hormones in the developing female rhesus monkey. *Endocrinology, 141,* 1325–1331.

Dees, W. L., Srivastava, V. K., & Hiney, J. K. (2001). Alcohol and female puberty: The role of intraovarian systems. *Alcohol Research and Health, 25,* 271–275.

Donohue, B., Allen, D. N., Maurer, A., Ozols, J., & DeStefano, G. (2004). A controlled evaluation of two prevention programs in reducing alcohol use among college students at low and high risk for alcohol-related problems. *Journal of Alcohol and Drug Education, 48,* 13–33.

Donovan, J. E., Jessor, R., & Jessor L. (1983). Problem drinking in adolescence and young adulthood: A follow-up study. *Journal of Studies on Alcohol, 44,* 109–137.

Donovan, J. E., Leech, S. L., Zucker, R. A., Loveland-Cherry, C. J., Jester, J. M., Fitzgerald, H. E., et al. (2004). Really underage drinkers: Alcohol use among elementary students. *Alcoholism: Clinical and Experimental Research, 28,* 341–349.

Engels, R. C., Knibbe, R. A., & Drop, M. J. (1999). Visiting public drinking places: An explorative study into the functions of pub-going for late adolescents. *Substance Use and Misuse, 34,* 1261–1280.

Engineer, R., Phillips, A., Thompson, J., & Nicholls, J. (2003). *Drunk and disorderly: A qualitative study of binge drinking among 18- to 24-year olds.* London: Home Office Research, Development and Statistics Directorate.

Fabiano, P. (2003). Applying the social norms model to universal and indicated alcohol interventions at Western Washington University. In H. W. Perkins (Ed.), *The social norms approach to preventing school and college age substance abuse: A handbook for educators, counselors, and clinicians* (pp. 83–99). San Francisco: Jossey-Bass.

Feldman, L., Harvey, B., Holowaty, P., & Shortt, L. (1999). Alcohol use beliefs and behaviors among high school students. *Journal of Adolescent Health, 24,* 48–58.

Fergusson, D. M., Lynskey, M. T., & Horwood, L. J. (1996). Alcohol misuse and juvenile offending in adolescence. *Addiction, 91*, 483–494.

Foxcroft, D. R. Ireland, D., Lister-Sharp, D. J., Lowe, G., & Breen, R. (2003). Longer-term primary prevention for alcohol misuse in young people: A systematic review. *Addiction, 98*, 397–411.

Frias, J., Rodriguez, R., Torres, J. M., Ruiz, E., & Ortega, E. (2000). Effects of acute alcohol intoxication on pituitary-gonadal axis hormones, pituitary-adrenal axis hormones, beta-endorphin and prolactin in human adolescents of both sexes. *Life Sciences, 67*, 1081–1086.

Fromme, K., Marlatt, G. A., Baer, J. S., & Kivlahan, D. R. (1994). The Alcohol Skills Training Program: A group intervention for young adults. *Journal of Substance Abuse Treatment, 11*, 143–154.

Gamela, J. F. (1995). Spain. In D. B. Heath (Ed.), *International handbook on alcohol and culture* (pp. 254–269). Westport, CT: Greenwood.

Gaughan, M. (2006). The gender structure of adolescent peer influence on drinking. *Journal of Health and Social Behavior, 47*, 47–61.

Geckova, A., & Van Dijk, J. P. (2001). Peer impact on smoking, alcohol consumption, drug use and sports activities in adolescents. *Studia Psychologica, 43*, 113–123.

Godfrey, C., Toumbourou, J. W., Rowland, B., Hemphill, S., & Munro, G. (2002). *Drug education approaches in primary schools.* West Melbourne, Australia: Drug Info Clearinghouse.

Gorman, D. M. (2002). "Science" of drug and alcohol prevention: The case of the randomized trial of the Life Skills Training program. *International Journal of Drug Policy, 13*, 21–26.

Governors Highway Safety Association. (2001). *Survey of the states: Underage drinking prevention.* Issue 3. Washington, DC: Author.

Grant, B. F., & Dawson, D. A. (1997). Age at onset of alcohol use and its association with *DSM-IV* alcohol abuse and dependence: Results from the National Longitudinal Alcohol Epidemiologic Survey. *Journal of Substance Abuse, 9*, 103–110.

Grunbaum, J. A., Kann, L., Kinchen, S. A., Williams, B., Ross, J. G., Lowry, R., et al. (2002). Youth risk behavior surveillance, United States, 2001. *Morbidity and Mortality Weekly Report, 51*, 1–64.

Haines, M. P. (1996). *A social norms approach to preventing binge drinking at colleges and universities.* Newton, MA: Higher Education Center for Alcohol and Other Drug Prevention.

Haines, M. P., & Barker, G. (2003). The NIU experiment: A case study of the social norms approach. In H. W. Perkins (Ed.), *The social norms approach to preventing school and college age substance abuse: A handbook for educators, counselors, and clinicians* (pp. 21–34). San Francisco: Jossey-Bass.

Haines, M. P., Perkins, H. W., Rice, R. M., & Barker, G. (2004). *A guide to marketing social norms for health promotion in schools and communities.* DeKalb, IL: National Social Norms Resource Center.

Harrington, N. T., & Leitenberg, H. (1994). Relationship between alcohol consumption and victim behaviors immediately preceding sexual aggression by an acquaintance. *Violence and Victims, 9*, 315–324.

Hawkins, J. D., Graham, J. W., Maguin, E., Abbott, R., Hill, K. G., & Catalano, R. F. (1997). Exploring the effects of age of alcohol use initiation and psychosocial risk factors on subsequent alcohol misuse. *Journal of Studies on Alcohol, 58*, 280–290.

Hayes, L., Smart, D., Toumbourou, J. W., & Sanson, A. (2004). *Parenting influences on adolescent alcohol use*. Research Report No. 10. Melbourne: Australian Institute on Family Studies.

Hellandsjø Bu, E. T., Watten, R. G., Foxcroft, D. R., Ingebrigtsen, J. E., & Relling, G. (2002). Teenage alcohol and intoxication debut: The impact of family socialization factors, living area and participation in organized sports. *Alcohol and Alcoholism, 37*, 74–80.

Hernandez, D. V., Skewes, M. C., Resor, M. R., Villanueva, M. R., Hanson, B. S., & Blume, A. W. (2006). A pilot test of an alcohol skills training programme for Mexican-American college students. *International Journal of Drug Policy, 17*, 320–328.

Hibell, B., Andersson, B., Bjarnason, T., Ahlström, S., Balakireva, O., Kokkevi, A., et al. (2004). *The ESPAD Report 2003: Alcohol and other drug use among students in 35 European countries*. Stockholm: Swedish Council for Information on Alcohol and Other Drugs (CAN) and the Pompidou Group at the Council of Europe.

Hingson, R., Heeren, T., Zakocs, R. C., Kopstein, A., & Wechsler, H. (2002). Magnitude of alcohol-related mortality and morbidity among U.S. college students aged 18–24. *Journal of Studies on Alcohol, 63*, 136–144.

Holder, H. D., Gruenewald, P. J., Ponicki, W. R., Treno, A. J., Grube, J. W., Saltz, R. F., et al. (2000). Effect of community-based interventions on high-risk drinking and alcohol-related injuries. *Journal of American Medical Association, 284*, 2341–2347.

International Center for Alcohol Policies (ICAP). (2000). *Life skills education in South Africa and Botswana*. Washington, DC: Author.

International Center for Alcohol Policies (ICAP). (2002). *Drinking age limits*, rev. ed. ICAP Reports 4. Washington, DC: Author. (Originally published in 1998)

International Center for Alcohol Policies (ICAP). (2004). *Alcohol education and its effectiveness*. ICAP Reports 16. Washington, DC: Author.

International Center for Alcohol Policies (ICAP). (2005). *Table: Minimum drinking and purchasing age laws*. Retrieved April 24, 2006, from http://www.icap.org/PolicyIssues/YoungPeoplesDrinking/AgeLawsTable/tabid/219/Default.aspx.

Jeffrey, L., Negro, P., Miller, D., & Frisone, J. (2003). The Rowan University social norms project. In H. W. Perkins (Ed.), *The social norms approach to preventing school and college age substance abuse: A handbook for educators, counselors, and clinicians* (pp. 100–110). San Francisco: Jossey-Bass.

Jennison, K. M. (2004). The short-term effects and unintended long-term consequences of binge drinking in college: A 10-year follow-up study. *American Journal of Drug and Alcohol Abuse, 30*, 659–684.

Jerez, S. J., & Coviello, A. (1998). Alcohol drinking and blood pressure among adolescents. *Alcohol: An International Biomedical Journal, 16*, 1–5.

Johanssen, K., Collins, C., Mills-Novoa, B., & Glider, P. (1999). *A practical guide to alcohol abuse prevention: A campus study in implementing social norms and environmental approaches*. Tucson: Campus Health Service, University of Arizona.

Johnson, H. L., & Johnson, P. B. (1995). Children's alcohol-related cognitions: Positive versus negative alcohol effects. *Journal of Alcohol and Drug Education, 40*, 1–12.

Johnston, L. D., O'Malley, P. M., Bachman, J. G., & Schulenberg, J. E. (2005). *Teen drug use down but progress halts among youngest teens*. University of Michigan News and Information Services. Retrieved April 24, 2006, from http://www.monitoringthefuture.org.

Kairouz, S., Gliksman, L., Demers, A., & Adlaf, E. M. (2002). For all these reasons, I do drink: A multilevel analysis of contextual reasons for drinking among Canadian undergraduates. *Journal of Studies on Alcohol, 63,* 600–608.

Kalafatelis, E., McMillen, P., & Palmer, S. (2003). *Youth and alcohol: 2003 ALAC youth drinking monitor.* Wellington: Alcohol Advisory Council of New Zealand (ALAC).

Kivlahan, D. R., Marlatt, G. A., Fromme, K., Coppel, D. B., & Williams, E. (1990). Secondary prevention with college drinkers: Evaluation of an alcohol skills training program. *Journal of Consulting and Clinical Psychology, 58,* 805–810.

Klein, R. F. (1997). Alcohol-induced bone disease: Impact of ethanol on osteoblast proliferation. *Alcoholism: Clinical and Experimental Research, 21,* 392–399.

Kono, Y., Yoneda, H., Sakai, T., Nonomura, Y., Inayama, Y., Koh, J., et al. (1997). Association between early-onset alcoholism and the dopamine D2 receptor gene. *American Journal of Medical Genetics (Neuropsychiatric Genetics), 74,* 179–182.

Kumpfer, K. L., Alvarado, R., Tait, C., & Turner, C. (2002). Effectiveness of school-based family and children's skills training for substance abuse prevention among 6–8-year-old rural children. *Psychology of Addictive Behaviors, 16*(4S), S65–S71.

Kumpfer, K. L., Alvarado, R., & Whiteside, H. O. (2003). Family-based interventions for substance use and misuse prevention. *Substance Use and Misuse, 38,* 1759–1787.

Kuntsche, E., & Kuendig, H. (2006). What is worse? A hierarchy of family-related risk factors predicting alcohol use in adolescence. *Substance Use and Misuse, 41,* 71–86.

Kuntsche, E., Rehm, J., & Gmel, G. (2004). Characteristics of binge drinkers in Europe. *Social Science and Medicine, 59,* 113–127.

Landry, M., Guyon, L., Bergeron, J., & Provost, G. (2002). Évaluation de la toxicomanie chez les adolescents: Développement et validation d'un instrument [Development and validation of an evaluation tool for drug addiction in adolescents]. *Alcoologie et Addictologie, 24,* 7–13.

Lang, A. R., & Michalec, E. M. (1990). Expectancy effects in reinforcement from alcohol. In W. M. Cox (Ed.), *Why people drink: Parameters of alcohol as a reinforcer* (pp. 193–232). New York: Gardner.

Leigh, B. C. (1999). Thinking, feeling, and drinking: Alcohol expectancies and alcohol use. In S. Peele & M. Grant (Eds.), *Alcohol and pleasure: A health perspective* (pp. 215–232). Philadelphia: Brunner/Mazel.

Lindsay, J. (2005, February). *Addressing youth drinking cultures now and in the future.* Paper presented at the Thinking Drinking: Achieving Cultural Change by 2020 conference, Melbourne, Australia.

Lloyd, C., Joyce, R., Hurry, J., & Ashton, M. (2000). Effectiveness of primary school drug education. *Drugs: Education, Prevention and Policy, 7,* 109–126.

Lo, C. C., & Globetti, G. (2000). Gender differences in drinking patterns among Hong Kong Chinese youth: Pilot study. *Substance Use and Misuse, 35,* 1297–1306.

MacAskill, S., Cooke, E., Eadie, D., & Hastings, G. (2001). *Perceptions of factors that promote and protect against the misuse of alcohol amongst young people and young adults.* Glasgow, UK: Center for Social Marketing, University of Strathclyde.

Martinic, M., & Measham, F. (in press). *Swimming with crocodiles: The culture of extreme drinking.* New York: Brunner-Routledge.

Mattern, J. L., & Neighbors, C. (2004). Social norms campaigns: Examining the relationship between changes in perceived norms and changes in drinking levels. *Journal of Studies on Alcohol, 65,* 489–493.

McBride, N., Farringdon, F., Midford, R., Meuleners, L., & Phillips, M. (2004). Harm minimization in schools: Final results of the School Health and Alcohol Harm Reduction Project (SHAHRP). *Addiction, 99,* 278–291.

McBride, N., Midford, R., Farringdon, F., & Phillips, M. (2000). Early results from a school alcohol harm minimization study: School Health and Alcohol Harm Reduction Project. *Addiction, 95,* 1021–1042.

McGue, M., Iacono, W. G., Legrand, L. N., & Elkins, I. (2001). Origins and consequences of age at first drink. II. Familial risk and heritability. *Alcoholism: Clinical and Experimental Research, 25,* 1166–1173.

Milgram, G. G. (2001). Alcohol influences: The role of family and peers. In E. Houghton & A. Roche (Eds.), *Learning about drinking* (pp. 85–101). Philadelphia: Brunner-Routledge.

Miller, E. T. (2001). Preventing alcohol abuse and alcohol-related negative consequences among freshmen college students: Using emerging computer technology to deliver and evaluate the effectiveness of brief intervention efforts. *Dissertation Abstracts International, 61,* 4417B.

Miller, E. T., Kilmer, J. R., Kim, E. L., Weingardt, K. R., & Marlatt, G. A. (2001). Alcohol skills training for college students. In P. M. Monti, S. M. Colby, & T. A. O'Leary (Eds.), *Adolescents, alcohol and substance abuse: Reaching teens through brief interventions* (pp. 183–215). New York: Guilford Publications.

Miller, P., & Plant, M. (2003). Family, peer influences and substance use: Findings from a study of U.K. teenagers. *Journal of Substance Use, 8,* 19–26.

Miller, W. R., & Rollnick, S. (2002). *Motivational interviewing: Preparing people to change.* 2nd ed. New York: Guilford.

Mohler-Kuo, M., Dowdall, G. W., Koss, M. P., & Wechsler, H. (2004). Correlates of rape while intoxicated in a national sample of college women. *Journal of Studies on Alcohol, 65,* 37–45.

Monti, P. M., Miranda, R., Jr., Nixon, K., Sher, K. J., Swartzwelder, H. S., Tapert, S. F., et al. (2005). Adolescence: Booze, brains, and behavior. *Alcoholism: Clinical and Experimental Research, 29,* 207–220.

Nahoum-Grappe, V. (2002). Les "botellons" [The "botellons"]. *Focus Alcoologie, 4,* 11.

Nash, S. G., McQueen, A., & Bray, J. H. (2005). Pathways to adolescent alcohol use: Family environment, peer influence, and parental expectations. *Journal of Adolescent Health, 37,* 19–28.

National Department of Education. (1997). *Curriculum 2005: Grades 1–9.* Pretoria, South Africa: Author.

National Health and Medical Research Council. (2001). *Australian alcohol guidelines: Health risks and benefits.* Canberra, Australia: Author.

National Research Council & National Institute of Medicine. (2004). *Reducing underage drinking: A collective responsibility.* Washington, DC: National Academy Press.

Organisation for Economic Co-operation and Development. (2006). *Portugal: Country statistical profile 2006.* Retrieved April 24, 2006, from http://stats.oecd.org/WBOS/ViewHTML.aspx?QueryName=196&QueryType=View&Lang=en.

Palinkas, L. A., Atkins, C. J., Miller, C., & Ferreira, D. (1996). Social skills training for drug prevention in high-risk female adolescents. *Preventive Medicine, 25,* 692–701.

Perkins, H. W. (1997). College student misperceptions of alcohol and other drug norms among peers: Exploring causes, consequences, and implication for prevention programs. In *Designing alcohol and other drug prevention programs in higher education: Bringing theory into practice* (pp. 177–206). Newton, MA: Higher Education Center for Alcohol and Other Drug Prevention.

Perkins, H. W. (2002). Social norms and the prevention of alcohol misuse in collegiate contexts. *Journal of Studies on Alcohol, 14*(Suppl.), 164–172.

Perkins, H. W. (2003). *Social norms approach to preventing school and college age substance abuse: A handbook for educators, counselors, and clinicians.* San Francisco: Jossey-Bass.

Perkins, H. W., & Berkowitz, A. D. (1986). Perceiving the community norms of alcohol use among students: Some researcher implications for campus alcohol education programming. *International Journal of the Addictions, 21*, 961–976.

Perkins, H. W., & Craig, D. W. (2002). *A multifaceted social norms approach to reduce high-risk drinking: Lessons from Hobart and William Smith Colleges.* Newton, MA: Higher Education Center for Alcohol and Other Drug Prevention.

Perkins, H. W., & Craig, D. W. (2003). Imaginary lives of peers: Patterns of substance use and misperceptions of norms among secondary school students. In H. W. Perkins (Ed.), *Social norms approach to preventing school and college age substance abuse: A handbook for educators, counselors, and clinicians* (pp. 209–223). San Francisco: Jossey-Bass.

Perkins, H. W., Meilman, P., Leichliter, J. S., Cashin, J. R., & Presley, C. (1999). Misperceptions of the norms for the frequency of alcohol and other drug use on college campuses. *Journal of American College Health, 47*, 253–258.

Perkins, H. W., & Wechsler, H. (1996). Variation in perceived college drinking norms and its impact on alcohol abuse: A nationwide study. *Journal of Drug Issues, 26*, 961–974.

Perry, C. L. (1987). Results of prevention programs with adolescents. *Drug and Alcohol Dependence, 20*, 13–19.

Plant, M., Bagnall, G., & Foster, J. (1990). Teenage heavy drinkers: Alcohol-related knowledge, beliefs, experiences, motivation and the social context of drinking. *Alcohol and Alcoholism, 25*, 691–698.

Plant, M., & Plant, M. (1992). *Risk-takers: Alcohol, sex, drugs, and youths.* London: Routledge.

Plant, M., & Plant, M. (1999). Primary prevention for young children: A comment on the U.K. government's 10-year drug strategy. *International Journal of Drug Policy, 10*, 385–401.

Poikolainen, K., Yuulio-Henriksson, A., Aalto-Setala, T., Marttunen, M., & Lonnqvist, J. (2001). Predictors of alcohol intake and heavy drinking in early adulthood: Five-year follow-up of 15–19-year-old Finnish adolescents. *Alcohol and Alcoholism, 36*, 85–88.

Prescott, C. A., & Kendler, K. S. (1999). Age at first drink and risk for alcoholism: A non-causal association. *Alcoholism: Clinical and Experimental Research, 23*, 101–107.

Richardson, A., & Budd, T. (2003). *Alcohol, crime and disorder: A study of young adults.* Home Office Research Study 263. London: Home Office.

Rocha-Silva, L. (1998). *The nature and extent of drug use and the prevalence of related problems in South Africa: National surveillance.* Pretoria: Human Sciences Research Council of South Africa.

Rose, R. J. (1998). A developmental behavior-genetic perspective on alcoholism risk. *Alcohol Health and Research World*, *22*, 131–143.

Rossow, I. (1996). Alcohol-related violence: The impact of drinking pattern and drinking context. *Addiction*, *91*, 1651–1661.

Saitz, R., Helmuth, E. D., Aromaa, S. E., Guard, A., Belanger, M., & Rosenbloom, D. L. (2004). Web-based screening and brief intervention for the spectrum of alcohol problems. *Preventive Medicine*, *39*, 969–975.

Sampson, H. W., Gallager, S., Lange, J., Chondra, W., & Hogan, H. A. (1999). Binge drinking and bone metabolism in a young actively growing rat model. *Alcoholism: Clinical and Experimental Research*, *23*, 1228–1231.

Sanchez-Sosa, J. J., & Poldrugo, F. (2001). Family and cultural influences on alcohol and young people. In E. Houghton & A. M. Roche (Eds.), *Learning about drinking* (pp. 57–83). Philadelphia: Brunner-Routledge.

Shedler, J., & Block, J. (1990). Adolescent drug use and psychological health. *American Psychologist*, *45*, 612–630.

Sheehan, M., & Ridge, D. (2001). "You become really close . . . you talk about the silly things you did, and we laugh": The role of binge drinking in female secondary students' lives. *Substance Use and Misuse*, *36*, 347–372.

Spear, L. P. (2004). Biomedical aspects of underage drinking. In *What drives underage drinking? An international analysis* (pp. 25–38). Washington, DC: International Center for Alcohol Policies.

Spoth, R. L., Guyll, M., & Day, S. X. (2002). Universal family-focused interventions in alcohol-use disorder prevention: Cost-effectiveness and cost-benefit analyses of two interventions. *Journal of Studies on Alcohol*, *63*, 219–228.

Spoth, R., Redmond, C., & Lepper, H. (1999). Alcohol initiation outcomes of universal family-focused preventive interventions: One- and two-year follow-ups of a controlled study. *Journal of Studies on Alcohol*, *13*(Suppl.), 103–111.

Stewart, C., & Power, T. G. (2002). Identifying patterns of adolescent drinking: A tri-ethnic study. *Journal of Studies on Alcohol*, *63*, 156–168.

Tapert, S. F., Brown, G. G., Kindermann, S. S., Cheung, E. H., Frank, L. R., & Brown, S. A. (2001). fMRI measurement of brain dysfunction in alcohol-dependent young women. *Alcoholism: Clinical and Experimental Research*, *25*, 236–245.

Toumbourou, J. W., Williams, I. R., White, V. M., Snow, P. C., Munro, G. D., & Schofield, P. E. (2004). Prediction of alcohol-related harm from controlled drinking strategies and alcohol consumption trajectories. *Addiction*, *99*, 498–508.

Traeen, B., & Kvalem, I. L. (1996). Sex under the influence of alcohol among Norwegian adolescents. *Addiction*, *91*, 99–106.

Turrisi, R., Wiersma, K. A., & Hughes, K. K. (2000). Binge-drinking-related consequences in college students: Role of drinking beliefs and mother-teen communications. *Psychology of Addictive Behaviors*, *14*, 342–355.

Unos 70.000 jóvenes sevillanos se congregan mediante SMS para celebrar la Fiesta de la Primavera [About 70,000 young sevillans come together using SMS to celebrate the Spring Festival]. (2004, March 20). *El Mundo* [Online]. Retrieved April 30, 2004, from http://elmundo.es/elmundo/2004/03/20/sociedad/1079751674.html.

U.S. Bureau of Census. (2004). *Current population survey: School enrollment*. Retrieved April 18, 2006, from http://www.census.gov/population/www/socdemo/school.html.

U.S. National Highway Traffic Safety Administration (NHTSA). (2005). *Traffic safety facts 2004: Alcohol*. Washington, DC: Author.

U.S. Substance Abuse and Mental Health Services Administration (SAMHSA). (2004). *2004 National Survey on Drug Use & Health.* Rockville, MD: Department of Health and Human Services.

Vakalahi, H. F. (2001). Adolescent substance use and family-based risk and protective factors: Literature review. *Journal of Drug Education, 31,* 1–28.

Virkkunen, M., & Linnoila, M. (1997). Serotonin in early-onset alcoholism. *Recent Developments in Alcoholism, 13,* 173–189.

Wagenaar, A. C., Murray, D. M., & Toomey, T. L. (2000). Communities Mobilizing for Change on Alcohol (CMCA): Effects of a randomized trial on arrests and traffic crashes. *Addiction, 95,* 209–217.

Wechsler, H., Lee, J. E., Kuo, M., Seibring, M., Nelson, T. F., & Lee, H. (2002). Trends in college binge drinking during a period of increased prevention efforts. Findings from 4 Harvard School of Public Health College Alcohol Study surveys: 1993–2001. *Journal of American College Health, 40,* 203–217.

Wechsler, H., Moeykens, B., Davenport, A., Castillo, S., & Hansen, J. (1995). The adverse impact of heavy episodic drinkers on other college students. *Journal of Studies on Alcohol, 56,* 628–634.

Wells, S., Graham, K., Speechley, M., & Koval, J. J. (2005). Drinking patterns, drinking contexts and alcohol-related aggression among late adolescent and young adult drinkers. *Addiction, 100*(7), 883.

Werner, M. J., Joffe, A., & Graham, A. V. (1999). Screening, early identification, and office-based intervention with children and youth living in substance-abusing families. *Pediatrics, 103,* 1099–1112.

Wood, M. D., Read, J. P., Mitchell, R. E., & Brand, N. H. (2004). Do parents still matter? Parent and peer influences on alcohol involvement among recent high school graduates. *Psychology of Addictive Behaviors, 18,* 19–30.

World Health Organization (WHO). (1986). *Young people's health—a challenge for society. Report of a WHO Study Group on young people and "Health for All by the Year 2000."* Technical Report Series No. 731. Geneva, Switzerland: Author.

World Health Organization (WHO). (1999). *Partners in life skills education: Conclusions from a United Nations Inter-agency Meeting.* Geneva, Switzerland: Author.

World Health Organization (WHO). (2003). *Value adolescents, invest in the future: Educational package.* Manila, Philippines: WHO Regional Office for the Western Pacific.

World Health Organization (WHO). (2004). *Global status report: Alcohol policy.* Geneva, Switzerland: Author.

8

Feasible Interventions for Minimizing Harm

This book does not pretend to make life easy for the policy-maker. It has highlighted the complexity of drinking: Alcohol can be enjoyed as well as misused, and can benefit as much as harm those who consume it. The duality of its nature makes alcohol unlike many other commodities and plays an important role in why people drink and in the outcomes they are likely to experience. Patterns of drinking shape both benefit and harm: Where people drink, what, how, when, how often, and with whom are all important influences. At the same time, drinking is much like many other behaviors—driving, skiing, sailing, riding, and even eating—because it is learned, it can be accompanied by responsible choices, and the potential for harm is preventable.

Although the harms related to certain drinking patterns can be quantified (and have been measured extensively, as outlined in the Annex), the benefits are often impossible to assess. How does one measure wellbeing, quality of life, "social lubrication," or just pure enjoyment? The complexity of the interaction between positive and negative consequences means that many of the benefits of alcohol consumption are largely omitted from any systematic analysis. This omission is a major issue in the assessment of the net outcome of drinking, and a satisfactory solution to the methodological conundrum it presents has not yet been found. Most interventions focus on reducing negative aspects of alcohol consumption: Although some governments are trying to reformulate policy into a positive mode (for example, the effort in the United Kingdom to move toward a "café culture" of drinking), this idea has as yet rarely translated into quantification of relevant quality-of-life measures, or into actual projects or their evaluation. Inevitably, this book likewise focuses mainly on problem reduction, a focus on the negative rather than the convivial. This is not true of all interventions—for example, those that encourage moderate and sensible drinking. We hope that refocusing on patterns of drinking will help refocus policy, research, and front-line projects.

Interventions around alcohol are best applied so as to minimize the potential for harm while at the same time maximizing any potential benefits. Weighing the costs and benefits of a particular intervention must, therefore, include all potential outcomes: effects on health-related harms and benefits, psychosocial ramifications, economic considerations, and also unintended consequences.

"Health is a state of complete physical, mental, and social wellbeing and not merely the absence of disease or infirmity" (World Health Organization, 2004). It would be well worth keeping this WHO definition of health in mind when reviewing interventions aimed at reducing harm. Arguably, the impact of any intervention must also extend beyond simply the "absence of disease or infirmity." Drinking is not a disease. It is a behavior and, as such, whether we like it or not, hinges largely on individual decisions and choice. Whereas diseases can be addressed with treatment, surgery, or immunization, such a clear-cut approach is not possible when it comes to drinking problems. There are too many factors involved, and a linear relationship with an intervention leading to a specific outcome is not possible.

As a result, interventions that purport to offer a simple solution are only avoiding the complexity of the problem. Drinking cannot be addressed in isolation and even less by simply focusing on alcohol itself and its availability. This approach disregards the myriad influences and contexts that surround and shape drinking. It addresses only the product, without taking into consideration how and why it is consumed.

A further reason why this book does not make life easier for the policy-maker is that, as shown in Chapters 4, 5, 6, and 7, there is a plethora of possible interventions. As we begin to disaggregate drinking, moving from total populations to thinking of drinking in terms of targeted populations, contexts, and behaviors, the real world of policy-making inevitably becomes more complex. So, what is the way forward for the policy-maker? What are the best choice and mix of interventions?

INTERVENTIONS TO CHANGE DRINKING

Interventions aimed at reducing the potential harm associated with drinking can be divided into two basic categories, which are by no means mutually exclusive and may be used in tandem to complement and strengthen each other. One is the population-level approach to prevention, consisting of across-the-board measures. These measures rely heavily on controlling the volume of drinking across entire populations. The other approach involves interventions that are applied in a targeted way, focusing on particular groups, behaviors, drinking patterns, or settings where the potential for harm is elevated. A comprehensive overview of targeted interventions is offered in Chapters 4, 5, 6, and 7. The split between whole-population and targeted interventions is not always neat, because some population-level measures (for example, health warning labels) can be aimed either at the whole drinking population or at subgroups (for example, pregnant women).

Regulations concerning the availability of alcohol are a necessary component of any balanced alcohol policy. There exists the need to ensure that there is oversight of where alcohol may be consumed and by whom. However, interventions must also be pragmatic; they need to consider the reality of people's drinking and consumer demands. Alcohol is there because people want it. What we can do, however, is to make drinking a safer behavior. Therein lies the real challenge.

ASSESSING INTERVENTIONS: APPROPRIATENESS, FEASIBILITY, AND IMPACT

It is conventional to begin discussion of intervention choice in terms of known impact: What is the evidence for whether it works or not? In other words, did the intervention achieve the desired aims, as set out by those designing it?

Effectiveness research is increasingly an important component of prevention, especially given the growing emphasis on evidence-based prevention programming. When done well, such research allows interventions that work to be separated from those that do not, and modifications to be made in order to improve particular approaches. However, it should be noted that the vast majority of policy measures and prevention programs are not evaluated, and that many approaches are designed or implemented in such a way as to make evaluation difficult or meaningless.

Evaluations of interventions to answer these questions, be they policy or prevention measures, have been approached in a variety of ways. These include experimental studies, time-series analyses, and natural experiments (Babor et al., 2003). Simply put, outcomes of interventions are measured by comparing what happens when a measure is implemented with what happens (or has happened in the past) in the absence of the intervention.

A critical feature of this type of design is the ability to control for confounding variables that may have an impact on outcomes and to ensure that the cultural contexts in both the experimental and the control settings are comparable. In reality, however, outside a laboratory setting where variables can be rigorously controlled, confounders are difficult to eliminate. This is especially true where cultural, individual, and social factors all play important and overlapping roles.

Ideally, the parameters for measuring the outcome and effectiveness of a particular approach are built into it from the outset. In other words, the very design of the approach already sets out what variables will be measured. For example, brief intervention measures to change problematic drinking patterns have to consider that follow-up will be needed to determine whether the interventions have worked.

There are several caveats to bear in mind when dealing with the assessment of effectiveness. What works in one culture may not work in another because of the different views on alcohol and its role in society, the political palatability of certain measures, and the extent of transferability of measures from society to society, for instance from the developed to the developing world.

It is also important to recognize that rigorous insistence on measurement may not always be possible, particularly when it comes to developing countries. There may be a lack of resources and technical skills to carry out evaluations; populations may be difficult to reach because of geographic isolation, high illiteracy rates, or absence of means for easy communication. In some cultures, there may be a reluctance to carry out assessment for fear of appearing critical of those who have initiated or implemented a program. Finally, when it comes to a basic economic decision between more prevention and evaluation, resources will almost invariably be allotted to prevention.

Whereas quantitative measures are certainly fairly straightforward to interpret, qualitative indicators are also important but more rarely taken into consideration. For instance, is it possible to quantify change in drinking culture? There needs to be some agreement among those who work in the prevention field and, particularly, those who attempt to assess various prevention efforts that there is a place for both qualitative and quantitative measures of effectiveness.

The complexity of assessing interventions means that many efforts are never formally evaluated. However, this raises an important issue that is largely ignored for political or other reasons. The lack of evaluation does not mean that a particular program is ineffective. It simply means that this particular program has not been evaluated, nothing more or less. Critics of various targeted intervention approaches often emphasize the lack of formal evaluation. It is important to remember that lack of evaluation is by no means proof that certain approaches *do not work*.

Selecting the Right Interventions

The first area on which to agree is what we might reasonably expect from an intervention. Clearly, a linear relationship between intervention and outcome would be the most desirable measure of success. For example, implementing intervention A should reduce harmful drinking pattern B. In reality, however, given the complexity of a behavior such as drinking and the involvement of a broad range of confounding factors, establishing such a cause-and-effect relationship is rarely possible.

Although a measured reduction in health and social harms is certainly the ultimate measure of effectiveness, it is overly limiting, because we know from research that achieving change is a process. A program or intervention can be evaluated by how it achieves steps along the continuum of change. Evaluation might therefore choose significant milestones and proxy indicators. For example, a first evaluation question might be whether the program can be implemented. What resources are required? Is it feasible to introduce and operate a particular program in a particular society? Has it been implemented as intended? What factors have facilitated or hindered its implementation? Does it deliver the product that it was designed to deliver? Does it reach its target population? Thus, we need to consider which prevention measures are easiest and most appropriate to implement. A measure that is costly to apply may not lend itself well to implementation under all circumstances.

The most desirable outcome in the long term is a change in the prevailing drinking culture that makes certain behaviors acceptable but not others, and inculcates a sense of appropriateness in drinking and the need for harm reduction in those at whom particular interventions are aimed. This is a protracted process but not an impossible task, relying on synergy between a range of approaches over time.

The Impact of Culture Change: An Example From Iceland

Concern about public drunkenness, endemic in the Icelandic culture and tradition, along with the momentum of the Temperance movement in Northern Europe and North America, led to a referendum on prohibition in Iceland in 1908. Prohibition was incrementally lifted on various beverage categories, but the prohibition on beer remained in effect until 1989.

After the Second World War, Icelandic society was no longer isolated from the rest of the world. Increased prosperity, travel, communications, and trade brought in ideas from other countries, permeating the local drinking culture. As Ólafsdóttir (1999) noted, "A part of this process was the formation of new drinking habits. Alcohol became used more frequently, and without almost every drinking situation resulting in intoxication" (p. 553).

This culture shift was accompanied by an erosion of support for the ideology of the welfare state and an increased emphasis on individualism and individual choice. Members of the new generations began to view the prohibitionist approach to alcohol policy as paternalistic. When the prohibition on beer was finally lifted in 1989, it was largely in response to a general shift in culture that included drinking patterns and a changed outlook on the relationship between individual and state, including personal responsibility.

Source: Ólafsdóttir (1999).

So, how to select, design, and implement interventions? In Chapter 3, we argued that the basis of all action in the alcohol field should be assessment—we offered the slogan "No intervention without assessment." We argued this on the basis that the complexity and variation in drinking should forewarn against "off-the-peg" solutions. In the parlance of social intervention planning, assessment is followed by the identification of suitable targets and goals. This includes *prioritization*—how important is the response? How urgently is it needed? Why is it important to act now rather than later? It includes *relevance*—is the proposed response the correct one? Could another response be more effective? If so, what would it be? It includes *feasibility*—are there any obvious obstacles to the initiative's implementation? And it includes *acceptability*—how acceptable is the intervention to the target group, stakeholders, decision-makers, and public? What obstacles might there be?

Selection and planning of programs also require specification of objectives, strategies for achieving these objectives, and specification of targets (behaviors,

Table 8.1 Intervention Planning and Choice

Objectives	Specific statements that describe what the intervention should accomplish.
Targets	The population, behavior, or context that is the object of the intervention; this should also include an indication of the required coverage of the intervention.
Outcomes	Changes occurring as a result of the intervention. Positive outcomes are sought, but there may be unintended outcomes.
Shortcomings	Negative outcomes and limitations of the intervention.
Obstacles to overcome	Societal, community, and other factors that may inhibit the introduction of the intervention, impede its implementation, or hinder its success.
Procedural requirements	The actions that need to be taken—and at which level—in order to introduce the intervention.
Resources for implementation	Required human and organizational resources.

contexts, and populations), together with consideration of the necessary resources. Human resources might, for example, be outreach workers or people with skills in advocacy work. Medical resources may include supplies needed for the intervention (for example, treatment facilities). Information resources can include administrative support or publishing equipment for producing informational leaflets and brochures. This kind of planning is summarized in the WHO's *Rapid Assessment and Response Technical Guide* (Stimson et al., 2003).

Table 8.1 offers an approach to selecting and designing interventions. The process is not solely oriented to positive outcomes: As with all social and health policies, there may be unintended and negative outcomes, and these need to be considered when deciding whether and/or how to introduce an intervention. For example, raising taxes on beverage alcohol to make it less accessible may have the undesired consequence of shifting demand to cheaper products of lower quality (Härstedt, 2004; Haworth & Simpson, 2004; Leifman, 2001; Nordlund & Österberg, 2000). Where pricing of beverage alcohol is high, noncommercial production, trade in illicit alcohol, and smuggling have been observed (European Commission, 1999; Nordlund & Österberg). Instead of reducing the demand for beverage alcohol, such measures may simply shift it to a different supply source.

Assessing how an intervention can be implemented includes identifying obstacles to be overcome. For instance, some interventions can effect changes, but rely heavily on enforcement in order to do so. Means have to be found to motivate and reward enforcement—and, for example, to minimize corruption. Interventions will also need to be appropriate to the country and target audience and require political and other support. There is only so far that governments can move while keeping all players and partners on their side.

Finally, there are differences between interventions in the procedural requirements needed for implementation. Some rely on legislative change, and all require resources to implement change. Responsibility for delivering interventions might lie with government departments, community organizations, consumer groups, producers and retailers, or professional and trade associations.

THE INTERVENTION MIX: SYNERGY IN PREVENTION

Perhaps the most important factor to keep in mind is that no intervention to reduce alcohol-related harm can be expected to be entirely successful on its own. It is unrealistic to expect that a single measure can stand alone. Effective prevention, like effective alcohol policy, rests on the synergistic implementation of a range of different approaches. Interventions that work rely on a mix of measures: some regulatory, addressing the population at large, and others aimed at individuals at risk, high-risk behaviors, or high-risk settings. They include educating individuals about drinking, while at the same time actively ensuring their safety. Ultimately, what works is a range of measures designed to achieve short-term as much as long-term results—instant rewards combined with an investment in the future.

Perhaps the best illustration of synergistic approaches to prevention is offered by efforts in many countries to reduce the harm caused by alcohol-impaired driving. A range of approaches—including the establishment of blood alcohol concentration (BAC) limits and legislation on legal drinking age, the active enforcement of these laws, and awareness-raising campaigns in schools, community centers, drinking establishments, and other public places—have played an important part in reducing harm associated with alcohol-impaired driving. Not only has there been a significant decrease in such injuries and fatalities, but also, in many countries, driving while intoxicated is generally regarded as inappropriate and unacceptable behavior. A culture shift has occurred, instilling in the minds of those who drive that drinking may not be a compatible behavior.

Much of the success of these interventions is due to the fact that reducing harm associated with alcohol-impaired driving is something on which all segments of society can agree. A concerted effort at the society, community, and individual levels stands a much better chance of success than single approaches that attempt to address an issue.

Table 8.2 examines a range of different prevention measures aimed at reducing the potential harm associated with drinking, many of which are discussed in this book. The table is intended to be used as a guide by those seeking to design, monitor, and implement alcohol policy measures that may be most suitable and practical within their particular contexts. It can be used as an aid in comparing and weighing various approaches against each other, to be updated and modified as best fits the particular circumstances in question.

For ease of reference, measures are grouped by intervention type, though policy-makers should be encouraged to think logically in terms of objectives and the strategies for achieving the objectives. For example, the reduction of alcohol-impaired driving might involve various strategies and measures—applied alone or, more probably, in combination.

Table 8.2 Feasible Interventions for Minimizing Harm

Among the many interventions that may be applied at the national or local levels and that target the population, groups, contexts, and behaviors associated with increased risk for harm, some may be implemented quickly and efficiently. These measures (highlighted) may often be implemented without major procedural or structural changes (such as changes in legislation) and many do not require intensive allocation of resources. The omission of other measures from selection does not imply that they are ineffective in minimizing harm around drinking, simply that their implementation may be more difficult. In fact, measures such as the setting of legal age limits for the consumption and purchase of beverage alcohol, random breath testing, or alcohol education are valuable tools with proven impact.

Intervention	Objectives	Target	Intended Outcomes	Unintended Outcomes	Shortcomings	Obstacles to Overcome	Procedural Requirements	Resources for Implementation
				Whole-Population Measures				
Total ban on sales	Elimination of alcohol from market	Whole population	Zero or minimal consumption Reduced abuse Reduced physical harm (chronic and acute) Reduced social cost	Rise in illicit production and trade; black market Rise in organized crime Increased availability of lower-quality beverages Reduced pleasure and benefits	Elimination of commercial sector Inconsistency with policies in neighboring countries Restricted consumer freedoms Reduced pleasure and benefits	Cultural resistance to/ acceptability of government control Consumer demand for alcohol Illicit trade Loss of revenue from taxation and pricing	Legislation for prohibition Institution of penalties for breaches	Government at national level Government at local level, where jurisdictions have autonomy Enforcement by police and customs Religious leaders and institutions

Taxation and pricing	Raise price, reduce overall consumption	Whole population	Reduced alcohol abuse and heavy drinking Reduced social cost Reduced physical harm (chronic and acute)	Reduced pleasure Reduced benefits Increased black market Increased cross-border trade Increased illicit production Increased consumption of low-quality beverages Social inequality of access/affordability	Loss of revenue Individual responsibility not encouraged Inconsistency with policies in neighboring countries	Cultural resistance Requires education for acceptance	Legislation Standards for taxation rates	Government at national level Government at local level, where jurisdictions have autonomy Adequate and efficient enforcement Collection of revenue Private sector needed for implementation Commercial market/products
Government monopoly of retail sales	Regulated access to alcohol	Whole population	Limited private sector involvement Increased government revenue Reduced alcohol abuse Reduced social problems	Limited free market and trade Impact on economy around production, distribution, and sale Restricted private sector Rise in illicit production and trade; black market	Inconsistency with policies in neighboring countries Restricted consumer freedoms Limited choice	Cultural resistance to/ acceptability of government control Harmonization of regional alcohol policies Traditionally unresponsive to consumer demand	Legislation	Government at national level Government at local level, where jurisdictions have autonomy Infrastructure for retail Enforcement through police force Customs and border control agencies for law enforcement and monitoring of cross-border trade and black market

continued

Table 8.2 (continued) Feasible Interventions for Minimizing Harm

Intervention	Objectives	Target	Intended Outcomes	Unintended Outcomes	Shortcomings	Obstacles to Overcome	Procedural Requirements	Resources for Implementation
Whole-Population Measures (continued)								
Government monopoly of retail sales (continued)				Rise in organized crime Shifts trade to neighboring jurisdictions Impact on social outcomes, such as drinking and driving across borders				
Restricted hours and days of sale	Limited access to alcohol	Whole population	Reduced consumption Reduced alcohol abuse Reduced social problems	Inconsistency with policies in neighboring countries Restricted consumer freedoms	Increased availability of lower-quality beverages Limited free market and trade Impact on economy around production, distribution, and sale Loss of revenue Shifts trade to neighboring countries	Cultural resistance to/ acceptability of government control Harmonization of regional alcohol policies Unresponsive to consumer demand	Legislation Institution of penalties for breaches of regulation	Government at national level Government at local level, where jurisdictions have autonomy Enforcement through police force Customs and border control agencies for law enforcement and monitoring of cross-border trade and black market

Restrictions on advertising and promotions	Reduce consumption by reducing enticement to purchase	Whole population May also target groups (e.g., sports audiences, and young people)	Reduced harmful drinking, especially among young people	Restriction of commercial freedoms Disregard of beneficial aspects of alcohol consumption Limited brand information Restriction on funds to TV/radio programming, sports, and arts from alcohol advertising/sponsorships	Does not take other influences into account (e.g., family and peer influences)	Consumer demand for alcohol Advertising practices in neighboring jurisdictions, the Internet, and the media	Legislated regulatory or self-regulatory framework	Government at national level Enforcement mechanism
Responsible drinking messages	Reduce consumption by alerting consumers to health hazards of immoderate consumption	Whole population Target groups (e.g., women and young people)	Reduce abusive drinking patterns and harm Encourage responsible drinking	None	Longer-term approach: awareness building and information Implementation best when combined with other measures (e.g., education)	Perception of industry motivation in messages Prevailing drinking culture	Legislated regulatory or self-regulatory framework	Producers of beverage alcohol Advertisers and the media

continued

Table 8.2 (continued) Feasible Interventions for Minimizing Harm

Intervention	Objectives	Target	Intended Outcomes	Unintended Outcomes	Shortcomings	Obstacles to Overcome	Procedural Requirements	Resources for Implementation
					Targeted Measures: Groups at Risk			
Minimum legal purchase/ drinking age	Elimination of drinking under legal age	Young people under the legal purchase and drinking age	Prevention of health and social problems among those below legal age; Adherence to law	Impact on social outcomes, such as drinking and driving across borders; Drives underage drinking underground; Criminalization of underage drinking	Legal purchase and drinking ages vary across countries; Inconsistency between age of majority and legal age of purchase; Incongruity with reality of drinking among young people; Does not teach responsible drinking patterns; Inconsistency of legal age across neighboring jurisdictions	Drinking culture among young people; Permissiveness of drinking under legal age; Lack of viable alternatives to drinking for many young people; Ignorance about drinking patterns and relationship to outcomes; Ignorance about legal age in many countries; Lack of enforcement	Legislation; Enforcement and implementation of punitive measures for breaches of regulation	Government at national level; Government at local level, where jurisdictions have autonomy; Educators, medical professionals, social workers, and others to pass information; Training, education, and awareness building (e.g., through public campaigns); Compliance among retailers and servers; Effective enforcement measures; Community support; Parents, guardians, and other adult role models

School-based education	Educate young people about alcohol and its effects; Reduced drinking under legal drinking age; Reduced problems among young people	Young people	Abstinence under minimum mandated age; Responsible and moderate drinking (as legally permissible); Raised awareness; Harm reduction	Raised interest in alcohol; Interest in alternative psychoactive substances	Evaluation suggests that behavior changes are not immediate; Longer-term approach: awareness building and provision of information; Implementation best when combined with other measures	Influence of parents and peers; Didactic approach may not resonate with young people; Active participation of young people needed; Does not reach marginalized groups due to attrition from schools (e.g., in many developing countries)	Education policy	Education system and school boards for integration into school curricula; Teachers, parents, and students; Training of teachers and educators; NGOs, beverage alcohol industry (e.g., social aspects organizations [SAOs]), and others to develop and sponsor programs; Community leaders; Funding for development of materials, training, and implementation
Life skills	Reduction of heavy or harmful drinking patterns	Young people	Behavior change and awareness building around responsible drinking		Does not focus exclusively on drinking; Longer-term approach: awareness building and information	Attrition from schools, especially in developing countries; Requires involvement of parents and others	Education or health policy	Can be integrated into existing programs and education measures; Community, educators, and religious leaders; Range of programs for young people

continued

Table 8.2 (continued) Feasible Interventions for Minimizing Harm

Intervention	Objectives	Target	Intended Outcomes	Unintended Outcomes	Shortcomings	Obstacles to Overcome	Procedural Requirements	Resources for Implementation
			Targeted Measures: Groups at Risk (continued)					
Life skills (continued)			Integration of responsible drinking with healthy lifestyles and decision-making Addressing hard-to-reach populations		Behavior changes may not be immediate	Requires commitment from teachers to learn/teach the program		Funding for development of materials, training, and implementation NGOs, beverage alcohol industry (e.g., SAOs), and others to develop and sponsor programs
Early identification and brief intervention	Early prevention of harm in those at risk	Nondependent problem drinkers	Modify harmful drinking patterns Reduce risk for social and physical harm	Patients lie to medical practitioners		Reluctance to undergo screening Ensuring follow-up Social stigma of drinking problems	Integration into health care system Referral for treatment, where appropriate	Any health care setting (e.g., pharmacy, emergency room, clinic, or doctor's office) Availability of screening instruments Training of practitioners in screening Treatment resources available Technology resources for Internet-based tools

Targeted Measures: Contexts

Server training	Reduced incidence of intoxication Reduced violence and public disorder Reduced potential for harm and injury Reduced liability for outlet owners and operators	Licensed premises and other public venues	Reduced violence Reduced public disorder Reduced alcohol-impaired driving Reduced intoxication Reduced liability for outlet owners and operators	Decreased sales Shifts heavy drinking to home or other venues	Ignores nondisruptive heavy drinkers Implementation best when combined with other measures (e.g., education and campaigns)	General support needed Cost for hospitality and retail sector operators	Possible linkage to licensing requirements Insurance and liability Self-enforcement needed	Retail and service sector outlet owners, managers, and staff Producers of beverage alcohol Incentives or penalties needed Training of staff Broad coverage of outlets and trade support Police presence National or regional government Community support
Restrictions on density of serving and retail outlets	Reduced access to alcohol	Entertainment and retail districts	Reduced incidents of violence and public disorder Reduced heavy drinking	Shifts heavy drinking to home or other venues Reduced revenue generation for businesses and communities	Reduced competition, selection, and choice	Consumer demand Resistance from retailers Political interests	Licensing and zoning laws	Community support Enforcement Changes in infrastructure (e.g., transportation)
Local accords and community action	Reduced social harm	Communities/ areas where harm indicators are high	Prevention of violence, crime, and disorder		Focus on immediate community concerns, not long-range goals	Lack of communication between sectors of community	Enforcement needed Repercussions for breach of accord	Community support and involvement

continued

Table 8.2 (continued) Feasible Interventions for Minimizing Harm

Intervention	Objectives	Target	Intended Outcomes	Unintended Outcomes	Shortcomings	Obstacles to Overcome	Procedural Requirements	Resources for Implementation
Targeted Measures: Contexts (continued)								
Local accords and community action (continued)			Efficient use of available resources Involvement of all segments of community; general support		May be motivated by political expediency			Involved police, media, local government, retailers and servers, insurance providers, community and religious leaders, educators, and others Mechanism for communication Leadership
Breath testing in high-injury-risk workplaces	Reduced risk for harm	Workplace	Reduced accidents and injury to self and others Increased awareness/ deterrence	May neglect low-profile issues	Needs to be supplemented by employee support programs	Cultural resistance	Legislation or voluntary codes and self-regulation by employers and professional groups	Employer support Resources for testing needed Implementation of penalties Employee training
Targeted Measures: Behaviors								
Social norms marketing	Reduction of heavy drinking	Extreme drinking (especially among youth)	Instilling realistic expectancies and attitudes toward drinking	Responsible drinking among young people Reduced incidence of abusive drinking patterns and harm	Longer-term approach: awareness building and information	Misperceptions of peer drinking behavior may be hard to overcome	Education or health policy	Educators, school boards, and university governance bodies Integration into school curriculum

		Reduction of health and social harm	Realistic expectancies and attitudes around drinking	Behavior changes may not be immediate	Drinking culture among young people, for example on college/university campuses		Funding for development of materials, training, and implementation
Social norms marketing (continued)	Reduced drinking and driving						
Random breath testing/ sobriety checkpoints	Driving under the influence of alcohol	Reduced irresponsible drinking Increased awareness Sober driving, driving below legal BAC limits Reduced accidents, injuries, and mortality from road traffic crashes Encourage designated drivers or alternative transportation	Limited access to outlets relying on driving Impact on rural economy Discriminatory targeting of enforcement (e.g., ethnic groups)	Infringement of personal freedoms Inconvenience to sober drivers Diversion of resources Implementation best when combined with other measures (e.g., education and awareness campaigns)	Broad-based support Cultural/societal views on individual freedoms Corruption around enforcement Access to alternative transportation helpful	Legislation	Government at national or local level Police enforcement Training of police; equipment and resources for implementation Campaigns to raise awareness Beverage alcohol industry: retailers and servers Community support

Clearly, every measure has its strengths and weaknesses, and no single approach is a panacea. What we have attempted to demonstrate is that the criterion for selecting a particular intervention is not just whether there is available scientific evidence for effectiveness. Other criteria include what is feasible, what can be realistically accomplished, and what can be implemented with the resources available. The key criteria for the selection of some measures over others are that they do not require procedural or structural changes, or intensive allocation of resources.

Not every available measure is listed here, and the outcomes (intended or otherwise) and mode of implementation may well differ from country to country. As well as being an aide-memoire to common interventions, Table 8.2 (together with the checklist in Table 8.1) serves as a useful reminder to policy-makers of some of the things that need to be considered when selecting, designing, and implementing interventions.

INTERVENTIONS AND PARTNERSHIPS

The debate in alcohol policies about which measures are most effective has become unnecessarily polarized in recent years. The advocates of population-level measures discount the value of targeted interventions, whereas proponents of targeted interventions are largely critical of across-the-board measures and their reliance on regulation and enforcement. As the drink-driving example shows, it is possible and, indeed, desirable for these two approaches to work in tandem.

The most successful efforts in reducing harm involve a combination of population and targeted intervention approaches, implemented at the society, community, and individual level. Although many individual programs have not been evaluated, the totality of their efforts has produced change. There is certainly a need for more rigorous evaluation and the resources to achieve that goal. A better understanding of what is achievable in countries with limited resources is also desirable. This requires better understanding of how various institutions and organizations can work together. Most of the interventions listed in Table 8.2 clearly require cooperation among a wide range of potential partners. Quite simply, interventions cannot be introduced in opposition to major organizations or groupings in the population. Many need active cooperation, support, and endorsement in order to be implemented and to work successfully. Reducing alcohol-related harms is "everybody's business"—including consumers, producers, retailers, educators, law enforcers, and governments. In the next chapters, we turn to the themes of partnerships and how to find common ground among the different key players.

REFERENCES

Babor, T. F., Caetano, R., Caswell, S., Edwards, G., Giesbrecht, N., Graham, K., et al. (2003). *Alcohol: No ordinary commodity. Research and public policy.* Oxford: Oxford University Press.

European Commission. (1999, February 17). *Communication from the Commission to the Council concerning the employment aspects of the decision to abolish tax- and duty-free sales for intra-community travellers.* Brussels, Belgium: Author.

Härstedt, K. (2004). *Vår gar gränsen?* [*Where do we set the limit?*] Stockholm: Statens Offentliga Utredningar.

Haworth, A., & Simpson, R. (Eds.). (2004). *Moonshine markets: Issues in unrecorded alcohol beverage production and consumption.* New York: Brunner-Routledge.

Leifman, H. (2001). Homogenisation in alcohol consumption in the European Union. *Nordisk Alkohol- & Narkotikatidskrift, 18*(English Suppl.), 15–30.

Nordlund, S., & Österberg, E. (2000). Unrecorded alcohol consumption: Economics and its effects on alcohol control in the Nordic countries. *Addiction, 95*(Suppl. 4), S551–S564.

Ólafsdóttir, H. (1999). The entrance of beer into a persistent spirits culture. *Contemporary Drug Problems, 26*, 545–576.

Stimson, G. V., Donoghoe, M. C., Fitch, C., Rhodes, T., Ball, A., & Weiler, G. (2003). *Rapid assessment and response: Technical guide, TG-RAR.* Geneva, Switzerland: WHO Department of HIV/AIDS, Department of Child and Adolescent Health and Development.

World Health Organization. (2004). *World Health Organization: Basic texts.* 44th ed. Retrieved August 18, 2005, from http://www.who.int/governance/en/.

9

Key Players and Partnerships

MAXIMIZING BENEFIT AND MINIMIZING HARM

Policies are generally intended to provide a framework within which benefits can be maximized and harms minimized. Policy design must be based on the best available evidence and a balance between rights and responsibilities of those whom the policies will affect—individuals, communities, governments, nongovernmental and civil society organizations, and the private sector. How the final balance is achieved may vary according to the particular area in question, societal views on the relationship between the individual and the state, and the public palatability of measures.

Different societies balance individual freedom and state control differently. Some are willing to accept considerable state control, if it seems to be for the public good. Others emphasize the freedom of the individual and disapprove of state intervention in their daily lives. Although there may be a general tendency within a given society toward one end of the spectrum or the other, the position taken also depends on the area being regulated. In the United States, for example, high value is generally placed on the freedom of businesses to operate relatively unfettered in the marketplace, with a general tendency toward deregulation of the commercial sector. At the same time, there seems to be a willingness to accept quite severe restrictions in other areas, particularly at the individual level, as compared with what is found in some other countries—for example, minimum drinking age, speed limits, or possession of cannabis. The notion of "less government," thus, does not necessarily equate with less regulation in every area of daily life.

The balance between what is required of the individual and what is expected of the state not only varies according to the area being regulated (taxes or minimum drinking age) but also changes over time, so that alcohol prohibition in the United States was publicly accepted for a short period. On the whole, however, the trend in most countries over the course of the twentieth century has probably been for a bigger role for government in regulating individual behavior. In some cases, the increased regulation has been dictated by technological change. As automobiles became more powerful and faster, so it became necessary to introduce licenses to drive them, which could only be obtained by passing a driving test. This was primarily introduced to protect the public from the possible dangerous behavior of bad drivers. In the case of cigarette smoking in public places, we have seen a move over time from virtually complete freedom for the smoker to a high level of restriction in many countries, aimed at protecting nonsmokers.

There is, however, another motivation for such regulation: to protect people from *their own* possibly dangerous behavior. This can be seen, for instance, in the requirement for the drivers of cars to wear seat belts, and it is the reasoning behind the restrictions on the availability of alcohol. Even in such cases, however, the argument is that society as a whole suffers if one of its members is injured or dies, let alone generates any resultant health costs that may have to be borne by the wider society. The availability of health care is not infinitely elastic, and, in many countries, it is available to large numbers of people for little or no direct payment, either through government funding or through employer-assisted contributions to health insurance. In whatever way, however, it represents a cost to society, and individuals have to accept that their right to live in a modern society relies on taking some responsibility for their own health. A compromise must thus be reached between unbridled individual pursuits and social obligations. Yet, other legal restrictions exist to express certain moral positions, and these, too, vary over time. In the United Kingdom, for instance, we have seen the decriminalization of homosexual behavior in the 1960s and, more recently, the criminalization of fox hunting with hounds. It is being oversimplistic to postulate a trend one way or another with regard to individual freedom.

As with other issues, alcohol consumption can be looked at in terms of the spectrum that lies between the collective exercise of responsibility at one end and individual responsibility at the other. The burden of responsibility for managing the risks can be thought of as lying with society as a whole, or the emphasis can be placed on individual freedom and individual responsibility for preventing and managing the harm. We need, therefore, to strike the right balance between allowing people to decide how to behave, while not allowing that behavior to damage the health and wellbeing of others. Within all this, there is a need also to examine the role of the beverage alcohol industry (manufacturers and distributors) in reducing the possible harms that can arise from the consumption of its products. We need to look at imposed government regulation and contrast it with self-regulation by the alcohol industry and by individuals. Ultimately, a balance is always found between these positions, for there will always be good arguments for some government regulation. Public demand for unencumbered access to alcohol must be met with the ability to protect at-risk populations (through information, treatment, and prevention) and to reduce the potential for high-risk situations. In particular, government should be responsible for protecting those who are not fully able to make their own choices—for example, children or minors—although even there, one has to achieve a balance of responsibility between the state and the family.

There is considerable variation among countries in the salience of alcohol: In some, there is almost total disregard at the political level, whereas in others, it is a high priority on the political and public agendas. Within society, views on alcohol vary not only among different sectors involved in the field of alcohol policy—governments, industry, the scientific community, and nongovernmental organizations (NGOs)—but also among various players *within* each sector. The challenge in developing alcohol policies is to create an approach broad enough in scope and emphasis to be capable of involving and satisfying societies, communities, and individuals.

ROLE OF GOVERNMENT

"Government" is not a single entity. Different departments within government have different perspectives on alcohol. For example, finance departments are likely to be conscious of their significant reliance on alcohol taxes and may be reluctant to raise them as a means of regulating consumption if there is a risk that total revenue will fall. Agriculture and industry departments may have a general inclination against regulation and may support the alcohol production and hospitality industries as important players in the economy. Tourism and entertainment departments may wish to support the role of alcohol beverages as a contributing factor to quality of life and leisure. Justice departments are likely to have a more ambivalent position, but given their likely involvement in regulation of bar opening hours, public order, and so on, they are more likely to align themselves with health departments.

Health departments, meanwhile, are likely to give more priority to controlling consumption as part of their wider remit to improve public health. Traditionally, the role of publicly provided health services has concentrated rather narrowly on the provision of treatment services (through hospitals) and primary care in the community. Essentially, the traditional model has looked more like an "illness service" than a health service. More recently, driven by increases in the elderly population and the growing demand for and cost of treating chronic conditions in many societies, the idea of a governmental role in encouraging the population to maintain good health has gained currency. However, in most countries the health improvement agenda is still a rather minor and nonprioritized part of the overall picture, attracting neither adequate funding nor prestige for practitioners.

The cost of publicly funded health services tends to increase at rates well beyond those of general inflation or other government programs. There are many reasons for this, including the relatively high staff intensity of services and the increasing real-term costs of technology and drugs. This tends to lead to resistance from other government departments, which may see their own budgets threatened. The result is (at least perceived) constant pressure on health budgets and difficulty in securing adequate funding for services that are not viewed as urgent or do not seem to offer quick and visible results.

Who—if Anyone—Leads on Policy?

There is much room for dispute as to which government department is "in the lead" on alcohol policy. In many cases, the real answer is "none." However, in a changing climate of concern about increased consumption and associated health (and public order) risks, it would seem easier for health departments to obtain a clear lead where they have the will to do so. In practice, particularly where there is a vacuum in policy, the ground can be taken by whichever player feels more strongly about a given issue; or, in the case of politicians, a new policy drive can emerge in response to lobbying or the need for a novel eye-catching initiative.

Politics and Politicians

The first question to address is whether politicians are interested in alcohol policy—and if they are not, how to get their interest. For example, in many developing countries, alcohol problems are not perceived as an important issue, owing to the severity of other social and economic predicaments. The policy strategies, programs, and interventions under such conditions must be pertinent to the needs of the people, who are more concerned about hunger and unemployment than about changing problem drinking patterns. To reach consensus on a sustainable alcohol policy under such conditions, coordination among a number of sectors and priorities is necessary. A sensible alcohol policy proposal should be able to alleviate, or at least not ignore, these macro problems.

Policy-making is a complex process of articulating diverse political, theoretical, and technical points of view. Based on science, tradition, religion, prejudices, or ideologies, these views often oppose each other with as much hostility as political factions. Achieving equilibrium among competing powers—important for reaching stable policy agreements—is never guaranteed. Any political agreement may eventually weaken and collapse.

In many developing countries, the lone advocates for alcohol policies are in the public health sector, particularly in the area of mental health, but their access to the decision-making levels is usually insignificant when compared with the influence of the business community, including producers or importers of alcohol beverages. Ultimately, the enactment of a policy depends on the politicians' response to the clashing evidence and opinions presented before them. Such response often reflects the volatile balance of political and economic forces, rather than scientific or empirical evidence.

What can be done to change the terms of debate on the low priority for health improvement policies and the difficulty of finding money for policies where the payoff is likely to be long term (and so, in political terms, invisible)? The main arguments may have to be pragmatic: first, the avoidable costs of alcohol-related injuries, the economic loss through sickness and absenteeism, and the increasing costs to health services of both acute treatment of alcohol-related incidents and continuing treatment of chronic conditions resulting from problem drinking; then social benefits of responsible drinking patterns. These arguments can be backed by the more general need to improve public health against a backdrop of longer life expectancy in many societies.

Social policies are inherently complex and interact with each other. Health improvement, thus, needs to be seen in a holistic way (of which alcohol is only one aspect) rather than as a set of isolated streams of policy initiatives. At the same time, governments are facing more general difficulties in exercising their traditional roles. Globalization and reductions in tariff barriers make it more difficult to enforce tax policies (including those on alcohol) that are at odds with the policies of neighboring countries.

The trend for governments to become more involved in micromanagement of society coincides with growing individualism and diminishing respect for authority. Changes in the nature of society, including more openness, also mean less coherent hierarchical structures of government administration. As a consequence, local administrations and agencies are gaining more acceptance and legitimacy, and voluntary and nonprofit bodies are finding a bigger role to play in forming and implementing public policy.

What does this mean for the role of government? Although the traditional rule-making role remains, the way in which rules are developed and enforced may require rethinking. The main threads for successful government action on alcohol seem to be the following: Create a climate in which people recognize the need for an effective alcohol policy; establish and promote a clear factual basis for the policy; develop measures openly and with full participation of all parties likely to be involved in policy delivery and implementation; then champion the policy and ensure that government's own health delivery services give the policy priority and, for example, provide effective support for other deliverers. Fundamentally, government is unlikely to act effectively on its own without the cooperation of a wider range of agencies and groups.

WHAT CAN SCIENTIFIC COMMUNITIES CONTRIBUTE?

The scientific community in the alcohol field draws its membership from many different scientific and professional disciplines. This includes medical practitioners and medical scientists, psychologists, epidemiologists and public health specialists, social scientists, pharmacologists and biochemists, geneticists, and others from a laboratory science background. The science of alcohol and alcohol problems is hardly free of personal and political considerations. The intensity of views on the causes, nature, and treatment of alcohol problems is far greater than one typically sees in other areas of scientific endeavor.

Major Scientific Groups Specializing in Alcohol Research

Alcohol epidemiology and public health scientists are prominent in many national and international societies. One example is the Kettil Bruun Society for Social and Epidemiological Research on Alcohol (KBS), named after a famous Finnish scientist and established in 1987. The society emphasizes the essential link between the level of alcohol consumption and harm. A leading theory underlying these scientists' views is the continuous distribution of consumption model proposed originally by Ledermann (1956). The model states that as alcohol consumption increases in the society, so does the presence of hazardous drinking and dependence. According to this view, a fundamental means to reduce alcohol problems in society is to control overall consumption.

The *alcohol policy community* is closely related to the public health group. It draws upon the scientific evidence that links the level and frequency of alcohol consumption to various types of alcohol-related harm. It is also concerned that public policy be developed with a keen eye on its implications for public health and welfare. There is considerable overlap between this group and the alcohol epidemiologists. Many scientists in this group have been prominent in the World Health Organization. Important examples of this group's scientific output are the books *Alcohol Policy and the Public Good* (Edwards et al., 1994), and *Alcohol: No Ordinary Commodity* (Babor et al., 2003).

The *biomedical alcohol societies* are a variety of professional organizations. These include, for example, the International Society for Biomedical Research on Alcoholism (ISBRA), the European Society for Biomedical Research on Alcoholism (ESBRA), and the Japanese Medical Society of Alcohol Studies (JMSAS). Members of such societies tend to focus on biological and neuropsychological processes and are primarily concerned with three main issues: the effect of alcohol at an individual level, the fundamental mechanisms by which repeated alcohol consumption causes dependence and various types of organ damage, and the risk factors that lead to alcohol use disorders. In recent years, many such societies have expanded their brief to encompass prevention, epidemiology, and public health. They are not especially wedded to a control of consumption approach. Instead, they hold the view that understanding the risk factors and effects of alcohol consumption offers a greater prospect of dealing with alcohol use disorders effectively and without undue impact on the rest of the community. Such societies have been criticized by some commentators for not contributing much to the policy debate and for keeping to what others consider a narrow paradigm of understanding.

The *International Council on Alcohol and Addictions (ICAA)* is a well-established international NGO, founded in 1907 and headquartered in Switzerland. It is a broad-based organization with members principally drawn from the social sciences, psychology, and clinical practice. Each year, ICAA holds international conferences as well as regional and special interest meetings. Its conferences are particularly popular among practitioners, and there is usually a substantial participation from middle-income and developing countries. In 1968, ICAA broadened its scope to include a range of drugs and addictive behaviors.

There is considerable variation in *national alcohol research societies.* Some societies, such as the U.S.-based Research Society on Alcoholism, focus almost entirely on alcohol. In many other countries, such societies also focus on addiction to prescribed and illicit drugs and tobacco. The pioneer society, the Society for the Study and Cure of Inebriety, was established in the United Kingdom in 1884. Now called the Society for the Study of Addiction (SSA), it is the parent society of *Addiction*, one of the highest-rating scientific journals in the field of addictions. The Australian Professional Society on Alcohol and Other Drugs (APSAD) is an example of a more recently founded society (it celebrated its 25th anniversary in 2006). Like the SSA, APSAD holds an annual scientific conference and attracts a wide audience from Australasia and the Asia–Pacific region.

Medical academies and colleges are primarily responsible for the training of medical practitioners in addiction medicine and for accrediting them as competent clinicians. For example, the Finish Society of Addiction Medicine provides specialist training and seminars to doctors and nurses, and encourages clinical research through awards. Another example is the Australasian Chapter of Addiction Medicine, which is part of the Royal Australasian College of Physicians. Possession of the Fellowship of the Chapter of Addiction Medicine is regarded as an essential qualification for the practice in specialty in Australia and New Zealand.

Scientists and Policy-makers

Alcohol scientists do not form a unified community. Indeed, this sector is often driven by disputes and antagonism. For example, in 2003, a national forum was planned in New Zealand to promote the exchange of research and opinion on alcohol policy and programs. The forum was organized by the Alcohol Advisory Council, the formal body in New Zealand that advises government on policy, service development, and access to services. The undertaking was designed to engage a range of actors and sectors concerned with alcohol and the prevention of alcohol-related harm. Those invited included scientists working in epidemiology, public health, and community studies; practitioners involved in medical disciplines, including psychiatry; representatives of injury prevention and domestic violence organizations; treatment and other service providers; and representatives of the alcohol beverage industry. However, an influential group of scientists within New Zealand considered it inappropriate to involve industry representatives in the development of national policy and programs on alcohol. As a result, the meeting was canceled a week before its set date and the opportunity for exchange of scientific information and opinion was lost.

This salutary tale raises the important issue of the role of scientists. Are they dispassionate seekers of truth or advocates for a particular policy perspective? The role of science may have changed from the objective exploration and testing of scientific theory to a greater attempt at making science "relevant" to policy and program development. Should the traditional gulf between the generation of knowledge on the one hand and decision-making on the other remain, especially in a politically charged area such as alcohol studies? This is an issue on which the scientific alcohol community is deeply divided, and where any attempt at resolution will be challenging.

THE RANGE AND ROLE OF NONGOVERNMENTAL ORGANIZATIONS IN ALCOHOL POLICY AND SERVICES

Nongovernmental organizations (NGOs) have historically played major roles across an array of service, policy, advocacy, and industry sectors. NGOs have been particularly influential in democratic countries and are considered an important linchpin of civil society. This is not the case in all countries. In developing and transitional countries, there may be a lack of tradition of such civil society activity, suspicion about the role and intentions of NGOs, and barriers to their operation.

Nongovernmental Organizations Working in the Alcohol Field

The NGO sector may be divided into three broad groups: organizations that function as service agencies, as advocacy and/or policy bodies, or as representatives of industry. A few examples of these broad NGO types demonstrate the breadth of this sector's activity as well as the sometimes complementary and divergent missions, values, and goals that various NGOs pursue.

Some alcohol NGOs are driven by service, treatment, support, education, and prevention. They are typically community-based and focus on treating persons with alcohol dependence or alcohol problems, providing counseling and offering support to clients' family members, and/or increasing public awareness about the potential consequences of alcohol-related health problems (for example, Alcoholics Anonymous and Alcohol Focus Scotland). These NGOs are connected to and often represented by umbrella service and professional associations (such as the Federation of Drug and Alcohol Professionals in the United Kingdom and the Alcohol Advisory Council of New Zealand). Through such organizations, public policy relating to alcohol laws and regulation is influenced at provincial and national policy levels, in both the legislative/parliamentary and executive/administrative branches of government.

A second category of NGOs has a primary interest in alcohol policy and advocacy. An example of one such NGO is the Indian Alcohol Policy Alliance (IAPA), organized in 2004 in New Delhi to provide "a forum for alcohol policy" and to disseminate "information on alcohol policies and best practice in policy advocacy" (Hariharan, 2005, p. 6). Another such NGO is the Alcohol Policy

Network (APN), a project of the Ontario Public Health Association in Canada. APN describes itself as "a network of over 1000 individuals and organizations across Ontario concerned about the impact of alcohol on our friends, families, and communities" (Alcohol Policy Network, 2005, para. 1).

The third group of alcohol NGOs is those considered to be "trade associations" representing one or more aspects of the "industry" (distillers, retailers, bartenders, and so on). Most of these associations are funded by the industry and/or through membership dues from individual and corporate members. A major element of such NGOs is to protect their constituencies from what they consider to be "overregulation." For example, the Web site of the American Beverage Institute (ABI) states, "The ABI is a restaurant trade association dedicated to protecting the on-premise dining experience—which often includes the responsible consumption of adult beverages" (American Beverage Institute [ABI], 2005, para. 1).

Also sponsored by the industry are the social aspects organizations (SAOs). A reflection of the industry's wish to play a more proactive role in alcohol-related social policy, SAOs promote the idea of responsible alcohol consumption and generally focus on four main topics: alcohol education, alcohol-impaired driving, sensible drinking for those who choose to drink, and self-regulation of industry marketing practices (Orley, 2005). Building partnerships is an important component of SAOs' activities. Today, over 30 SAOs exist, based mainly in Europe and North America, but also in Africa and Australasia (Orley). Examples of social aspects organizations include the Industry Association for Responsible Alcohol Use (ARA) in South Africa, Enterprise and Prévention in France, and the Century Council in the United States.

NGOs: Synergy or Clash of Cultures?

When reviewing the purposes and stated philosophies of the different types of alcohol NGOs, there often seem to be relatively few points where "positive" synergy among the organizations is likely. This is particularly apparent in how the organizations representing the first and second categories of NGOs—the service, treatment, and education agencies and alcohol policy/advocacy organizations—and the third group, the trade and industry representative organizations, view each other.

This perspective is voiced from the industry viewpoint by the American Beverage Institute: "We [ABI] also expose and vigorously counter the campaigns of modern-day prohibitionists who seek to target these sensible adults in an effort to reduce per capita consumption of adult beverages" (ABI, 2005, para. 2). Nor is the rhetoric from the service, treatment, and education and policy/advocacy sectors much kinder in expressing their impression of the industry. The U.S.-based Center for Science in the Public Interest (CSPI) stated in the description of its Alcohol Policies Project, "The alcoholic-beverage industry's relentless marketing and powerful political influence, coupled with ineffective governmental alcohol policy, contribute to . . . [an] ongoing public health and safety epidemic" (Center for Science in the Public Interest, 2003, para. 3).

Given the current climate of conflicting and even competitive perspectives and widely divergent goals that characterize the various segments of the alcohol NGO community, promoting positive synergy and collaboration will be difficult. This is not to say that no efforts are being made to bridge the "alcohol NGO divide." Some of the alcohol studies and policy organizations have established working, and funding, relationships with industry; and some major players in the alcohol industry have funded and/or mounted prevention and responsible use campaigns. Too often, however, such collaborations and strategies are viewed as having inherent "conflicts of interests" (for example, an alcohol policy organization that receives funding from an industry source may be seen by others in its sector as "selling out") or being "self-serving" (for example, when a beverage producer or trade association launches an awareness campaign through the media, it may be viewed as "manipulating a gullible consumer audience").

Is there leadership in the NGO community that can effectively promote common ground and serve as a convener of a forum for interaction and collaboration among the various components of the alcohol NGO sector? A meeting of NGOs and professional associations convened by WHO in April 2006 did not succeed in resolving this issue in a comprehensive way, because only NGOs from the first and second categories were invited. Whether any of the existing international "umbrella" alcohol policy or study organizations can assume this challenge of sector leadership remains to be seen.

THE PRIVATE SECTOR:
PROFIT MOTIVE AND SOCIAL RESPONSIBILITY

The debate over the role of the beverage alcohol industry rages in almost every public policy discussion of alcohol. Although the industry—composed of producers, retailers, and the hospitality sector—asserts a role in helping prevent harmful use of its products, others contend that the profit motive is in inherent conflict with public health goals. Controversy over involvement of the private sector in public policy development is by no means confined to the alcohol field. It is argued that the profit motive of business in general makes it an inherently unacceptable partner in public policy issues (see, for example, Drummond, 2005). At the same time, it may be argued that business represents an important stakeholder, whose interests go well beyond short-term profits to embrace the wellbeing of the consuming public as well as the economic viability of the enterprise.

The origins of this debate can be traced back to the 1960s, when the activist Saul Alinsky codified strategies and tactics to guide groups seeking to harness fears about the role of business in public policy. His famous book, *Rules for Radicals*, sought to establish a clear contrast between activist and the establishment (Alinsky, 1971/1989). Perhaps, his last rule summarizes them all: "Pick the target, freeze it, personalize it, and polarize it" (p. 130). Alinsky's polarization approach has been challenged by the many successful partnerships among governments, the private sector, and civil society based upon mutual commitment to goals that simultaneously build business, social, health, and economic value. The role of business in these efforts has been variously labeled as *corporate citizenship, corporate social responsibility,* or *sustainability.*

Discussions about the appropriate role for the beverage alcohol industry in public health debates mirror the polarization versus partnership debate. For some, any role for the beverage alcohol industry in the formulation and implementation of alcohol policy is inappropriate. The claim stems from the belief that the industry's commercial interests are in direct conflict with public health aims. This paints the picture of an industry that is exclusively profit-driven and preoccupied with encouraging consumption, often through "aggressive" marketing and promotions (for example, "Drinking It In," 2002). Therefore, alcohol policy should be formulated "without interference from commercial interests" (Jenkins & Hines, 2003; Lantos, 2001; World Health Organization Regional Office for Europe, 2005). Under this view, the role of the industry should be exclusively confined to ensuring that its products are safe and that its marketing is wholly responsible, whereas wider considerations are the preserve of the "public health" community (Barry, 2002).

In contrast, much of the global beverage alcohol industry believes it has a business interest and a legitimate role in helping to prevent harmful use of its products. The industry is increasingly composed of larger enterprises, many of which take a long-term view of business success. They recognize that they need to preserve their "license to operate" and that harmful use of alcohol is a negative factor that affects their reputation. The industry members also look to attract the best talent they can find in a market where competition is intense. They know they will not attract, retain, and motivate talented individuals if it is perceived that the industry is unethical. Companies selling alcohol for on-premise or off-premise consumption want the drinking environment to be a pleasurable and positive experience that customers will repeat. Drunkenness, violence, and other undesirable behaviors in the selling and serving environment are hardly conducive to this. These and other considerations drive the beverage alcohol industry to the conclusion that responsible consumption by consumers is not only the right thing to do—it is in the industry's commercial interest (Allied Domecq, 2005; Asahi Breweries Group, 2005; Diageo, 2005; Heineken NV, 2004; SAB Miller, 2005; V&S Group, 2003; Worldwide Brewing Alliance, 2003).

The beverage alcohol industry argues that it cannot be expected to support policies that directly affect its interests, but in which it has had no say. But, perhaps more importantly, industry may contribute perspectives on policy that result in more effective policy outcomes. For example, the formulation of policy on advertising and marketing can benefit from the vast knowledge held by the industry and experience gained by its self-regulation. This is the case in other areas, such as policy governing the sale of beverage alcohol in the retail environment, where regulation and targeted interventions have potential synergistic effects.

Industry Initiatives to Reduce Harmful Alcohol Use

For over 75 years, the beverage alcohol industry has sponsored initiatives designed to reduce the harmful use of alcohol, an effort that has intensified over time. Today, these contributions include a wide range of initiatives, such as discouraging alcohol-impaired driving (including designated driver programs); schools-based education and college/university campus education; training of bar staff and others who serve alcohol on how to handle drunk customers and how to deal with individuals under the legal drinking age; labeling of units of alcohol, information on serving sizes, and "Drink responsibly" messages; and provision of information about drinking alcohol via Web sites and other sources. Below are two examples of industry interventions.

The BARS Program

The BARS Program (BARS Program, n.d.) is the largest service in the United States that provides retailer training in ensuring that staff comply with legal minimum age limits when selling age-sensitive products, such as alcohol and tobacco. The program works with thousands of convenience stores, restaurants, bars, and grocery stores in every state.

The BARS Program takes training into the store. Twice each month, BARS sends checkers, aged 21 to 25 years, into client store locations to conduct mock purchases of cigarettes and beer. If an identification (ID) with proof of age is requested prior to ringing the sale, the employee receives a Green Card. If not, a Red Card is given. Within 24 hours, every store visit is reported to the store's management.

The trademarked Green and Red Card system is the proven method to ensure that employees properly monitor sales of alcohol and tobacco. With consistent training visits and follow-up reporting to management, employee behaviors are changed and asking customers for IDs becomes an automatic part of sellers' job. In the United States, many retailers have a policy to request IDs of individuals who look younger than age 30. The BARS Program makes this happen with every transaction. Clients of the BARS Program report that 95% of employees request IDs as proof of age after 1 year of being in the program. The investment in training pays for itself. Licensees save $5 in fines for every dollar spent using the BARS Program (BARS Program, n.d.).

"I'll Be Des" Campaign

"I'll Be Des" is a designated driver campaign developed and implemented by the Portman Group (n.d.) in the United Kingdom. The campaign is active especially during summers and the winter holiday season, with informational materials available year-round. It evolved from the October 1999 initiative aimed at 18- to 40-year-old football fans and backed by all major national football organizations and professional football players. Since 2000, the campaign widened its scope to the general public and joined forces with key stakeholders in the licensed trade, road safety, and health sectors at local and national levels. According to the Portman Group, although the campaign is relevant to all regardless of age and sex, "Des is aimed particularly at 18- to 40-year-old male drivers who are the group most at risk of being involved, injured, or killed in a drink-drive accident" (Portman Group, n.d.). Campaign elements include branded materials for display and use by licensees, law enforcement, and health professionals; a Web site with information about the program, the program's message, and contact information; advertising and promotions in print media; various activities at local level (for example, National Pubwatch supported the campaign by running full-page advertisements promoting the "Don't drink and drive" message in the quarterly *Newsletter*, which reached thousands of licensees and their customers). A November 2003 study undertaken by the market research company, Vision 21, and the Royal Automobile Club (RAC) Motoring Services revealed that two thirds of 18- to 30-year-olds had not only heard of this designated driver campaign but also acted as a Des. In 2001, the campaign won the Prince Michael International Road Safety award. "I'll Be Des" is supported by both the U.K. Department for Transport and the British Beer and Pub Association (BBPA).

In the last few years, leading beverage alcohol companies have entered new arenas, notably by applying their skills and expertise to understanding consumer motivations and communicating with consumers to address specific harmful uses of alcohol. This often takes the form of combining a responsible drinking message and a branded broadcast advertisement.

In the field of advertising and marketing, there remain significant differences in opinion between the industry, which believes in responsible marketing through self-regulation, and many in the public health community who see industry self-regulation as a conflict of interest and prefer marketing to be independently regulated. Irrespective of this debate, there has been expansion of and continual improvement in self-regulatory codes and systems over the years. Increasingly, self-regulatory codes govern the full range of consumer marketing from advertising to Web sites and other technological means of communication. Most codes contain provisions that cover the following points:

- not targeting minors and those below the legal purchasing age;
- restricting use of media and sponsorship of events frequented by minors;
- not encouraging excessive consumption or portraying abstinence in a negative way;
- not suggesting any association between drinking and potentially dangerous activities, such as driving; [and]
- not creating the impression that drinking alcohol is a requirement for sexual or social success.

In recent years, leading beverage alcohol companies have sought to define their broader "social responsibility." This takes different forms depending on the company and country. Increasingly, however, the process begins with identification of stakeholders. Usually, the stakeholders include employees, to whom the company promotes responsible drinking practices and policies in the workplace; the company's supply chain, whom it encourages to use responsible retailing practices; and its consumers, to whom it commits to promote, market, and sell its products in a wholly responsible manner.

There will, of course, be limitations on the role of the beverage alcohol industry in policy development and efforts to reduce harmful use of alcohol, although there is no clear consensus on this. It may be unacceptable to many in other sectors for the industry to have direct involvement in research to understand underage drinking or in programs to teach the young about responsible consumption, as there is a danger that these activities could be misunderstood or misused (Seltzer, 1997). Conducting or supporting scientific research more generally is also controversial. On the one hand, some expect industry to devote financial resources to support such research, although, on the other hand, such contributions would leave industry open to the accusation (whether or not correct) that it is attempting to manipulate the science for its own commercial ends.

PUBLIC SUPPORT FOR ALCOHOL POLICIES

There are many examples of alcohol policy interventions by governments that have failed because they did not gain sufficient support from society as a whole. One lesson from the U.S. experience with Prohibition is that consumers will always find ways of circumventing controls if alcohol policies are not considered acceptable by society (Musto, 1997; Thornton, 1991). That is also true of consumers today when they are confronted with higher taxes or extreme restrictions on alcohol availability in one country by comparison with its neighbors. Both measures may lead to smuggling, to consumers trading down to lower-priced drinks, or to an increase in home or illicit production of alcohol beverages (Nordlund & Österberg, 2000).

Leaving consumers out of policy development may mean that they do not "buy in" to the end results and that consumer response to policy interventions may have unanticipated consequences (Ringold, 2002). It is imperative that policy-makers factor in the "gut response" of individuals and the public before intervening (Martinic & Leigh, 2004). This is particularly true at a time when the power of the state to "control" what consumers do is declining in many parts of the world. Similarly, what citizens expect from governments has changed greatly over recent decades. Experience in the Nordic countries suggests that citizens who used to accept state interference with their lifestyle choices as a way of protecting the public good now may see it as "obsolete paternalism" (Sulkunen, Sutton, Tigerstedt, & Warpenius, 2000, p. 12).

It appears from large-scale opinion research in a number of countries, including Australia, the United Kingdom, and the United States, that most citizens support some constraints on drinking behavior—typically, where drinking may lead to harm—but prefer a more relaxed approach to the availability and consumption of alcohol (Bromley & Ormston, 2005; Harwood, Wagenaar, & Bernat, 2002; McAllister, 1995; Pendleton, Smith, & Roberts, 1990). Consumers are, in general, less supportive of policy measures that they see as eroding personal freedoms.

The surveys also highlight the importance of taking cultural and historical attitudes to alcohol into account. For example, in the United States, the majority of adults disapprove of alcohol consumption by those aged under 21 (the minimum legal age to buy alcohol in that country), even in very controlled environments (Harwood et al., 2002). Meanwhile, in Scotland, only 17% of adults think it is "always wrong" or "mostly wrong" for 17-year-olds to drink small amounts of alcohol at home with their parents; and drinking by youths is legally permitted in the United Kingdom, within controlled circumstances, from the age of 5 (Bromley & Ormston, 2005). Clearly, policy measures and messages that might gain public support in the United States might not be effective or popular in Scotland for reasons of law, culture, history, and public perception.

Rights, Responsibilities, and Responsible Drinking

The European Charter on Alcohol attempted to set out a number of basic rights to which individuals should be entitled in relation to alcohol consumption, starting with the statement that "[a]ll people have the right to a family, community and working life protected from accidents, violence and other negative consequences of alcohol consumption" (World Health Organization Regional Office for Europe, 1995, p. 1). However, as pointed out by MacAvoy and Mackenzie (2005), the charter could be made more relevant to consumers and to society as a whole by including an acknowledgment of the potential social and health benefits of alcohol, a recognition of the right to individual pleasure, and a statement regarding the need for individuals to assume responsibility for their own behavior with regard to alcohol consumption. The ultimate goal of involving consumers in alcohol policy development and implementation must be to ensure that individuals accept that the right to live in a modern society brings with it a greater personal responsibility for their own health and for wellbeing of others.

Control measures that generally appear to have widespread public support include not only tough enforcement of drink-driving legislation but also enforcing laws on serving intoxicated customers and requiring compulsory training for licensees and serving staff. Research in the United States suggests that, for every dollar spent on such enforcement programs, between US$90 and US$280 could be saved in the costs of traffic crashes (McKnight & Streff, 1994). More could be done to build on existing initiatives in this area and to introduce them in countries where they do not currently exist.

Marketing and Social Marketing: Lessons From Industry

From a health promotion perspective, it is frustrating to communicate messages about the risks associated with excessive drinking and not necessarily see corresponding changes in behavior. The instinctive response may be that educational approaches "do not work." Yet, looking at health promotion from a marketing perspective, the response would be "You are not delivering the right message, or you are delivering the right message in the wrong way. Find a message that is relevant and motivating to that particular consumer group." From an anthropological perspective, many innovations or changes are not accepted by the public because there is no perceived advantage or benefit to the consumer— no "felt need to change" (Naylor, 1996). Finding positive incentives, not just communicating negative messages, is very important (Daube, 1999).

Research and evaluation of programs or activities that have attempted to involve consumers in developing positive messages or incentives for change are limited. However, market research during development of a responsible drinking campaign in Ireland (Diageo Ireland, 2005) indicated that it is possible to come up with effective responsible drinking messages if understanding consumer motivations and beliefs relating to responsible drinking is put at the heart of the campaign development process. In audience research, 75% of consumers said the ads were "the kind that made you think" and 57% said they would reconsider how they drank as a result of viewing the campaign.

Seeking out expertise from marketing specialists may not be commonplace for those working in health promotion. In the world of marketing, however, "consumer insights" are key. This means identifying the drivers for different choices and using this knowledge to reach particular groups of consumers. Commercial marketers have skills that can be of benefit to health promotion workers and regulators. It makes sense to involve them when considering how to communicate with consumers:

> The commercial world of advertising is of course far ahead. . . . Perhaps health promotion should take not just the occasional leaf from their book, but a few chapters. . . . We should throw away some of the shackles that for so long have made us embarrassed about the very prospect that in promoting health we also might promote something that is pleasurable. (Daube, 1999, pp. 39, 43, 47)

BRINGING IT TOGETHER AT THE COMMUNITY LEVEL

Although communities can be decisive and influential in their contributions, this tier of involvement is, perhaps, the least powerful in a mix where the big players are, on the one hand, formal regulators and enforcers and, on the other hand, the alcohol beverage industry at producer, retail, and membership organization levels.

Can local communities make a difference by themselves? The evidence is that they can. However, it also demonstrates that partnership with other players delivers outcomes and payoffs beyond what each actor could have achieved in isolation.

Clearly, communities can be self-starters in influencing local alcohol policy and interventions. An illustration of this is the Mothers Against Drunk Driving (MADD) phenomenon, which began in the United States in 1980 (Mothers Against Drunk Driving, 2005). A common denominator in examples of spontaneous community involvement in the policy debate is pain—through injury or death, loss of public amenity, loss of trade, and community-borne costs. However, effective community action requires the existence of local leaders—individuals with some knowledge of handling the "who," "what," "how," and "when." Where such leadership is lacking, a process of capacity building may be needed. This may be seen within a synergy perspective as building capacity for community networks and state–society relations, with government, the private sector, and communities as the main players (Woolcock, 2000, p. 24). Within this view, the policy prescriptions include co-production, complementarity, accountability, transparency, reducing inequality, and increasing participation and linkages.

Engaging the Community, Government, and Industry

The Queensland Safety Action Projects provide an example of one model used to facilitate engagement between community, government regulators, and industry. These projects began in Surfers Paradise, Queensland, Australia, in 1994 as a response to the community's growing disenchantment with the increasing loss of amenity occasioned by drunkenness and violence in the central business district, which was also the nightclub precinct. The aim was to reduce violence in and around the nightclubs by identifying and addressing all major contributing factors. Action researchers who developed the interventions found it useful to flesh out project planning within a tripartite regulatory model that focuses on formal regulation and law enforcement at the state level, on informal controls and persuasion at the local community level, and on self- and peer regulation by licensees in drinking venues (Ayres & Braithwaite, 1992; Homel, Carvolth, Hauritz, McIlwain, & Teague, 2003).

Fundamental to this model was the assumption that a regulatory system responsive to varying retail industry conditions depends on the interrelationship of three main subsystems: formal regulation, informal regulation (mobilizing the community sector), and self-regulation by retailers and industry associations. The Ayres and Braithwaite (1992) regulatory approach commends the following: regulation that addresses industry context and culture, combining persuasion and sanctions; support of community sector engagement to help safeguard against regulatory capture (when a regulatory body becomes dominated by the interests of the group it oversees) and corruption; and enforced self-regulation, where measures such as codes of practice are developed by industry but publicly enforced with the help of community sector mechanisms if practice falls short of the code (Homel et al., 2003).

How Do Communities Get Involved?

Community Involvement

The most common ways for communities to contribute to the local policy equation include the following:

- *reactive input*, such as letters to editors (for example, one statewide network of local papers in Australia has a "ticks and crosses" column for praise and shame directed at local actors and organizations);
- *consultation* rounds to inform a particular government policy or practice;
- *appointed advisory positions* to government departments or projects, which provide an ongoing community voice;
- *project steering and reference groups* that mobilize community involvement and are usually facilitated by a project officer employed by local government, a university, or a national or regional government department; [and]
- *informal regulation role* through monitoring and providing constructive checks and balances (positive and negative) to the other partners in a tripartite regulatory approach, involving government and alcohol beverage retailers and producers.

Involvement of the community has often come from key groups, such as the local government authority or working groups, the chamber of commerce or other local business associations, and advocacy groups in the health and welfare sector (for example, alcohol and drugs or women's issues groups). Holder (2003) outlined an important mechanism to which the community may contribute in bringing about change in problem environments and outcomes:

> [P]olicies can be used to shape the community [environment] in a way which discourages undesired behaviors, for example, the identification and modification of community settings where heavy drinking peer groups can gather. The effectiveness of such policy strategies which go beyond those already tested (largely for tobacco and alcohol) are unknown but the intent to create a comprehensive community prevention intervention will require a mix of (a) evidence based program components and (b) tested or potential policy strategies. (p. 31)

There are many examples of different ways in which communities have become involved in alcohol policy and local interventions.

- *Local accords* were first developed in Australia, following the pioneering work in responsible hospitality interventions undertaken by the state health department in Queensland through the Patron Care program, begun in January 1980 (Carvolth, 1983). Accords involve regulatory enforcers, industry, and the community sector in identifying issues that contribute to lack of safety and developing a set of agreements, where each party consents to actions it will take as part of the safety process. Ideally, all participants must deliver the goods (for example, responsible hospitality policy and practice, responsible labeling, advertising and promotions, balanced and adequately enforced legislation, safe environs, lighting and visibility, and adequate transport arrangements). Accords are a case in which process and partnering are as important as product and outcome. Local communities have contributed productively to the development of accords in Australia (Felson, Berends, Richardson, & Veno, 1997; New South Wales Department of Gaming and Racing, 2004), New Zealand (Crime Prevention Unit, Department of the Prime Minister and Cabinet, Alcohol Advisory Council of New Zealand, & New Zealand Police, 2000), and further afield.

- *Local government acting as manager of alcohol licensing* (New Zealand) allows decisions to be made, contributed to, and monitored locally (see, for example, Wellington City Council, n.d.). New Zealand is one country that has effectively devolved responsibility for licensing to the local level. This provides a greater chance for local knowledge and concerns to be brought to bear, although without proper safeguards, such arrangements may increase the chance of regulatory capture and corruption.

- *The Lahti Project* was the first evaluated community-based intervention of its kind in Finland (Holmila, 2000). This project, led by the action research team, employed a reflexive problem prevention approach in which the community was kept informed of results in each phase and guided the shape of the next phase in the intervention.

- *The Model Community Responsible Beverage Service Covenants* approach has been employed in more than one jurisdiction (the United Kingdom and United States). This approach is, in many ways, a variation of the local accords schemes and, as with the accords, brings all the key players together during development and implementation of the covenant. Model community responsible beverage service covenants have been developed notably in the State of California, United States (Mosher, 1991), and, through the *Code of Good Conduct Schemes*, in the United Kingdom. These schemes involve retailers, pubs, and clubs and are run locally by a partnership of the industry, police, and licensing panels led by the local authority. They are state-mandated and coordinated in such a way as to be responsive to actual community needs. The schemes will also involve contributions by alcohol beverage producers to a fund and the development of social responsibility initiatives (United Kingdom Prime Minister's Strategy Unit, Cabinet Office, 2004).

- *Local alcohol management plans in indigenous areas* (Australia) have been created under the Meeting Challenges, Making Choices (MCMC) initiative by the Queensland state government, where the local community justice group has the role of developing a workable plan for alcohol availability and controls (Queensland Government, n.d.). These relatively recent developments are the latest attempts to address the significant alcohol-related violence in indigenous communities in Queensland. The plans have sometimes been accused of being too influenced by the state government and have demonstrated a mix of positive and neutral results.

- *Sporting clubs alcohol policies* (Australia). Sporting clubs have been seen as useful settings for shaping the attitudes and alcohol consumption norms and practices of young players. Such approaches include the national Good Sports program (Australian Drug Foundation, n.d.) and the Up Sport Without Drowning in Grog project in Queensland (Queensland Government Department of Health and Department of Emergency Service and Sport, n.d.), where community members and volunteer club officials use guidelines to develop, implement, and support clubs' alcohol policies. Clubs also have the opportunity of being accredited by Good Sports.

TOWARD PARTNERSHIP

Governments are responsible for imposing regulation on society. In this, they must strike a balance between the rights of an individual to drink for pleasure and their duty to help protect that individual and the wider society from any unacceptable risks and costs. But achieving this balance is complicated by the fact that governments almost always have a degree of financial dependence on the tax they get from the sales of alcohol, as well as from the employment that the industry generates. Maximizing the revenue stream has to be balanced against the wish of governments to maximize harm reduction by means that will often reduce sales. All this is further complicated in some countries where the governments own some of the largest drinks companies. The "government sector," therefore, cannot really be thought of as a monolith entity with one coherent policy. When we are talking of partnerships between the various sectors, we have to be aware about which part of the government sector should be involved—law enforcement, health, or taxation authorities, for instance. Each part will have its own agenda, which may, at times, be in conflict with others in the same sector.

Nor can the "industry" be considered a single entity with a unified position. Although maximizing profits is an underlying objective throughout, the implications of this may be different, depending on the interpretation of the meaning of "profit maximization." What companies do to achieve long-term profitability might well be different from what they do for short-term profit. Therefore, within the industry, there will be those who practice responsible marketing with a view to improve the health of the company over the long term, even if this means sacrificing some profits in the short term. There may be, however, some companies who forego responsible practice to make a quick profit. Even within one company, there may be tensions between the marketing division, which concentrates on maximizing sales, and those working in the public relations or corporate responsibility divisions. Thus, it can be hard to identify a single coherent "industry voice" and to arrive at a consensus industry view as this sector tries to negotiate some kind of partnership with other stakeholders.

The nonprofit sector is no more likely than the others to have a unified position with regard to alcohol. The various NGOs have their own different agendas. Some are, implicitly at least, against any form of alcohol consumption. Others focus on trying to prevent particular problems, such as alcohol-impaired driving or underage drinking, and distinguish between acceptable moderate drinking and unacceptable alcohol misuse.

Given these complications, how should the various parties approach each other? There is an increasing recognition that an adversarial approach between the key players involved in policy and program development is not the most efficient or effective way of proceeding. The interests of the various parties will certainly not be identical, but this does not mean that agreement cannot be reached in important areas. Collaboration rather than conflict should be the underlying principle governing the process.

Many different kinds of partnership can exist, combining the skills and resources of a wide range of collaborators. Administratively, such partnerships may be led by government bodies (for example, public sector programs with private sector participation), or by independent nonprofit bodies implementing strategies on behalf of governments or at least with their approval. Some may be industry led, but with government and NGO involvement or approval. Each sector has its own strengths, and partnerships should be able to harness them in order to carry forward agreed-upon components of a policy for harm minimization. Chapter 10 in this volume further explores the potential for intersector partnership.

The prime goal of effective public policy is to promote social wellbeing. Because alcohol is a commodity with a potential for harm as well as good, it is reasonable to expect it to be regulated so that its beneficial effects are maximized and its harmful effects minimized. In this, it is far from unique. Many other commodities, from motor vehicles to pharmaceuticals, require similar balancing acts. The purpose of regulation is not to restrict access to these commodities per se, but to make them as widely available as possible—consistent with the wellbeing of society. Sadly, those affected adversely by alcohol, such as motor vehicle casualties and alcoholics, are always likely to be with us. The trick is to find a way of keeping harm to a minimum, while not unreasonably restricting the freedom of society as a whole.

REFERENCES

Alcohol Policy Network (APN). (2005). *Welcome to ALPONET.* Retrieved November 14, 2005, from http://www.apolnet.ca/AboutUsHome.html.

Alinsky, S. (1989). *Rules for radicals: A pragmatic primer for realistic radicals.* New York: Vintage. (Originally published in 1971)

Allied Domecq. (2005). *Our social report 2005.* Bristol, UK: Author.

American Beverage Institute (ABI). (2005). *About us.* Retrieved November 14, 2005, from http://www.abionline.org/aboutUs.cfm.

Asahi Breweries Group. (2005). *Asahi Breweries Group corporate social responsibility report.* Tokyo, Japan: Author.

Australian Drug Foundation. (n.d.). *Good sports.* Melbourne. Retrieved August 15, 2005, from http://www.goodsports.adf.org.au/.

Ayres, I., & Braithwaite, J. (1992). *Responsive regulation: Transcending the deregulation debate.* New York: Oxford University Press.

Babor, T. F., Caetano, R., Casswell, S., Edwards, G., Giesbrecht, N., Graham, K., et al. (2003). *Alcohol: No ordinary commodity. Research and public policy.* Oxford: Oxford University Press.

Barry, J. (2002, October 16). *Alcohol in Ireland: A lot of damage done, more to do.* Paper presented at the Alcohol, Ethics, and Society Conference, Dublin, Ireland.

BARS Program. (n.d.). *Program statistics.* Retrieved February 28, 2006, from http://www .barsprogram.com/prostats.htm.

Bromley, C., & Ormston, R. (2005). *Part of the Scottish way of life? Attitudes towards drinking and smoking in Scotland—findings from the 2004 Scottish Social Attitudes Survey.* Edinburgh, UK: Scottish Executive, Social Research Substance Misuse Research Programme.

Carvolth, R. J. (Ed.). (1983). *National Drug Institute innovations: Proceedings of the National Drug Institute, Brisbane, Australia.* Canberra: Australian Foundation on Alcoholism and Drug Dependence.

Center for Science in the Public Interest (CSPI). (2003). *About the Alcohol Policies Project.* Retrieved November 14, 2005, from http://www.cspinet.org/booze/pdbooze.htm.

Crime Prevention Unit, Department of the Prime Minister and Cabinet, Alcohol Advisory Council of New Zealand (ALAC), & New Zealand Police. (2000). *Alcohol accords: Getting results. A practical guide for accord partners.* Retrieved December 1, 2005, from http://www.ndp.govt.nz/alcohol/AlcoholAccords_GettingResults.pdf.

Daube, M. (1999). Pleasure in health promotion. In S. Peele & M. Grant (Eds.), *Alcohol and pleasure: A health perspective* (pp. 37–47). Philadelphia: Brunner/Mazel.

Diageo. (2005). *Celebrating life, everyday, everywhere: Corporate citizenship report 2005.* London: Author.

Diageo Ireland. (2005). Unpublished market research. Research carried out for Diageo Ireland by Millward Brown, January 2005, based on 500 face to face interviews.

Drinking it in: Marketing and promotion of alcohol to young people. (2002). *The Globe, 2,* 3–4.

Drummond, C. (2005). The alcohol industry has a conflict of interest in alcohol research and policy. *Addiction, 100,* 128–129.

Edwards, G., Anderson, P., Babor, T. F., Casswell, S., Ferrence, R., Giesbrecht, N., et al. (1994). *Alcohol policy and the public good.* New York: Oxford University Press.

Felson, M., Berends, R., Richardson, B., & Veno, A. (1997). Reducing pub hopping and related crime. In R. Homel (Ed.), *Policing for prevention: Reducing crime, public intoxication, and injury* (pp. 115–132). Crime Prevention Studies, No. 7. Monsey, NY: Criminal Justice Press.

Hariharan. (2005). Indian Alcohol Policy Alliance launched. *The Globe, 2,* 5–6.

Harwood, E. M., Wagenaar, A. C., & Bernat, D. H. (2002). *Youth access to alcohol survey: Summary report.* Minneapolis, MN: Alcohol Epidemiology Program.

Heineken NV. (2004). *Living our responsibility.* Amsterdam, the Netherlands: Author.

Holder, H. D. (2003, February). Strategies for reducing substance abuse problems: What research tells us. Paper presented at National Drug Research Institute Symposium 2003, "Preventing substance use, risky use and harm: What is evidence-based policy," Fremantle, Australia.

Holmila, M. (2000). The Finnish case: Community prevention in a time of rapid change in national and international trade. *Substance Use and Misuse, 35*, 111–123.

Homel, R., Carvolth, R., Hauritz, M., McIlwain, G., & Teague, R. (2003, February). Cleaning up the nightclub act through problem-focussed, responsive regulation. Paper presented at National Drug Research Institute Symposium 2003, "Preventing substance use, risky use and harm: What is evidence-based policy," Fremantle, Australia.

Jenkins, J., & Hines, F. (2003). *Shouldering the burden of corporate social responsibility: What makes business get committed?* Working Paper Series No. 4. Cardiff, UK: Centre for Business Relationships, Accountability, Sustainability and Society (BRASS).

Lantos, G. P. (2001). The boundaries of strategic corporate social responsibility. *Journal of Consumer Marketing, 18*, 595–630.

Ledermann, S. (1956). Alcool, alcoolisme, alcoolisation. In *Données scientifiques de caractère physiologique, économique et social* (Vol. 1). Paris: Presses Universitaires de France; Institut National d'Études Démographiques, Travaux et Documents, Cahier 29.

MacAvoy, M., & Mackenzie, M. (2005). Government regulation, corporate responsibility and personal pleasure: A public health perspective from New Zealand. In M. Grant & J. O'Connor (Eds.), *Corporate social responsibility and alcohol: The need and potential for partnership* (pp. 81–82). New York: Routledge.

Martinic, M., & Leigh, B. (2004). Toeing the line: Risk and alcohol policy. In M. Martinic & B. Leigh, *Reasonable risk: Alcohol in perspective* (pp. 143–176). New York: Brunner-Routledge.

McAllister, I. (1995). Public attitudes to the regulation of alcohol. *Drug and Alcohol Review, 14*, 179–186.

McKnight, A. J., & Streff, F. M. (1994). Effect of enforcement upon service of alcohol to intoxicated patrons of bars and restaurants. *Accident Analysis and Prevention, 26*, 79–88.

Mosher, J. F. (1991). *Responsible beverage service: An implementation handbook for communities*. San Rafael, CA: Marin Institute for the Prevention of Alcohol and Other Drug Problems.

Mothers Against Drunk Driving (MADD). (2005). *MADD milestones*. Retrieved August 15, 2005, from www.madd.org/aboutus/0,1056,1179,00.html.

Musto, D. F. (1997). Alcohol control in historical perspective. In M. Plant, E. Single, & T. Stockwell (Eds.), *Alcohol: Minimizing the harm. What works?* (pp. 10–25). New York: Free Association Books.

Naylor, L. L. (1996). *Culture and change: An introduction*. Westport, CT: Bergin & Garvey.

New South Wales Department of Gaming and Racing. (2004). *Liquor accords: Local solutions for local problems*. Sydney, Australia: Author.

Nordlund, S., & Österberg, E. (2000). Unrecorded alcohol consumption: Economics and its effects on alcohol control in the Nordic countries. *Addiction, 95*(Suppl. 4), S551–S564.

Orley, J. (2005). Corporate social responsibility in practice within the beverage alcohol industry. In M. Grant & J. O'Connor (Eds.), *Corporate social responsibility and alcohol: The need and potential for partnership* (pp. 103–113). New York: Routledge.

Pendleton, L. L., Smith, C., & Roberts, J. L. (1990). Public opinion on alcohol policies. *British Journal of Addiction, 85*, 125–130.

Portman Group. (n.d.). *"I'll be Des" campaign.* Retrieved February 28, 2006, from http://www.portmangroup.org.uk/campaigns/57.asp.

Queensland Government. (n.d.). *Meeting challenges: Making choices—alcohol restrictions.* Retrieved August 15, 2005, from http://www.alcoholimits.qld.gov.au/community/restricted.php.

Queensland Government Department of Health and Department of Emergency Service and Sport. (n.d.). *Up sport without drowning in grog.* Brisbane, Australia: Authors.

Ringold, D. J. (2002). Boomerang effects in response to public health interventions: Some unintended consequences in the alcoholic beverage market. *Journal of Consumer Policy, 25*, 27–63.

SAB Miller. (2005). *Corporate accountability.* London: Author.

Seltzer, C. C. (1997). "Conflicts of interest" and "political science." *Journal of Clinical Epidemiology, 50*, 627–629.

Sulkunen, P., Sutton, C., Tigerstedt, C., & Warpenius, K. (Eds.). (2000). *Broken spirits: Power and ideas in Nordic alcohol control.* NAD Publication No. 39. Helsinki, Finland: Nordic Council for Alcohol and Drug Research.

Thornton, M. (1991). *The economics of prohibition.* Salt Lake City: University of Utah Press.

United Kingdom Prime Minister's Strategy Unit, Cabinet Office. (2004). *Alcohol harm reduction: A strategy for England.* Retrieved August 15, 2005, from http://www.strategy.gov.uk/work_areas/alcohol_misuse/index.asp.

V&S Group. (2003). *V&S responsibility 2003.* Stockholm: Author.

Wellington City Council. (n.d.). *Liquor licensing.* Retrieved August 15, 2005, from http://www.wellington.govt.nz/services/liquor/index.html.

Woolcock, M. (2000). Social capital: The state of the notion. In J. Kajanoja & J. Simpura (Eds.), *Social capital: Global and local perspectives* (PAGES). Helsinki, Finland: Government Institute for Economic Research.

World Health Organization Regional Office for Europe. (1995). *European charter on alcohol.* Copenhagen, Denmark: Author.

World Health Organization Regional Office for Europe. (2005). *Alcohol policy in the WHO European Region: Current status and the way forward.* Copenhagen, Denmark: Author.

Worldwide Brewing Alliance. (2003). *Global social responsibility initiatives.* London: British Beer & Pub Association.

10

Finding Common Ground: Conflict of Interest or Interest in Partnership?

A recent study by two deans of the RAND Graduate School observed that public-private partnerships "are the rage in the government, business, and nonprofit worlds alike" (Klitgaard & Treverton, 2003, p. 6). At the international level at least, the response in the past decade to the participation of the private sector in policy-making has been a resounding "yes." This view has been perhaps best exemplified (and encouraged) by the creation by Secretary-General of the United Nations (UN) Kofi Annan of a "Global Compact" among business, governments, civil society, and the UN. First announced in 1999, the Global Compact is a voluntary initiative designed "to promote responsible corporate citizenship so that business can be part of the solution to the challenges of globalization" (Global Compact, 2005b, para. 2). Private companies that wish to participate do so by declaring their acceptance of 10 principles in the areas of human rights, labor standards, the environment, and anticorruption. By 2005, the compact had over 2,400 participants and nearly 50 country networks, and, in September 2005, it was announced that a new governance framework would be adopted to provide "greater focus, transparency, and sustained impact" (Global Compact, 2005a, p. 1; see also Nowrot, 2005). The new structure will include a nonprofit foundation that will have the ability to receive voluntary contributions and fund Global Compact events and publications.

The underlying principles of the Global Compact are also reflected in the activities of organizations such as the Copenhagen Centre, an international institution established by the Danish government in the late 1990s to promote voluntary partnerships among business, government, and civil society. One of the center's reports described such partnerships, which are "aimed at meeting the dual challenges of social cohesion and economic competitiveness," as "one of the most important trends emerging throughout Europe as we enter the 21st century"

(Nelson & Zadek, 2000, p. 5). Most of these "social partnerships" are designed to improve access to the labor market, particularly for marginalized groups, but the assumptions on which they are based are applicable to other areas as well:

> [T]he quest for partnership presupposes that despite potential conflicts between members there is enough to be shared for positive gain. Turning adversaries into partners that cooperate despite conflicts is one of the achievements that come about as a result of a civil society freely operating in a political democracy. (Evers, 2003, p. 43)

Public-private partnerships are also increasing in the public health arena. In 2004, Nishtar (2004) identified 91 transnational public-private partnership arrangements in the health sector, the great majority of which were dedicated to infectious disease prevention and control. The author underlined a number of generic "ethical challenges" that might be of particular salience in the context of alcohol policy, including potential conflicts of interest and concerns that partnerships might inappropriately "redirect national and international health policies and priorities" (Nishtar, 2004, p. 4). Observing that public-private partnerships seem both "unavoidable and imperative," the author cautioned that "the driving principles for such initiatives [should] be rooted in 'benefit to the society' rather than 'mutual benefit to the partners' and should center on the concept of equity in health" (p. 5). Once the ultimate priority of societal benefit is recognized, however, the public sector needs to "recognize the basic legitimacy of the private sector and the profit motive that drives it. It is also essential for the public sector to respect the organizational autonomy and priorities of the nonprofit sector" (p. 6).

A number of initiatives at the national level demonstrate the feasibility and desirability of partnerships in many situations. In the United Kingdom, for example, there is an alliance between the pharmaceutical industry and the National Health Service (NHS). The 2005 edition of *NHS and Pharmaceutical Industry Working Together for Patients* recognizes that the "history of joint working between the pharmaceutical industry and the NHS is patchy, with examples of excellent partnerships but also of mistrust, ideological differences, and bad behaviours" (Colin-Thomé, 2005, p. i). For the past several years, however, the response has been to seek to expand and improve partnerships, not to eliminate them. The U.K. Department of Health has made it clear that "[i]deological boundaries or institutional barriers should not stand in the way of better care for NHS patients" and that by "constructing the right partnerships, the NHS can harness the capacity of private and voluntary providers to treat more NHS patients" (Department of Health, 2000, p. 96).

The ground rules identified for collaboration between pharmaceutical companies and the NHS are familiar. They include "trust, mutual benefit, added value, reliability, consistency, and integrity" (Association of the British Pharmaceutical Industry [ABPI], 2005, p. 4). To assist NHS primary care organizations in managing their relationship with pharmaceutical companies, the 2005 framework includes a checklist of questions that should be addressed. Many of these issues would be equally relevant to cooperation between the drinks industry and the public sector, such as, Who has been consulted prior to initiating the joint project, and how? Is there an open and transparent decision-making process? What are the potential conflicts of interest? On completion of the project, how will it be evaluated in terms of patient benefits? Participants are also required to declare any interests in the project, including personal ("you [or your spouse] receive direct payment for services or hold shares in the relevant company or a competitor"), nonpersonal ("your unit benefits by receiving funding from the company"), and specific ("you have undertaken work or given advice on other products made by the relevant manufacturer") interests (ABPI, 2005, pp. 5–7). Of course, similar questions can also be asked for projects run by the public sector, which is certainly not immune to the promotion of personal interests.

Another national initiative of interest is the Fair Labor Association (FLA), which grew out of a 1996 task force created by U.S. President Bill Clinton, known as the Apparel Industry Partnership (AIP). AIP was a response to growing concern and publicity about sweatshop conditions in many suppliers of U.S. clothing makers, and it brought together businesses, trade unions, human rights groups, religious organizations, and consumer groups under the political aegis of the U.S. government. The FLA was created in 1999 as an independent, nonprofit monitoring body that promotes labor rights through multi-stakeholder coalitions of companies, universities, and nongovernmental organizations (NGOs). FLA company members agree to adopt a workplace code of conduct and set up a system of internal monitoring; they also agree to independent external monitoring of their workplaces. The association issues an annual report on the practices of each of its company members.

The pharmaceutical, alcohol, and other industries have been criticized by some health advocates and special interest groups for exerting too much influence on both research and policy-making, and health advocacy groups have been criticized themselves for not having a disinterested view in science—for example, criticism (Goldin, 2006) of articles by the National Center on Addiction and Substance Abuse (CASA; Foster, Vaughan, Foster, & Califano, 2006) on underage drinking revenues. It would be disingenuous to suggest that partnerships are always possible or desirable or that the influence of business on society is always benign. A typical opinion is the following, which describes a one-day conference held in Washington, DC, in 2003:

A backlash against academic science collaborating with industry has been building for years, inspired by instances of suppression of research unfavorable to corporate sponsors, hidden conflicts of interest, distorted clinical trials, and retaliation against uncooperative scientists. . . . The meeting is a good candidate for landmark status in the mounting concerns about the erosion of scientific independence under stretched academic budgets, the lure of corporate funds, and government pressures for closer relations between the two sectors as a source of economic growth. (Greenberg, 2003, p. 302)

A more nuanced view was offered by Nelson (2000):

> Partnerships are not a panacea for solving complex problems. Indeed, in some cases they are inappropriate. Even when they do have potential, the process of creating and sustaining mutually beneficial partnerships is not easy. This is especially the case for cross-sector partnerships between business, government, and civil society. (p. 24)

PUBLIC-PRIVATE PARTNERSHIPS, RESEARCH, AND POLICY

The debate over public-private partnerships raises two separate yet related issues. The first is the issue of the role of industry in funding for and influencing the agenda of scientific research. The second is the broader question of whether industry in general, and the beverage alcohol industry in particular, has a legitimate role to play in contributing to the formulation of public policy on areas within the industry's expertise.

The issue of research is perhaps best addressed by insisting on rigorous scientific standards, transparency, and disclosure of any personal conflict of interest. In the context of developing sound alcohol policy at the national and international levels, it is imperative, at the very least, that decision-making is based on the best available facts. These facts in turn should not only be based on unassailable research methodology, vetted by peer review, but also encompass the widest possible scope of relevant information. As noted in the *Dublin Principles of Cooperation Among the Beverage Alcohol Industry, Governments, Scientific Researchers and the Public Health Community*, policies should be based upon "the fullest possible understanding of available scientific evidence," which includes "a better understanding of the use, misuse, effects, and properties of alcohol and the relationships among alcohol, health, and society" (National College of Ireland, 1998, I.A, II.B).

The key to ensuring that such research is not skewed or biased is transparency, and it appears now to be common practice to require that researchers disclose the sources of funding for their research and any possible conflicts of interest that might affect their findings. The requirement for such disclosure is set out clearly in the Dublin Principles (National College of Ireland, 1998, II.D.1, II.D.2). Of course, the best checks on biased research are peer review and public scrutiny, as is the case with any scientific claim.

One should also bear in mind that potential bias is inherent in all scientific research that depends for its funding on outside sources:

> The argument has been advanced that funding from the drinks industry is some-how so tainted that it corrupts any research endeavor and should be rejected. It is difficult to understand, however, why money from the drinks industry is any more corrupting than money from the pharmaceutical, food, car, or chemical

industries, each of which also has profit-making as its primary corporate goal. And, if the profit motive can bias research, then certainly the possible ideological bias of governments—for example, [that] alcohol or high energy consumption is in itself undesirable—must be equally suspect. (Hannum, 1998, p. 335)

Even if the integrity of research can be safeguarded by particular vigilance regarding both funding sources and scientific method, the broader issue remains: Should the industry that makes and profits from producing beverage alcohol be permitted or even encouraged to participate in developing alcohol policies?

Some critics accuse beverage alcohol companies of the amoral (at best) pursuit of profit through advertisements and products designed to appeal to vulnerable drinkers. On the other hand, some government and NGO advocates appear motivated as much by ideological or moralistic reasons as by public health concerns, and individual rights are often totally absent from the debate. In the public health context, for example, it has been noted that "many NGOs even in the developing countries are little more than lobby groups with a particular interest, which may or may not be aligned to public good" (Nishtar, 2004, p. 4). There is a danger that zealous advocates who claim the high moral ground in debates over health and other issues may be more interested in intellectual purity than effectiveness—for example, witness the less than successful promotion by the U.S. government of simplistic calls for sexual abstinence, instead of supporting nuanced sex education and ensuring the availability of products to prevent unwanted pregnancies and the spread of sexually transmitted diseases. Similarly, a government that chooses to fund research to determine the linkages (if any) between alcohol and crime exhibits a different bias than one that might fund a study on the linkages (if any) between alcohol and health or longevity.

Although these extreme positions probably describe accurately some participants in the alcohol policy debate, they are unlikely to lead to policies that even attempt to discover a "win-win" or mutually acceptable solution to alcohol-related problems.

CONFLICT OF INTEREST AND COOPERATION

Interpreting *conflict of interest* too broadly is likely to eliminate any possibility of cooperation or collaboration among social groups. Management and labor would bargain only as adversaries; consumer groups, which are interested in low prices, could not talk to producers interested in maximizing profits; public health advocates would do their best to prohibit "bad" or require "good" behavior—regardless of an individual's right of choice—rather than working with others to educate and persuade. Although government should, in theory, be the final arbiter of many of these conflicting interests, a responsive and democratic government should seek to minimize conflict and maximize consensus, not just choose which side is "right" in complex debates over health, safety, individual rights, and the proper degree of latitude to be given to the "free" market.

It would be possible to develop much safer automobiles, restrict the amount of fat and sugar in processed foods, extract natural resources while fully protecting the environment, and allow drugs to reach the market only when it is absolutely certain that they will have almost no negative side effects. However, each of these goals conflicts in part with other social goods, ranging from the recognition of individual rights and preferences to countervailing demands on the public treasury. Government mandates often set a floor below which companies may not go, requiring that certain health, safety, and other protections are met. But that minimum floor is unlikely to be raised, so long as governments (or health or environmental advocates) view the private sector as inevitably adversarial and morally corrupted by profits.

Beverage alcohol is not unique among widely used consumer goods in being potentially harmful, and public health efforts to minimize that harm are not qualitatively different from efforts to persuade people to eat healthier foods or drive more responsibly. Given the vulnerability of some individuals or segments of the population (such as children), the private sector should not be left on its own to produce the fastest cars, the fastest food, or the strongest and cheapest drinks. At the same time, just as collaboration among various public and private sources and industry self-regulation have incrementally produced safer cars and healthier food, collaboration and self-regulation can produce more responsible advertising and products in the drinks and hospitality industries.

Defining *conflict of interest* in a useful way would not prohibit all contact among those whose interests differ, nor would it draw arbitrary lines between some profit-making industries that are allowed to contribute to policy-making (such as automobiles, pharmaceuticals, and energy) and those that may not make such contributions (as some critics would propose for the drinks industry). Of course, strict guidelines to ensure transparency of competing interests and the fullest possible disclosure of relevant financial and other ties between regulators and industry are essential. There is also a danger that government officials or regulators may become too beholden to private interests whose economic power is great.

This danger is particularly keen with respect to developing countries, whose ability to withstand the entreaties or threats of large local or transnational companies may be suspect. However, the answer to undue influence by the private sector is to strengthen government, not to pretend that "neutral" bodies such as the World Health Organization or public health NGOs can step in and inevitably choose the correct path to follow. Corruption is a two-way process, and weak government officials may be seduced by international organizations as easily (if not quite as directly) as by large companies. In addition, the alcohol industry is likely to be less significant to the economies of developing countries than industries concerned with agriculture, armaments, or the extraction of natural resources.

The Global Corporate Citizenship Initiative of the World Economic Forum (WEF) recently identified a number of problems and lessons (as they relate to economic development) in partnerships between business and other sectors. Among the obstacles to successful partnerships are lack of trust and mutual understanding;

different ways of operating; different timeframes; lack of clarity and communication; lack of appropriate skills and competencies; and operating in a hostile political, social, and economic context (World Economic Forum [WEF], 2005, pp. 37–38). Although noting that "[t]here is no simple checklist or blueprint for successful partnership building," the initiative identified seven "success factors" in creating effective partnerships, including the following: openness, transparency, and clear communication to build trust and mutual understanding; clarity of goals and ground rules; application of professional rigor and discipline to the undertaking; respect for differences in approach and objectives of different partners; and focus on achieving mutual benefit in a manner that enables the partners to meet their own objectives as well as common goals (WEF, 2005, p. 40). These factors would appear to be as relevant to the alcohol industry as to any other, although unequal bargaining power remains a potential obstacle to achieving a partnership that is truly mutually beneficial.

CORPORATE SOCIAL RESPONSIBILITY

Few (if any) within the alcohol industry would argue that self-regulation is sufficient to deal with the negative consequences of what all observers agree can result from alcohol misuse. Consumer groups, public health workers, and policy-makers may feel that they have cause to be skeptical of well-meaning pronouncements from CEOs if they are contradicted by questionable marketing techniques. However, self-interest and an increasing sense of corporate social responsibility have made drinks companies more likely to take seriously interests other than just the financial "bottom line." This broader obligation of business—that overall performance of a company should be based on its combined contribution to economic prosperity, environmental quality, and social capital—has come to be called "the triple bottom line" (Logan & O'Connor, 2005). The willingness of governments—as exemplified by the UN's Global Compact and many other initiatives— to see businesses as potential partners rather than solely as adversaries or revenue sources has also enhanced the cooperative spirit increasingly evident around the world, at least among many of the largest transnational companies.

The motivations for the willingness on the part of (some) private businesses to cooperate with those who have other priorities are mixed; long-term economic survival, fear of consumer backlash, and potential financial liability for alcohol abuse may well be as significant as any sense of social responsibility. But just as consumer and health groups have a right to expect that their views be considered seriously by industry, so does industry have an equivalent right to acceptance of the legitimacy of its goals. When acceptance and respect are absent, whether due to an ideological distrust of for-profit enterprises, moral disapproval of drinking, or both, partnership will not work.

Although partnerships may not be a panacea, they are rapidly becoming an important way of addressing a multitude of problems, given the increasing interrelationship and global reach of not only the private sector but also government and civil society. Today, government regulation is a necessary but insufficient means of restraining actors who may often work at cross purposes, as government attempts to create conditions that benefit society as a whole. *Corporate social responsibility* has become much more than a phrase for many companies, in part because they recognize that, in the long term, responsible behavior is likely to contribute to their financial goals as well (see Grant & O'Connor, 2005). Finally, the Internet and its many offshoots have made it easier for nongovernmental or civil society groups to exchange information and mount campaigns than ever before.

THE PROMISE OF PARTNERSHIP

Though this chapter focuses on partnerships between industry (producers and distributors) and national governments, effective partnerships are much more varied. Local police and "problem" pubs or off-licenses often can cooperate to reduce public disorder. Schools or other institutions concerned primarily with young people might engage local sellers in ways of decreasing juvenile misuse of alcohol. International institutions can assist local bodies with educational and other materials, and international exchanges on "best practices" might bring valuable lessons to one country or region from another.

Vague calls for "partnership" among the alcohol industry, civil society, and government are not likely to lead to a significant increase in communication or collaboration. But a willingness not only to listen to other views, but also to allow meaningful participation of all those affected by alcohol policy, is much more likely to lead to effective actions that will curb the misuse of alcohol products without threatening the very existence of the companies that produce them. Alcohol policy partnerships, like other partnerships, must be based on a certain degree of trust and perceived mutual benefit, no matter how that benefit is defined by the various parties. They also must include a commitment by all parties—particularly by industry—to the highest level of transparency and ethical standards, so that all involved can be judged by what they do and not just by what they say.

Many other commercial sectors are beginning to explore the advantages of partnership, and there is no persuasive reason why the drinks industry should be different. Past mistrust will not be easy to overcome, but by not expecting or demanding too much from any single stakeholder, unproductive antagonism might shift to productive partnership in which differing interests need not always lead to conflict.

REFERENCES

Association of the British Pharmaceutical Industry (ABPI). (2005). *NHS and pharmaceutical industry working together for patients.* London: Author.

Colin-Thomé, D. (2005). Foreword. In Association of the British Pharmaceutical Industry (ABPI), *NHS and pharmaceutical industry working together for patients* (p. i). London: Author.

Department of Health. (2000). *The NHS plan: A plan for investment, a plan for reform.* London: Author.

Evers, A. (2003). Origins and implications of working in partnership. In L. Kjaer, P. Abrahamson, & P. Raynard (Eds.), *Local partnerships in Europe: An action research project* (pp. 43–50). Copenhagen, Denmark: Copenhagen Centre.

Foster, S. E., Vaughan, R. D., Foster, W. H., & Califano, J. A. (2006). Estimate of the commercial value of underage drinking and adult abusive and dependent drinking to the alcohol industry. *Archives of Pediatrics and Adolescent Medicine, 160,* 473–478.

Global Compact. (2005a). *The Global Compact's next phase.* Retrieved February 3, 2006, from http://www.unglobalcompact.org/docs/about_the_gc/2.3/gc_gov_framew.pdf.

Global Compact. (2005b). *What is the Global Compact?* Retrieved November 16, 2005, from http://www.unglobalcompact.org.

Goldin, R. (2006, May 8). *Another crazy Columbia alcohol study.* Statistical Assessment Service at George Mason University. Retrieved August 1, 2006, from http://www.stats.org/stories/another_crazy_columbia_may08_06.htm.

Grant, M., & O'Connor, J. (Eds.). (2005). *Corporate social responsibility and alcohol: The need and potential for partnership.* New York: Routledge.

Greenberg, D. S. (2003). Conference deplores corporate influence on academic science. *Lancet, 362,* 302–303.

Hannum, H. (1998). Condemning the drinks industry rules out potentially useful research. *British Medical Journal, 317,* 335–336.

Klitgaard, R., & Treverton, G. F. (2003). *Assessing partnerships: New forms of collaboration.* Arlington, VA: IBM National Endowment for the Business of Government.

Logan, D., & O'Connor, J. (2005). Corporate social responsibility and corporate citizenship: Definitions, history, and issues. In M. Grant & J. O'Connor (Eds.), *Corporate social responsibility and alcohol: The need and potential for partnership* (pp. 5–28). New York: Routledge.

National College of Ireland. (1998). *The Dublin Principles: Principles of cooperation among the beverage alcohol industry, governments, scientific researchers and the public health community.* Dublin, Ireland: Author.

Nelson, J. (2000). The leadership challenge of global corporate citizenship. *Perspectives on Business and Global Change, 14,* 11–26.

Nelson, J., & Zadek, S. (2000). *Partnership alchemy: New social partnerships in Europe.* Copenhagen, Denmark: Copenhagen Centre.

Nishtar, S. (2004, July 28). Public–private "partnerships" in health: A global call to action. *Health Research Policy and Systems, 2.* Retrieved November 17, 2005, from http://www.health-policy-systems.com/content/pdf/1478-4505-2-5.pdf.

Nowrot, K. (2005). *The new governance structure of the Global Compact: Transforming a "learning network" into a federalized and parliamentarized regulatory regime.* Policy Papers on Transnational Economic Law 47. Halle, Germany: Transnational Economic Law Research Center.

World Economic Forum (WEF). (2005). *Partnering for success: Business perspectives on multistakeholder partnerships.* Geneva, Switzerland: Author.

Conclusions

Alcohol can benefit as well as harm those who consume it. This dual nature puts it apart from many other commodities and plays an important role in why and how people choose to drink. The way alcohol is consumed—patterns of drinking—shape the likely outcome of consumption. At the same time, drinking is a learned behavior like many others. It can be molded to involve responsible decision-making and to minimize potential harm. In selecting alcohol policies, societies must decide how to encourage some behaviors and discourage others, while maintaining what they perceive as an appropriate balance between state and individual responsibility.

Good alcohol policy is the art of the possible. In an ideal world, seeking to reduce risk levels to zero, it might be appropriate to advise some sections of the population—such as pregnant women and anyone intending to drive a motor vehicle—not to drink at all. However, as we all know, the world is far from ideal. The reality is that some people do drink irresponsibly and may end up causing harm to themselves and others. All reasonable people would agree that efforts should be made to prevent that harm from occurring.

There is a considerable body of literature on measures that appear most effective because they can be shown to have an impact on consumption or harm, or both. In this book, our focus has been on those initiatives that are also *feasible*. Traditionally, the centerpiece of many alcohol policies has been the population-level regulation of consumption through restrictions on alcohol availability (for example, by making it more expensive or by limiting when, where, and by whom it may be obtained). However, even if many of these population-level measures might have a positive impact on alcohol-related harm, they are sometimes difficult to introduce and could have detrimental unintended effects. This volume argues that population-level measures *alone* are inadequate: They are insensitive to cultural variations and needs of at-risk individuals and groups, their implementation requires elaborate political negotiation, and they are frequently unpopular, at least in part because they are perceived to be discriminatory. Thus, in the real world, they may be less appropriate and hence less effective than more targeted interventions. Again, the distinction is between policy ideals and what will actually work as a practical policy. It is far better to acknowledge that people will want to have the freedom to choose whether or not to drink, without being unduly restricted in doing so, and provide information to them about responsible drinking. It is far better to acknowledge that some people will drink irresponsibly and to develop policies that will minimize the harm they do to themselves and others. It is far better, therefore, to develop policies that maintain the benefits of responsible drinking and minimize the harm of irresponsible consumption. A successful design for alcohol policies that is both realistic and sustainable relies on balancing population-level measures with targeted interventions.

It might be argued that such an approach is too opportunistic and lacking in predetermined scientific validation. There is an element of truth to both charges, but neither is sufficient to discredit the approach. Social policy should certainly have a strong ethical framework, but it will need to be pragmatic in looking for culturally appropriate opportunities when it comes to implementation. Similarly, scientific analysis needs to be the servant of policy, not its master. Evidence-based policy is an aspiration, but feasible policy is a prerequisite for action.

In reviewing the many possible policy options set out in Table 8.2 (Chapter 8), it is important not to take a narrow view that considers only those measures for which there currently exists scientific evidence of effectiveness. Evidence-based policy needs to be set in a context of what is likely to work. A broader view looks at both intended and unintended consequences, evaluates the negative impact of policies as well as their benefits, and assesses the feasibility of introducing them in terms of costs, support, and cultural appropriateness.

The three underlying themes of this book are that *patterns of drinking* are the best way to understand alcohol's place in society, that *targeted interventions* are the most sensitive to cultural differences, and that *partnerships* offer the best opportunity to develop policies that reflect the values of society as a whole. That is what is meant by looking at drinking in context. Alcohol is a commodity, certainly; it is special, not just because it has the potential to cause harm but also—more importantly—because it has the capacity to contribute in a significant way to people's wellbeing. But it is drinking behavior that matters most, because it is the way people behave that determines whether they will drink responsibly or irresponsibly, whether they will experience benefits or harm. In selecting the best alcohol policies, societies are faced with choices about how to encourage some behaviors and discourage others. In many countries, alcohol is here to stay. Putting drinking into context is how we learn to live with it best.

Afterword

NORMAN SARTORIUS

The editors of this book decided to invite a small group of experts with experience in the field of public health, as well as representatives of the International Harm Reduction Association, the World Federation for Mental Health, and the Institut de Recherches Scientifiques sur les Boissons, to give them advice and comments on the materials that were to be included in this volume. The group met twice. Prior to its second meeting, the group had an opportunity to read the manuscripts that were ready at the time. The group worked well together and felt that it was consulted fairly and that its comments were taken into account in finalizing the text.

The group's main aim was to respond to the editors' request to suggest a new way of approaching the phenomena of drinking and problems that can be related to them. The group quickly agreed that the book should acknowledge the prevailing notions about alcohol policies rather than try to discuss, support, or oppose them. Instead, the group felt that the book should (a) emphasize the usefulness of the exploration of the social, cultural, and economic contexts of drinking in developing specific interventions aiming to prevent problems related to it; (b) concentrate on interventions of proven usefulness in the prevention or reduction of problems of public health importance and related to the drinking of alcohol; and (c) help to identify and involve partners who could effectively participate in such efforts.

Possibly as a result of these suggestions, the book's three central chapters address the issues of preventing or reducing problems related to the consumption of alcohol and driving, the role of drinking alcohol in the genesis of social disorder, and problems related to alcohol drinking by young people. These are issues that are of great concern around the world—in developed and developing countries alike. They are also issues where it is possible to take effective action by introducing interventions that can make a significant difference.

There are, of course, other issues that the group felt might have been chosen as a focus of discussion. Drinking of alcohol during pregnancy was one that received prominence in this respect, and it is addressed in the book, although not in as much detail as the three that were selected. Several other problems identified in introductory chapters of the book might have been included using similar criteria—and, perhaps, will be in a subsequent volume, which might follow if this one proves to be useful.

Drinking alcohol is part of the sociocultural fabric in many countries. It is an example of human behavior that can give pleasure, but can also be related to serious social and health problems that cannot be easily prevented or even reduced. The strategy that the group proposed as the main axis of this volume—namely, selecting problems related to drinking that are of major public health importance and can be addressed by interventions of proven efficacy—might be a way to go about resolving these problems. Whether this strategy will produce tangible public health benefits will have to be carefully evaluated to help in steering further action.

Nothing in this book is intended to belittle traditional approaches to alcohol policy. Rather, the goal is to acknowledge the place of these approaches and, at the same time, to look beyond them toward the early and energetic implementation of a series of carefully selected interventions addressing major problems related to drinking, tailored to fit the sociocultural settings in which they are to be applied, and carried out in partnership with all those who have put the improvement of health and wellbeing at the center of their agenda.

Annex

Alcohol and the Global Burden of Disease: Methodological Issues

There is vast and convincing evidence that some drinking patterns are associated with physical harm, and that they may adversely affect the family, the community, and the society at large. At the same time, there is the experience, supported by equally convincing evidence, that alcohol consumption is highly prevalent and even increasing in many societies in many cultures. At first glance, there seems to be a contradiction between the data provided by research and the experience that reflects people's behaviors. This contradiction, however, disappears if one accepts that many people like to consume alcohol, and that the vast majority of those who drink neither experience nor cause harm. This observation is as obvious as it is largely ignored in the health-related alcohol literature and in alcohol research.

ALCOHOL AND THE BURDEN OF DISEASE

There is clear evidence that some drinking patterns may pose a risk to health and social life and may be associated with chronic diseases, and injuries, as well as acute and chronic social problems. According to legend, the first sake was produced around 2000 b.c. in China. When it was offered to King Wu, he liked it so much that he was drunk for several days. He then immediately ordered its prohibition, saying, "Sake is so good that people will surely be unable to limit their drinking and will ruin themselves and the country" (Shinfuku, 1999, p. 113). It took another 4,000 years to systematically compare the health consequences of drinking alcohol with other health hazards.

In the 1990s, the World Bank (1993) and the World Health Organization (WHO; Murray & Lopez, 1996) conducted their landmark study on the contribution of a range of different causes to the global burden of disease (GBD). The impact of this work on public health in general and on health priority setting in particular was unprecedented: A way was found to include information on mortality and nonfatal disability in a single measure, a common "metric" was defined that allows a comparison of the public health impact of all diseases using the same measure, it became possible to estimate the combined health effect of the most common risk factors for health, and the best information available was used to estimate the actual burden of disease worldwide.

Table 13.1 Estimated Attributable Burden of 10 Leading Risk Factors in 2000

Risk Factor	DALYs (millions)	Percent of total
Underweight	138	9.5
Unsafe sex	92	6.3
High blood pressure	64	4.4
Smoking and oral tobacco	59	4.1
Alcohol	**58**	**4.0**
Unsafe water, sanitation, and hygiene	54	3.7
High cholesterol	40	2.8
Indoor smoke from solid fuels	39	2.6
Iron deficiency	35	2.4
Overweight	33	2.3
Total burden	**1,455**	**42.1%**

Source: WHO (2002).

However, great care needs to be exercised to avoid misinterpretation. First, alcohol is not a disease but rather a risk factor that may contribute to a number of diseases and social problems. WHO, in its *World Health Report 2002* (WHO, 2002), published estimates of the contribution of major risk factors to the GBD in year 2000. Alcohol consumption was identified as one of the leading causes of mortality and disability, contributing 58 million (or 4%) of total disability adjusted life years (DALYs) lost globally, ranking it among the top five risk factors for disease burden (see Table 13.1). This finding is quoted widely in the health-related literature on alcohol, and it is the basis for many recommendations on how to reduce the burden caused by alcohol consumption.

Second, the calculations of alcohol's contribution to the disease burden should differentiate between heavy and abusive drinking, on the one hand, and drinking that is low or moderate, on the other. As discussed in detail in Chapter 2, drinking patterns consist of a number of dimensions, all of which contribute in different ways to both harm and benefit. Given that some patterns of drinking confer benefit, not harm, a more accurate estimation of the burden attributable to alcohol might be derived from a focus on alcohol abuse, not simply "alcohol." In fact, it has been shown that the benefits conferred by moderate alcohol consumption actually contribute to reducing the disease burden and social cost (for example, Ashley, Rehm, Bondy, Single, & Rankin, 2000; English et al., 1995; Scragg, 1995; Single, Robson, Xie, & Rehm, 1996).

GBD METHODOLOGY: AN OVERVIEW

The method used to assess the public health impact of diseases and injuries rests on the concept of disease burden, which is measured in terms of DALYs. For a given disease or injury, the burden is an estimation of the total number of years in DALYs that are lost due to premature death or disability. More specifically, for fatal diseases, the method measures the number of years lost due to premature death (as compared to the life expectancy at the time when death occurred). For nonfatal diseases, the number of years is estimated by multiplying the time an "average" patient is sick by a disability factor, ranging between 0 and 1, that is specific to each disease. The more disabling a disease, the closer to 1 is the disability factor.

In order to estimate total DALYs for a given disease, the following parameters must be known (or estimated): the number of patients who die from the disease (mortality); the number of new cases per year (incidence); the average duration of the disease; and the disability factor characteristic of the disease. Typically, a disease may manifest itself in different degrees of severity. Therefore, different disability scores may have to be assigned, depending on whether the manifestation of the disease is light, moderate, or severe. In such situations, it is important to estimate the distribution of the severity in a population (the proportion of the patients for whom the manifestation is light, moderate, or severe). In the GBD studies, different sets of parameters were estimated for 14 different geographical regions and, separately, for males, females, and different age groups.

Numerous diseases or injuries arise from exposure to a risk factor or a hazard of some sort, and the assumption is that these cases would probably not have occurred in the absence of such exposure. It is important to identify and measure that exposure; the introduction of DALYs makes it possible to measure the burden attributable to the major risk factors.

To calculate the disease burden caused by a particular risk factor, a number of parameters (in addition to those mentioned above) are needed. The methodology for risk assessment is based on the "attributable fraction," defined by Miettenen (1974) as "the proportion of the disease in the specific population that would be eliminated in the absence of the exposure." To estimate the attributable burden for a given risk factor, it is necessary to know the *relative risk* for each cause of death and disability related to the exposure (such as alcohol use), the *prevalence of the risk*, and the *level of exposure*. For example, if the rate of patients who consume alcohol and who suffer from epilepsy is 130% of the rate of epilepsy patients who do not use alcohol,[1] then the relative risk for epilepsy of alcohol users is 1.30.

The *prevalence of the alcohol risk* is the proportion of the population who use alcohol; *level of exposure* refers to whether the alcohol use constitutes low, hazardous, or harmful drinking. Definition of these levels vary and have been used to establish a relationship between drinking level and relative risk for various diseases (see Tables 13.2A and 13.2B, for example). Table 13.3 lists the alcohol-attributable fractions for the most important acute consequences of alcohol consumption (English et al., 1995; Gutjahr, Gmel, & Rehm, 2001).

The methodology developed and used for estimating the burden of disease is complex. A prerequisite for evidence-based decision-making in health, however, is that the strengths and the limitations of the evidence on which the decisions rest

Table 13.2A Drinking Level and Increased Relative Risk for Selected Disease States by Gender

| Disease | Level of Drinking, relative risk | | | | | |
| | Low[a] | | Hazardous[b] | | Harmful[c] | |
	Female	Male	Female	Male	Female	Male
Cancer						
Lip and oropharyngeal	1.45	1.45	1.85	1.85	5.39	5.39
Esophageal	1.80	1.80	2.38	2.38	4.36	4.36
Liver	1.45	1.45	3.03	3.03	3.60	3.60
Laryngeal	1.83	1.83	3.9	3.9	4.93	4.93
Female breast	1.08	—	1.30	—	1.66	—
Epilepsy	1.34	1.23	7.22	7.52	7.52	6.83
Hypertension	0.85	1.02	1.27	1.43	1.79	2.05
Cardiac arrhythmias	1.51	1.51	2.23	2.23	2.23	2.23
Esophageal varices	1.26	1.26	9.54	9.54	9.54	9.54
Liver cirrhosis (unspecified)	1.26	1.26	9.54	9.54	9.54	9.54

[a] Drinking up to 20 grams of pure alcohol per day for females and up to 40 grams per day for males.

[b] Drinking on average between 20 and 40 grams of pure alcohol per day for females and between 40 and 60 grams per day for males.

[c] Drinking on average 40 grams per day or more of pure alcohol for females and 60 grams per day or more per day for males.

Source: Gutjahr et al. (2001); and English et al. (1995).

Table 13.2B Drinking Level and Decreased Relative Risk for Selected Disease States by Gender

| Disease | Level of Drinking, relative risk | | | | | |
| | Low | | Hazardous | | Harmful | |
	Female	Male	Female	Male	Female	Male
Diabetes	0.92	0.99	0.87	0.57	1.13	0.73
Coronary heart disease	0.82	0.82	0.83	0.83	0.88	0.88
Stroke	0.59	0.69	0.51	0.95	7.72	1.79
Cholelithiasis (gallstones)	0.82	0.82	0.68	0.68	0.50	0.50

Source: Gutjahr et al. (2001); and English et al. (1995).

are well understood, particularly if the decisions have far-reaching consequences (such as the choice of interventions that affect a whole population). In interpreting the indicators of the GBD, one should be aware of the strengths and weaknesses inherent in the underlying methodology. The most important limitation of this approach is its *disease* perspective, which ignores the positive aspects of alcohol

Table 13.3 Alcohol-Attributable Fractions of Injuries

Disease	Attributable Fraction*	
	Female	Male
Traffic crash injuries	0.00–0.34	0.18–0.43
Suicide, self-inflicted injuries	0.02–0.10	0.02–0.15
Victim assault	0.16–0.47	0.16–0.47

* Range of alcohol-attributable fractions, where minimum and maximum estimates are shown.

Source: Gutjahr et al. (2001).

consumption—by far the most important reason why people drink. Although the evidence provided in the estimates is no doubt valid, it is selective, so that some of its conclusions, as far as interventions are concerned, are questionable.

Methodological Problems in Measuring the Burden of Disease

- In establishing the cause of a disease, several criteria around the relationship between risk and outcome must be satisfied. These include temporality, strength, consistency, biological gradient, plausibility, and experimental evidence (WHO, 2002). However, the methodology applied in calculating the burden of disease associated with alcohol falls short of satisfying all of these criteria.

- Calculations of the global burden depend largely on aggregate measures of volume for a particular country, or its per capita alcohol consumption. Much of this information is derived from sales data, which take into account only recorded and commercial alcohol. Furthermore, survey data are used to divide the information on volume into age and gender categories for the population. In estimates of the burden of disease attributable to alcohol, only 52% of countries for which per capita consumption data were available also had available survey data. For the remaining 48%, estimates were made on the basis of survey data from neighboring countries, matched according to cultural and geographic similarities.

- For many developing countries included in the GBD study (Murray & Lopez, 1996), the estimates used for alcohol consumption are based on per capita consumption by country, cirrhosis death rates (excluding cirrhosis deaths attributable to hepatitis B), and deaths coded to alcohol dependence. For many countries, particularly in the developing world, estimate data for disease and death rates are highly heterogeneous and of inconsistent quality.

- The usual practice in the literature on attributable burden is to assume that relative risks are general, meaning that risks studied in one population can be applied to many other populations, albeit with caution. In the field of alcohol research, most such studies have been undertaken in a few industrialized countries, and it is highly unlikely that the exposure–risk relations can be simply transferred to other cultures in the developing world (Warner-Smith, Lynskey, Hall, & Monteiro, 2001).

- Drinking volume is but one dimension of drinking patterns. Other dimensions affect health outcomes differently. For example, heavy episodic drinking seems to be more frequently related to acute outcomes than is chronic drinking. However, data on the other aspects of patterns of drinking are still very scarce and difficult to compare across cultures (Rehm, Gmel, Room, & Frick, 2001). In an effort to remedy this, a scale was constructed that allowed countries to be classified according to drinking pattern. However, such a classification system presupposes that patterns remain constant over time. There is evidence that drinking patterns, particularly among some groups, such as young people, are changing (see Chapter 7 for an overview).

- Biological mechanisms have not been determined for all relationships. For example, although meta-analysis of morbidity and mortality studies finds a detrimental effect of drinking on breast cancer, the underlying mechanism linking alcohol with breast cancer is not understood.

- Relative risk for each cause of death or condition is often calculated on the basis of survey data, which may have a weak foundation. Social harms in particular, such as child abuse, public disorder, or vandalism, may occur where heavy drinking is prevalent, but actual causality has not been established.

- Some data collection methods that feed into final statistics on the burden attributable to alcohol do not specify whether alcohol is directly, indirectly, or only marginally related to an outcome. Such classification criteria are likely to skew the burden attributable to alcohol.

- The main estimates presented in the GBD study (Murray & Lopez, 1996) are for burden resulting from single risk factors, with the assumption that all others are held constant. When two risk factors affect the same disease or injury, the net effects may be less or more than the sum of their separate effects. The size of these joint effects depends on the amount of prevalence overlap (for example, how much more likely people who smoke are to drink alcohol) and the biological effects of joint exposure (for example, whether the risks of alcohol are greater among those who smoke). However, the premise that risk factors, such as drinking, can be seen in complete isolation from any others is an oversimplification of a complex problem.

DRINKING: NO ORDINARY RISK FACTOR

It has been argued that alcohol is not "a run-of-the-mill consumer substance" because it can cause a range of medical, psychological, and social harm (Alcohol and Public Policy Group, 2003; see also Babor et al., 2003). Public health responses, then, "must be matched to this complex vision of the dangers of alcohol as they seek better ways to respond to the population-level harms" (Alcohol and Public Policy Group, 2003, p. 1344). Following this line of thought, one should add that drinking is not an ordinary risk factor—not just because of its potential for harm, but because of the potential benefits it may confer. When one examines Table 13.1, it becomes clear that, with the exception of alcohol, other risk factors listed by WHO do not carry potential benefits. This is not simply a semantic issue. Not only does drinking alcohol have the potential to increase the risk for a number of diseases and injuries, both intentional and unintentional, but drinking also significantly reduces the risk of ischemic heart disease and ischemic stroke, as well as a number of other conditions, which are discussed at length in Chapter 2.

Moreover, the impact of alcohol consumption goes far beyond the disease aspect. It is well known that alcohol is linked to a number of social problems. However, although alcohol may be involved, the relationship is far from clear, and it cannot be argued that alcohol actually *causes* these problems. Furthermore, people like to drink because of the psychosocial benefits of drinking and its contribution to wellbeing. None of these dimensions of the positive and negative consequences of alcohol consumption are covered in the GBD model. This observation in no way diminishes the usefulness of the model. However, a warning is indicated against the indiscriminate promotion of preventive interventions that are exclusively disease-oriented. The costs and benefits of an intervention should be judged on the desirability of all its outcomes and not only of a subset, as well as by how feasible the intervention may be to implement. For example, preventing people's access to alcohol may reduce some negative health-related outcomes, but it will reduce the physical and psychosocial benefits as well. Hence, those who drink may not be prepared to renounce the psychosocial benefits associated with drinking, and their attempts to obtain alcoholic beverages illegally may cause more social harm than the prohibition prevents.

THE QUALITATIVE DIMENSIONS OF DRINKING

Alcohol consumption constitutes an integral part of social life in many cultures. Drinking for pleasure has many dimensions (Heath, 1999): sociability, relaxation, marking social boundaries (for example, "drinking like us"), framing of leisure (setting a boundary between work and nonwork), celebration, transcendence ("communicating with the gods"), social credit (buying a few drinks for friends or neighbors), signaling of status, competitive drinking, or creative drinking.

It is remarkable that the main reasons why people drink are largely ignored in the literature dealing with the (public) health aspects of alcohol consumption. Even when reference is made to positive health aspects of alcohol consumption, factors are usually highlighted with a potentially protective role of moderate drinking for certain *diseases* (for discussion, see Chapter 2; see also Gunzerath,

Faden, Zakhari, & Warren, 2004). However, it is unlikely that anyone consumes alcohol specifically in order to be protected from those diseases.

Positive Reasons for Drinking

In a traditional comic *kyogen* play produced during the Muromachi era in Japan (1333–1573), 10 virtues of sake, the Japanese rice wine, were praised (Shinfuku, 1999):

1. Provides a friend when alone
2. Produces harmony for all people
3. Allows ordinary people to greet nobles with ease
4. Justifies meeting with friends
5. Provides companionship while traveling
6. Promotes long life
7. Is the king of 100 medicines
8. Helps sorrow to disappear
9. Aids recovery from fatigue
10. Warms the body in the cold

More recently, in addition to the somatic health benefits conferred by moderate drinking on certain individuals (Gunzerath et al., 2004), three general areas of benefit have been identified: *psychosocial benefits* (such as subjective health, mood enhancement, stress reduction, and mental health), *social benefits* (such as sociability and social cohesion), and *cognitive and performance benefits* (such as long-term cognitive functioning, creativity, and income earned; Brodsky & Peele, 1999). People drink in part in anticipation of some of these immediate positive outcomes of drinking ("alcohol expectancies"). These include several of the factors identified some seven centuries ago in Japan: greater sociability and talkativeness, increased energy, relaxation and tension relief, pleasure, happiness, and altered consciousness (Leigh, 1999).

In its recent *Global Status Report on Alcohol*, WHO stated,

The consumption of alcoholic beverages can be studied from a number of viewpoints, ranging from the viewpoint of an economist to that of a cultural anthropologist. When viewed from a public health perspective, alcoholic beverages can potentially be an agent of illness and mortality. Depending on the consumption pattern, use of alcoholic beverages can elevate the drinker's risk of health problems (traffic and other accidents, chronic illness such as cirrhosis and cancer, and mental disorders such as alcohol dependence) as well as social problems (inability to cope with work, family and other roles, and harm to those in the drinker's surrounding environment). Against this burden, there is some evidence that small amounts of alcohol may play a protective role in heart disease. (WHO, 2004a, p. 22)

The inclusion of only the potential protective role of alcohol in heart disease offers just one aspect of the benefits associated with drinking (Gunzerath et al., 2004). Using the term *health* as a synonym for *disease* also implies that the psycho-social benefits of alcohol consumption are unrelated to health. It is difficult to reconcile this view with the broader and more inclusive definition of health where it is defined as "a state of complete physical, mental, and social wellbeing and not merely the absence of disease or infirmity" (WHO, 2004b). The evidence shows that, although alcohol may constitute a risk to all three dimensions of health, it may equally contribute to an individual's physical, mental, and social wellbeing.

WHO's constitutional definition of health (2004b) is seen by many as too broad and no more than an aspiration at best. However, if one accepts this perspective, one has to admit that alcohol consumption is a multivariate phenomenon, transcending the (narrow) boundaries of health. Preventive interventions must take psychosocial factors into account, whether classified under the heading of *health* or elsewhere.

Table 13.4 summarizes the impact of alcohol on health, taking into account the physical, mental, and social aspects—WHO's tri-axial construct. The table is not meant to be exhaustive. However, it is an attempt to point to the main dimensions, both positive and negative, and to list illustrative examples. The effectiveness of preventive interventions can only be assessed meaningfully and convincingly if their impact on all relevant consequences of drinking is taken into consideration. Equally important for the assessment of the effectiveness of any interventions is an understanding of how such interventions affect drinking patterns, which in turn determine both positive and negative outcomes of drinking.

ACCOUNTING FOR BENEFIT

The approach of considering both positive and negative dimensions is common-place in many areas of health and social research. In the field of alcohol, however, this view has, until recently, been the exception rather than the rule. For many decades, the most quoted indicator for alcohol-related problems has been the per capita consumption of ethanol across a population, and interventions have been uniformly aimed at reducing consumption. Although there is ample evidence that per capita consumption of ethanol correlates with the number of alcohol-related problems in a society, it is equally true that it also correlates with the pleasure and potential health benefits associated with moderate alcohol consumption. Hence, per capita consumption of ethanol can be thought of as an indicator of the quality of life of a population as much as an indicator of alcohol-related problems. It is by no means a coincidence that the per capita consumption of alcohol generally increases in societies with strong economies (Mäkelä, 2003) and that countries traditionally associated with a more relaxed and pleasure-oriented lifestyle and integrated drinking patterns (for example, the Mediterranean countries) also have higher levels of per capita consumption than their Nordic counterparts.

Table 13.4 Harms and Benefits for Physical, Mental, and Social Health Associated With Alcohol Consumption[a]

	Physical Health	Mental Health	Social Health
Harms			
	Alcohol dependence	Dementia	Absenteeism
	Neurological damage	Alcoholic psychosis	Suicide, depression
	Liver cirrhosis		Family disruption
	Esophageal and laryngeal cancer		Crime and violence
	Colorectal cancer		Unwanted/unintended sexual activity
	Breast cancer		Social costs of chronic harm
	Ischemic stroke		Social costs of acute harm
	Fetal alcohol syndrome (FAS)		
	Alcoholic gastritis		
	Intentional and unintentional injuries (for example, related to traffic crashes, workplace injuries, falls, or assault)		
Benefits			
	Type II diabetes mellitus	Improved cognitive function and memory (especially in elderly)	Quality of life
	Coronary heart disease	Vascular dementia	Sociability and social integration
	Hemorrhagic stroke	Wellbeing, pleasure, relaxation	Reduced mortality and morbidity across populations
	Pancreatitis		Symbol of adulthood and maturity
	Osteoporosis		
	Macular degeneration		
	Cholelithiasis (gall bladder disease)		

[a] Harm is generally related to heavy drinking patterns, whether sustained or episodic, whereas benefits are associated with moderate patterns of consumption.

The quantitative assessment of harm and benefits associated with alcohol hinges upon the existence of mathematically based methods that allow a formal cost–benefit analysis. With regard to the costs, the definition and measurement of the burden of diseases in terms of DALYs in the early 1990s marked an impressive achievement in epidemiological research. In contrast, there has been little progress in defining and measuring pleasure and other positive correlates of moderate alcohol consumption. The Quality of Life (QoL) project, launched by

**Table 13.5 Correlation of Different Facets of Life
With Overall Quality of Life**

Facet	Correlation (r)
1. Positive feelings	0.749
2. Activities of daily living	0.678
3. Energy and fatigue	0.676
4. Negative feelings	0.602
5. Work capacity	0.567
6. Self-esteem	0.564
7. Leisure activities	0.537
8. Personal relationships	0.531
9. Pain and discomfort	0.530
10. Sleep and rest	0.528

Source: Orley (1999).

WHO (WHO Quality of Life Group, 1998), is the broadest effort yet to develop a universal QoL instrument. Pleasure and other positive feelings are important ingredients in pertinent calculations. This instrument has not been systematically applied to the field of alcohol research. Nor does an equivalent to DALYs exist when it comes to the psychosocial dimensions. Nevertheless, it provides some insight into the relationship between drinking and quality of life. It identifies six axes along which quality of life should be measured: physical health, psychological (mental) health, level of independence, social relationships, environment, and spirituality (religion, personal beliefs). These are further broken down into 24 specific facets generally associated with quality of life. Among these, the most common association is with positive feelings. Table 13.5 shows the correlation of different facets of life with overall quality of life (Orley, 1999). Moderate consumption of alcohol seems to contribute to a number of these.

CONCLUSIONS

Positive and negative factors and their impact on health and wellbeing are constantly weighed against one another in different areas of life. The balance of their relative weights ultimately informs what policy measures are applied, their possible impact on the population, and, where appropriate, what intervention and prevention measures make the most sense and are likely to be most palatable to those they target.

For example, traffic crashes caused by motor vehicles are responsible for high mortality, injuries, and human suffering. On the other hand, people rely on cars, enjoy driving them, and enjoy economic benefits that are related to driving. These factors all contribute to subjective wellbeing. In selecting interventions to reduce the harm due to road traffic crashes, this balance has to be taken into account.

So, for example, it is to be expected that increasing purchase prices (for example, through taxation) should reduce the demand for vehicles, limiting their production and, in turn, reducing the number of motor vehicle crashes. At the same time, however, it would curtail the perceived benefits. No one seems even to have considered introducing measures aimed at reducing car production with a view to reduce death and injuries caused by motor vehicle crashes. No formal cost–benefit analyses have had to be carried out to reach this conclusion. The same argument holds for many lifestyle-related determinants of disease (for instance, no one has proposed increasing the prices of chairs to counteract sedentary lifestyles, which may lead to high blood pressure and pose a risk for cardiovascular diseases).

The argument may be well taken that alcohol is no ordinary commodity (Babor et al., 2003), but, equally, it is no ordinary risk factor either. Like other commodities, it carries with it benefit and harm, but more benefit than some in a range of different dimensions. The question is why the health benefits associated with drinking, as well as the obvious pleasure and other positive feelings associated with it, are being systematically overlooked, ignored, or denied. As Heath wrote (1999),

> Permission for pleasure has not been among the many aspects of culture that have been subject to cross-cultural investigation. Writings about norms, values, hedonism, and social control have nibbled at the edges of this subject, but it rarely has been confronted clearly and directly. (p. 66)

Attempts have been made to differentiate cultures in terms of an "Apollonian–Dionysian" dichotomy. In this view, Dionysians esteemed pleasure, sought it in a variety of ways, and embraced it if they found it. Apollonians, by contrast, were suspicious of pleasure, held it to be dangerous, and deplored any quest for it as risky. Perhaps the world of alcohol research and public health may also be divided in this way. No doubt reality is too complex to fit into such a simple model. However, the time may have come to "throw away some of the shackles that for so long have made us embarrassed about the very prospect that in promoting health we also might promote something that is pleasurable" (Daube, 1999, p. 47).

NOTE

1. The *theoretical minimum risk distribution* is defined as the distribution of exposure that would have the lowest associated population risk. The question whether abstinence or moderate drinking should be taken as the yardstick has been discussed inconclusively in the literature (Rehm et al., 2001).

REFERENCES

Alcohol and Public Policy Group. (2003). Alcohol: No ordinary commodity. A summary of the book. *Addiction, 98*, 1343–1350.

Ashley, M. J., Rehm, J., Bondy, S., Single, E., & Rankin, J. (2000). Beyond ischemic heart disease: Are there other health benefits from drinking alcohol? *Contemporary Drug Problems, 27*, 735–777.

Babor, T. F., Caetano, R., Caswell, S., Edwards, G., Giesbrecht, N., Graham, K., et al. (2003). *Alcohol: No ordinary commodity. Research and public policy.* Oxford: Oxford University Press.

Brodsky, A., & Peele, S. (1999). Psychosocial benefits of moderate alcohol consumption: Alcohol's role in a broader conception of health and well-being. In S. Peele & M. Grant (Eds.), *Alcohol and pleasure: A health perspective* (pp. 187–207). Philadelphia: Brunner/Mazel.

Daube, M. (1999). Pleasure in health promotion. In S. Peele & M. Grant (Eds.), *Alcohol and pleasure: A health perspective* (pp. 37–47). Philadelphia: Brunner/Mazel.

English, D. R., Holman, C. D. J., Milne, E., Winter, M. G., Hulse, G. K., Codde, J. P., et al. (1995). *The quantification of drug-caused morbidity and mortality in Australia.* Canberra, Australia: Commonwealth Department of Human Services and Health.

Gutjahr, E., Gmel, G., & Rehm, J. (2001). Relation between average alcohol consumption and disease: An overview. *European Addiction Research, 7*, 117–127.

Hanson, D. J. (2005). *Alcohol and health.* Retrieved April 30, 2006, from http://www2.potsdam.edu/hansondj/AlcoholAndHealth.html.

Heath, D. B. (1999). Drinking and pleasure across cultures. In S. Peele & M. Grant (Eds.), *Alcohol and pleasure: A health perspective* (pp. 61–72). Philadelphia: Brunner/Mazel.

Leigh, B. C. (1999). Thinking, feeling, and drinking: Alcohol expectancies and alcohol use. In S. Peele & M. Grant, (Eds.), *Alcohol and pleasure: A health perspective* (pp. 215–231). Philadelphia: Brunner/Mazel.

Mäkelä, P. (2003). Trends also in thinking and presentation. Comment on chapter 3: Alcohol consumption. Trends and patterns of drinking. *Addiction, 98*, 1353–1354.

Miettenen, O. S. (1974). Proportion of disease caused or prevented by a given exposure, trait, or intervention. *American Journal of Epidemiology, 99*, 325–332.

Murray, C. J. L., & Lopez, A. D. (Eds.). (1996). *Global burden of disease and injury: A comprehensive assessment of mortality and disability from diseases, injuries, and risk factors in 1990 and projected to 2020.* Cambridge, MA: Harvard School of Public Health and World Health Organization.

Orley, J. (1999). Pleasure and quality of life. In S. Peele & M. Grant (Eds.), *Alcohol and pleasure: A health perspective* (pp. 329–340). Philadelphia: Brunner/Mazel.

Rehm, J., Gmel, G., Room, R., & Frick, U. (2001). Average volume of alcohol consumption, drinking patterns and related burden of mortality in young people in established market economies of Europe. *European Addiction Research, 7*, 148–151.

Scragg, R. (1995). A quantification of alcohol-related mortality in New Zealand. *Australian and New Zealand Journal of Medicine, 25*, 5–11.

Shinfuku, N. (1999). Japanese culture and drinking. In S. Peele & M. Grant (Eds.), *Alcohol and pleasure: A health perspective.* (pp. 113–119). Philadelphia: Brunner/Mazel.

Single, E., Robson, L., Xie, X., & Rehm, J. (1996). *Costs of substance abuse in Canada: Highlights of a major study of the health, social and economic costs associated with the use of alcohol, tobacco and illicit drugs.* Ottawa: Canadian Centre on Substance Abuse (CCSA).

Warner-Smith, M., Lynskey, M., Hall, W., & Monteiro, M. (2001). Challenges and approaches to estimating mortality attributable to the use of selected illicit drugs. *European Addiction Research, 7,* 104–116.

WHO Quality of Life Group. (1998). The World Health Organization Quality of Life Assessment (WHOQOL): Development and general psychometric properties. *Social Science and Medicine, 46,* 1569–1584.

World Bank. (1993). *World development report 1993: Investing in health.* New York: Oxford University Press.

World Health Organization (WHO). (2002). *World health report 2002: Reducing risks, promoting healthy life.* Geneva, Switzerland: Author.

World Health Organization (WHO). (2004a). *Global status report on alcohol 2004.* Geneva, Switzerland: Author.

World Health Organization (WHO). (2004b). *World Health Organization: Basic texts,* 44th ed. Retrieved August 18, 2005, from http://www.who.int/governance/en/.

Index